KT-478-632

DISPOSED OF
BY LIBRARY
HOUSE OF LORDS

THE NEED FOR HEALTHCARE

In many countries health systems, among them the British NHS, face severe underfunding and rising demand. Governments respond with programmes of health system reform, nearly always arguing that their favoured proposals will satisfy 'the need for healthcare'. They rarely explain in depth how one would identify and define this need.

The Need for Healthcare analyses the empirical and logical foundations of the concept of 'needs'. Beginning from current British health policy and a critical review of recent philosophical discussions about needs, the author suggests criteria for a satisfactory theory of needs.

The study offers an analysis of the relationship between needs, drives, free will and recent debates about the mind–brain, and challenges some central assumptions of contemporary healthcare economics and health policy. It is therefore relevant for those interested in healthcare ethics, health policy and healthcare management.

Rod Sheaff is a Fellow at the Health Services Management Unit, Manchester University. He has had working, research and consultancy experience both in the British NHS and many overseas health systems. He is the author of *Marketing for Health Services* (1991).

SOCIAL ETHICS AND POLICY SERIES
Edited by Anthony Dyson and John Harris
Centre for Social Ethics and Policy,
University of Manchester

EXPERIMENTS ON EMBRYOS
Edited by Anthony Dyson and John Harris

THE LIMITS OF MEDICAL PATERNALISM
Heta Häyry

PROTECTING THE VULNERABLE
Autonomy and Consent in Health Care
Edited by Margaret Brazier and Mary Lobjoit

MEDICAL CONFIDENTIALITY AND LEGAL PRIVILEGE
Jean V. MacHale

ETHICS AND BIOTECHNOLOGY
Edited by Anthony Dyson and John Harris

LIBERAL UTILITARIANISM AND APPLIED ETHICS
Matti Häyry

CONTEMPLATING SUICIDE
The Language and Ethics of Self Harm
Gavin J. Fairbairn

THE NEED FOR HEALTHCARE

Rod Sheaff

London and New York

First published 1996
by Routledge
11 New Fetter Lane, London EC4P 4EE

Simultaneously published in the USA and Canada
by Routledge
29 West 35th Street, New York, NY 10001

Routledge is an International Thomson Publishing company

© 1996 Rod Sheaff

Typeset in Garamond by Routledge
Printed and bound in Great Britain by
T J Press (Padstow) Ltd, Padstow, Cornwall

All rights reserved. No part of this book may be reprinted or
reproduced or utilized in any form or by any electronic,
mechanical, or other means, now known or hereafter
invented, including photocopying and recording, or in any
information storage or retrieval system, without permission in
writing from the publishers.

British Library Cataloguing in Publication Data
A catalogue record for this book is available from the British Library

Library of Congress Cataloguing in Publication Data
Sheaff, Rod
The need for healthcare/Rod Sheaff.
p. cm. – (Social ethics and policy)
Includes bibliographical references and index.
1. Medical policy–Moral and ethical aspects. 2. Medical care–needs
assessment. 3. Need (Philosophy). 4. Right to health care. 5. Medical
policy–Great Britain. I.Title. II. Series: Social ethics and policy series
RA394.S55 1996
362.1'01–dc20
95–25911
CIP

ISBN 0–415–10111–5(hbk)
ISBN 0–415–10112–3(pbk)

CONTENTS

ILLUSTRATIONS

FIGURES

TABLES

PREFACE

Although a single author's name appears on the binding, few texts of this kind are purely the work of one person. Their contents stem in large measure from the nominal author's reactions to the opinions that many previous commentators have already expressed about the subjects discussed in the following pages, not to mention the criticisms, objections and questions that these commentators have anticipated. A small proportion of these intellectual debts are recorded in the text in the usual way. To them ought to be added at least the names of Ian Gough, David Grimes, Joan Higgins, Jim Kemeny, Hans Maarse, Nicolai Nevolin and John Torrance; and of my parents, to whom I owe my interest in ethics. Nevertheless I suspect that none of these (mainly unwitting) contributors would wholeheartedly endorse the positions outlined below. In philosophical and theoretical terms there is probably something to offend almost everyone in the pages that follow; and whatever mistakes of fact or reasoning remain in such a text are one of the few areas in which an author really can claim some originality.

1

WHY A THEORY OF NEEDS?

§1 NEEDS AND HEALTH POLICY

Hardly a change in British health policy has taken place since 1938 without announcements from the government, and sometimes from other people too, that the new policy is intended to meet the need for healthcare better than before. Recently, for example, 'Significant changes have been made to the way family health, community and hospital services are organised. The purpose of the reform was to give the National Health Service a much greater capacity to address the health needs of the country' (William Waldegrave's Foreword to Department of Health 1991: iii). Never mind that the latest policy – for instance, the new 'internal market' – reverses large elements of the preceding policy which were also legitimated in terms of the very same needs. Health service managers are increasingly joining clinicians and other health workers in using the language of needs to justify local changes in health services – changes that typically redefine what types of healthcare will be available and often ration access to it. When healthcare needs are invoked, policy debates, technical problems in healthcare management, epidemiology and healthcare ethics meet wider but more technical philosophical questions head on. Yet with a few honourable exceptions these interfaces around the concept of 'the need for healthcare' are under-analysed. The quality of most debate about health system reform is evidence of that. One way to attempt such an analysis is to begin by examining how the concept of 'needs for healthcare' has been used in British health policy and managerial contexts. This will furnish a set of questions about needs for healthcare, from which a fresh attempt at critical analysis can begin, with the aim of leading towards a more coherent, explicit and valid understanding of what health needs and healthcare needs there

1

really are (if any). The conclusions will have obvious implications for controversies about both health policy and clinical practice.

In UK government circles talk about health 'needs' began in earnest during the debates around the Beveridge Report and consequent legislation, including the 1946 NHS Act. The 1944 white paper on the NHS stated that under the proposed national health service 'every man, woman and child can rely on getting all the advice, treatment and care which they need ... and that ... their getting shall not depend on whether they can pay for them, or any other factor irrelevant to the real need' (Ministry of Health 1944). Official policy documents have reiterated statements of this kind, even during and after the Thatcher governments' attempts to shift the post-war consensus on health and welfare policy. For example,

> The Secretary of State recently [1993] restated the key of objectives of the NHS as being ... to provide a health service for all, on the basis of clinical need, regardless of ability to pay ... to ensure that treatment and care are targeted to meet local needs.
> (Department of Health 1993: 5)

In between, similar words were printed in support of the 1959 Mental Health Act, the RAWP report (Department of Health and Social Security 1976), the Royal Commission (Royal Commission on the National Health Service 1979), the current main NHS policy documents *Working for Patients* (Department of Health 1989a), *Health of the Nation* (Department of Health 1991), *Caring for People* (Department of Health 1989b), *The Patient's Charter* and WHO policy (WHO 1978: 44; WHO 1979: 43). One thing that these formulations all do is invoke the idea of needs as a characteristic of individuals or populations and as grounding an entitlement to healthcare, independently of commercial or financial considerations.

Among these individually oriented uses of the word 'needs' are various euphemisms, for instance in referring to severely (mentally or physically) disabled people as 'people with special needs'. On occasions NHS policy documents also betray a sense of distance between their authors and the needs of the care groups that they discuss. In this case it is homeless young people:

> Sometimes all that is needed is an emergency centre where a young person can talk through the reasons why they ran away; sometimes more continuing support and contact is needed. A project may help reconcile the child with their families. For

2

other children ... reconciliation with their families is is not an alternative. They need help in getting themselves established and building their own networks of support.

(John Bowis, Parliamentary Secretary to
the Department of Health, quoted in
Department of Health Press Release 1994: 1)

Not only individuals have health needs, if official policy documents are to be believed. So do whole organisations. The Acheson report on public health in England noted that, besides various public health shortcomings, 'Nor were the needs of health authorities whose responsibilities included hospitals always· fully met by community physicians' (Department of Health 1988: 6). Now that many NHS bodies are being encouraged to perceive themselves as businesses one encounters such expressions as 'The approach to the business needs' (NHSME IMG 1993).

The RAWP report attempted to define the healthcare needs of geographically distinct populations in ways that allow direct comparison (DHSS 1976: 13–46). However, the assumption that whole populations or nations have health needs is not an aberration of this one report. The Acheson report is also replete with references to 'the health of the population' and 'the health of the public' (Department of Health 1988). More recently NHS managers have been told that 'District Health Authorities will be responsible for assessing the health needs of their populations and arranging for those needs to be met' (NHSME 1993a: 1). The Black report, and subsequent research in similar vein (DHSS 1980; Wilkinson 1986), attribute distinct healthcare needs to different social classes, ethnic groups and smaller sub-populations again.

More abstractly, some official documents speak of 'needs' existing as entities in themselves, not explicitly belonging either to individual people nor to populations: 'Countries differ in their perception of the need for a medically qualified public health expert in their arrangements for the discharge of the public health function' (Department of Health 1988: 10). Or again: 'Hospitals and other units will be responsible for providing efficient and effective health services to meet the needs identified by health authorities' (NHSME 1993a: 1). Many official publications expressly assume that clinicians can make some sort of expert or privileged judgement about the existence or validity of such claims, discriminating 'real' needs from other kinds. To a battery of other criticisms Roy Griffiths made in his report on

3

NHS management he added: 'Nor can the NHS display a ready assessment of the effectiveness with which it is meeting the needs and expectations of the people it serves' (Griffiths 1983). In response, and as part of health authorities' new role after 1991, NHS managers began to attempt to define health and healthcare 'needs' more specifically and concretely. Several internal NHS guidance papers define healthcare need in terms of the population's ability to benefit from healthcare (Stevens and Raftery 1994: i 5; Mawhinney and Nichol 1993):

> The population's ability to benefit is the aggregate of individuals' ability to benefit but, for any health problem, depends on the incidence of (different degrees of severity) of the condition and the prevalence of its effects and complications .... The ability to benefit does not mean that every outcome is guaranteed to be favourable. But it does mean that there is only a need where there is a potential benefit i.e. where the intervention and/or the care setting is effective . . .. The benefit measured should include:
>
> i)   clinical status compared to that without the intervention.
> ii) reassurance, both to the individual and professional, that avenues of potential benefit have been explored i.e. confirming the diagnosis.
> iii) supportive care and the relief of pressure on other carers.
>
> Health care includes prevention and promotion, diagnosis and treatment, continuing care, rehabilitation and terminal care – all taken with the context of their setting.
>
> (NHSME 1991: 5)

This is certainly more specific than previous official definitions but whether it is any clearer the reader can judge for herself. This idea of need as the under-supply specifically of those existing health services that hold out promise of health 'benefits' is more formally theorised in Donabedian's earlier texts. He defined health 'needs' as the states of health or illness that the patient or physician sees are likely to make demands on the medical care system (e.g. Donabedian 1973).

As the problem of scarcity of healthcare resources has become too pressing for the elimination of 'non-beneficial' treatment to solve, the concept of 'need' has acquired another use, as a criterion for comparing different individuals' claims on health services that are rationed.

Caring for People announces that 'in future the Government will encourage the targeting of home-based services on those people whose need for them is greatest' (Department of Health 1989b). At managerial level, James describes how one district health authority has tried (rather inconclusively) to include criteria of need in making multi-criteria decisions about its budgetary allocations and purchasing decisions (James 1993: 13–15).

Sooner or later in most discussions about needs someone mentions 'equity'. One way to link it with the above debates is by redefining 'equity' in terms of needs, for instance as providing similar services for people with similar needs (Bamford 1993: 36; Wall n.d.: 12). Barry links the ideas of 'needs' and 'justice' with the concept of citizenship in a similar way, analysing (but not necessarily endorsing) the concept of 'citizenship' as concentrating on citizens' needs, regardless of the causes of those needs. Then claims about needs sustain an argument for minimum incomes, and hence of redistribution to achieve it, on grounds of justice (cf. Barry 1990: 38). The state's putative moral authority to satisfy individuals' objective needs on these grounds then does not depend on these citizens' subjective choices (cf. Barry 1990: 49). Radical critics of both current healthcare and the whole social system have often taken up the language of needs more enthusiastically. For example:

> some of the most basic needs of the mentally disabled – above all, the needs for housing, for occupation, and for community – are not satisfied by the market system of resource allocation that operates under capitalism. These needs are at present not even satisfied, systematically and appropriately, for normal people who labour without the further disadvantage of a mental or other disability.
>
> (Sedgwick 1982: 329)

Such debates are not restricted to the British health system. They are occurring in the USA, and now in much of Europe, in particular the Netherlands and Sweden (e.g. Dunning 1992), as health system reform returns to the political agenda. Neither is rhetoric of needs restricted to health policy debates. Wiggins quotes examples from British transport and atomic energy policy documents (Wiggins 1985: §3). Although the concept's justificatory uses are obviously not limited to healthcare, a preliminary task must be to analyse how 'need' is being used in these health policy debates.

§2 THE LANGUAGE AND LOGIC OF 'NEEDS'

What is being said or implied in these assertions (ch1§1) about needs for healthcare? Typically the policy documents noted above use 'need' implicitly to recommend a state of affairs (e.g. resource use) or an action. This use occurs not only in health policy debates but also in more everyday uses of the word (cp. Anscombe 1973: 179; McCloskey 1975: 7). It occurs even in passive constructions using the verb 'to need'. Thomson analyses 'The president needs to be shot' as being equivalent to 'someone ought to shoot the president' (Thomson 1987: 8). Expressions such as 'this kidney machine needs cleaning' are intelligible as extensions, metaphors or ellipses for such claims as 'We need this kidney machine to be cleaned'.

A recommendation presupposes a reference to whatever it is that is recommended (McInnes 1978: 239) – a counterfactual reference when whatever is recommended (here, 'a need') does not exist already. It is striking that British health policy documents nearly always use the word 'needs' as a noun. Like the passive construction, this usage defines 'needs' in a rather depersonalised way, in terms of what states of affairs are needed but in abstraction from the questions of who needs them or will realise them. By contrast everyday English no less often uses 'need' as a full verb and as a modal or auxiliary verb (Thomson 1987: 3–9), a usage also occurring in health policy documents. To recommend a state of affairs is implicitly to recommend the actions that bring it about; and to recommend an action is implicitly to recommend the states of affairs that it creates. What an action produces is a new state of affairs and a state of affairs is only maintained, or *a fortiori* created, by people taking the appropriate course of action (which might in certain circumstances be deliberately to do nothing). The noun usage of 'need' is readily explained in terms of the verb usage as a hypostasised form of the verb used to characterise whatever a person needs as that which he needs. 'A need' is initially definable as 'that which an agent needs' (compare 'a drink' or 'a sight'). Conversely, since 'to need' is a transitive verb its use is both grammatically and logically incomplete without a specification of what the object or action ('the need') is that a person needs. This suggests (*pace* McCloskey 1975: 2–4) that noun uses and verb uses of 'need' are logically inseparable. The use of the noun 'a need' implies the availability of a logically equivalent expression formulation using the verb 'to need'; and the latter explicitly implies the existence of both a subject who (or which) needs and that there is some state of affairs which this subject needs. In general the word 'needs' requires only a grammatical, not a human, subject although health policy documents usually attribute health needs and healthcare needs only to individual people, organisations, local and national populations and the 'public'.

To recommend something as a need is an act of speech (or of writing or other means of communication) involving three social roles. It presupposes a speaker who recommends the action or state of affairs as a 'need', and a listener to whom the recommendation is addressed. The listener's role can be filled by an individual or group or, when one is thinking about one's own needs, reflexively by the speaker himself. Attributions of need additionally imply a third role, that of the subject to whom the need is attributed. Normally this subject is a person and a third party (e.g. 'He needs to re-establish himself in London') or several of them ('They need') although it can also be the speaker ('I need . . . ') or listener ('You need . . . ') or both ('We need . . . ').

In recommending a particular health policy the documents quoted above often contrast 'real' health or healthcare needs with other, implicitly only 'apparent' or 'spurious', health needs. A favourite healthcare example is to contrast needs with addictions or harmful dependencies (e.g. on tobacco or sweet foods) (Thomson 1987: 24, 28). The distinction implies that claims about needs are corrigible, hence criticisable. This in turn implies that the word has specific empirical criteria.

Together these characteristics imply that claims about needs (including health and healthcare needs) typically involve four different assertions:

1 A claim that a person or other subject in fact satisfies the empirical criterion of having a need. This criterion is some sort of yet to be analysed relation between a person or other subject having the need and the state of affairs or action that they need. This relation is often, *inter alia*, one of lacking, say, healthcare or whatever else would satisfy the alleged need. As Thomson says, this is only a 'conversational implicature', not a logically binding implication (Thomson 1987: 11–12). Nevertheless it is an implicature that is typical of everyday usage and of health policy discussions.

2 Since the first claim is corrigible, an assumption that the speaker critically endorses it. Having examined whether the claim is logically coherent and whatever evidence proves to be relevant to it, the speaker discovers that the empirical criteria for the relation

do indeed give that person (or group or organisation, etc.) a reason for acting, irrespective of whether they give anyone else a reason for so acting.

3 As many health policy documents illustrate (ch1§1), the utterer uses 'needs' to endorse that person's or group's claim to whatever is putatively needed (Thomson 1987: 112), not only in the sense of agreeing that as a matter of fact they have a reason for trying to get it but in the further sense that the speaker also agrees on his own account that they ought to get what they putatively need (cf. Fitzgerald 1978: 208).

4 An assertion addressed to the listener (or reader or . . .) for him to assent to, that he also has reason to accept that the person or group to whom the need is attributed ought to get what they need.

Together these four elements comprise what Wiggins and others call the 'absolute' (i.e. non-hypothetical, seemingly unconditional) use of the word 'needs'. The documents also show that at least some senses of the word 'need' are moral uses. Some moral judgements presuppose or imply judgements about needs. These moralised uses of 'needs' are, says Wiggins, a special case of the absolutist use, for instance to identify areas wherein interests have a particular claim to be concerns of social justice (Wiggins 1985: §13) or for state protection. In other documents, 'needs' are simply concrete benefits to individuals, not necessarily moral benefits, and the corresponding claims about needs are not a priori exclusively moral claims. They might express, for example, what Fulford calls 'medical values' (Fulford 1989: 104,109).

Some British health policy statements say that people only have a healthcare need where they can receive a 'health gain' (see ch4§1). Such assertions use the term 'healthcare need' to mean 'that healthcare which is instrumentally necessary for improving health' (cf. Thomson 1987: 3, 10; Wiggins 1985: 153–4). In healthcare rationing contexts especially, this instrumental sense of 'needs' is used to make a tacit contrast between the healthcare that is needed, in the sense of necessary for some further purpose such as restoring a person's health, and healthcare that is superfluous for that purpose, even frivolous or luxurious (Thomson 1987: 2). This sense of the word 'need' appears to come closest to its use in (unphilosophical) clinical decision-making about the relative urgency of treating different patients, and in assessing the patient's 'interest', to the doctor, for teaching and research purposes (West 1993: 48). Of course this hypothetical use of 'need' implies that there exist some further ends that (healthcare) means are needed to realise. It is common to say that a person needs healthcare (or anything else) as a means to some further end, without endorsing that end at all (e.g. 'he needs the money for paying someone to murder his wife'). In this case, the speaker is making only the first two of the four assertions listed above.

Of course health officials' English and, still more, everyday English does not limit itself to these two main uses of 'needs'. It exhibits more flexible, richer nuances and rarer, more eccentric usages such as the literary archaism of using 'needs' as an adverb ('Go, since I needs must die, and give the world the lie'). The reader can doubtless recall still more exotic uses of 'needs'. It would be desirable if an account of needs could accommodate such aberrant uses as this and as the philosophers' question 'Do I need to survive?' (Doyal and Gough 1991: 54). (The difficulty in thinking of occasions outside philosophical debates for asking that question gives warning of its eccentricity.) However, it is not necessarily fatal to an analysis of needs to regard the occasional deviant use as a rhetorical extension of one of the main uses, not as a new and problematic theoretical category.

'Need' in the sense of 'necessary means' is a simpler use of 'needs' than the 'absolute' sense. Analysis of the latter is laden with philo-sophical problems: conceptual, logical, epistemological, ontological and ethical. Healthcare ethics is still underdeveloped both in respect of theories of needs generally and specifically in respect of theories of the need for healthcare. Although they are rare, such analyses are not entirely unknown. A first step must be to consider critically how far the analyses that are available can help us in analysing the need for healthcare, and in what way.

2

WHAT KIND OF THEORY OF NEEDS?

§1 NEEDS IN ETHICAL THEORY

A theory of needs for healthcare presupposes both a theory of health and a general theory of needs, in which needs for healthcare are embedded as a specific case. However, some writers have doubted whether a tenable general theory of needs can be produced. If it cannot, the possibility for a theory of needs for healthcare disappears with it. Confronting these objections to the concept of 'needs' *per se* will at least focus more exactly what makes for a defensible account of needs.

One objection, often voiced by economists, libertarians and some social market thinkers, argues that the concept of 'needs' is theoretically redundant, replaceable without loss of meaning (and with gains in clarity and links to existing economic theory) by the concepts of 'preference' or 'desires' or, through these, by the concept of 'demand' (Acton 1971: 70; Condren 1978: 252; Green 1986: 100; and analogously in the political domain, McInnes 1978: 234). These objections, however, presuppose that anyone who attempts to formulate or substantiate opinions about health, healthcare and health systems can properly do so only through the medium of an economic discourse originally devised for the analysis and legitimation of markets. That objection presupposes that the current discipline of economics constitutes a scientific account of how market economies work; an extremely dubious assumption. It also begs some of the most important health policy questions, ignoring (indeed, pre-empting) the point that a main use of the concept of 'needs' is for criticising or legitimating specific forms of health system organisation (including markets) in terms that do not simply and question-beggingly presuppose a market paradigm.

Perhaps this is one reason (but only one; see below) that critics have objected to the idea of 'needs' as a licence for authoritarianism (cp. McInnes 1978: 232, 235, 237–8, 243; Flew 1981: 129). If in a healthcare context 'needs' means 'demands which in the opinion of a doctor require medical attention' (Culyer 1976: 20, 47, 50)', organisational questions arise about which demands for healthcare (and other goods) are to be recognised, whose demands are to be recognised, and by whom. Recalling the Soviet experience or even western European welfare bureaucracies, these critics assume that the concept of 'needs' too readily legitimates an inflexible, unresponsive, bureaucratised and egalitarian welfare state as the administrative answer to these questions.

A variation on this objection is that rather than the interests of a state bureaucracy, the concept of 'needs' actually legitimates professionals' demands or experts' misconstruals of the solutions to (healthcare or other welfare) consumers' practical problems as being in the interests of these consumers themselves (Boulding 1967: 465, 478; Flew 1978: 117, 120, 134–7; Smith 1980: 2, 7, 65f, 85; and cp. Culyer 1976: 15, 19, 30). In using the concept of 'needs', welfare professionals' prime motives, critics say, are to sustain and develop the services that they favour or in which they work:

> The consumer is constructed to act according to a model. This construction occurs within a process of predetermining and constructing 'needs' . . . on the one hand, 'we' provide according to 'their' needs, yet on the other hand 'we' tell 'them' their needs.
>
> (Grace 1991: 339)

Grace sees this as a marketing process in which the 'customer' is induced to choose, according to particular desires and wants imputed by the professional service providers (Grace 1991: 335, 339). This applies as much to so-called 'community needs' as to individuals' needs: 'Community need does not pop out of nowhere; it is not emitted in response to a survey as if the whole process of questioning does not contribute to the construction of the "responses" ' (Grace 1991: 332).

These three objections ground a fourth: that the concept of 'need' is inherently and question-beggingly an anti-market conception. Applying the concept of 'need' to healthcare (and other social policy or welfare questions) leads the person who does so uncritically towards administrative or legal and away from market-oriented theorisations or policy solutions.

Alternately (because it is inconsistent with claiming that the concept of 'needs' is question-begging or a misformulation of economic concepts), a fifth objection is that the concept of need is vacuous. Any supporter of needs theory would have to agree that in many uses statements about 'needs' are as vague and vacuous as 'motherhood and apple pie' moralising (James 1993: 12; McInnes 1978: 232–9; Green 1986: 96). Claims about needs are inexact (Culyer 1976: 46, 107) and 'a mechanism to camouflage imperatives under an empirical guise' (Fitzgerald 1978: 200–1).

If these criticisms were valid, what they would imply is that health policy debates should not use the concept of 'needs'. They do not show that there is no point in analysing the concept of 'need'. A concept having as much influence in health policy debates as 'need' has (see ch1§1) deserves analysis for that reason alone even if the only outcome is to puncture an illusion, to explain it away and to draw lessons from the mistakes that it embodies. If the concept of 'need' is not irretrievably incoherent, however, an analysis of it can do more; to retrieve from the concept what well-founded empirical content it has, to amend whatever deficiencies there are in this content, and to identify points at which the concept of 'need' might be made more logically coherent. The only conclusive answer to the critics is to try to generate a concept of 'need' that is neither vacuous nor question-begging, nor an ideological cosmetic for professional or welfare-state 'authoritarianism', nor theoretically redundant. Following chapters attempt this, working at the levels both of ethical theory and of applying the results to substantive healthcare ethics and health policy issues. Insofar as they succeed, they refute the objections noted above.

There are two main approaches to the preliminary task of theorising needs in general. One starts scientifically, usually from biology but sometimes from psychology, eventually seeking the ethical significance of the substantive findings of these sciences. The other starts in a more conventionally philosophical way by analysing 'our' concepts or substantive moral judgements about needs, then working back to whatever assumptions are logically necessary to sustain and systematise these, including biological, psychological and other empirical assumptions.

The simplest philosophically based approach attempts to classify 'our' intuitions and linguistic usages about 'needs' inductively. Bradshaw classified needs as 'normative', 'felt', 'expressed' or 'comparative' (Bradshaw 1972), to which Clayton added the categories of 'approved' and 'latent' needs (Clayton 1983: 21). In the Hegelian–Marxist tradition, Heller differentiates objective (or 'real') from false

12

needs (Heller 1976). Many writers classify some needs as 'basic' (e.g. Gray 1992: 37; Sadurski 1983: 419). Nearly all count physical needs ('biological' or 'survival' needs for food, water, etc.) as 'basic' and many include health among basic needs (e.g. Doyal and Gough 1991, and Daniels 1985; but not Montagu 1961). Loewy counts healthcare only as a 'secondary' basic need (Loewy 1990: 20). Wiggins defines 'basic' needs more broadly as those needs whose lack would harm a person who lacked them, this harm arising either through the working of laws of nature, through invariable environmental facts or because of the human constitution (Wiggins 1985: 158). Wiggins differentiates vital from non-vital needs by moral criteria; non-vital needs may without injustice be sacrificed to the aggregated weight of other interests (Wiggins 1985: 180). As for vital needs,

> Nobody's bad, entrenched, non-substitutable need, or as one might say (exploiting the ambiguity in the adjective that was surely made for just this purpose) nobody's vital interest must be sacrificed by society to the mere desire of anybody else, or of any however large group of other people.
>
> (Wiggins 1985: 164)

Classifications, however, do not in themselves constitute an explanatory theory of needs, only a constituent of it. One, characteristically neo-Aristotelian, approach to such a theory addresses the question of how all a person's needs relate to each other, and how they relate to other people's needs and other 'values'. This invokes an account of moral experience or of a person's moral biography (e.g. Midgley 1980: 341) to correct the taxonomists' tendency to produce fragmented lists of needs. This account of needs situates them as a special instance of more generic moral standpoint with its own philosophical or theological grounding, independent of a theory of needs. For instance, Wiggins argues that needs claims are one candidate for and part (but only part) of what constitutes a claim of rights (Wiggins 1985: 169–70,173); Solomon sees them as a consideration of justice (Solomon 1993: 153, 235).

Another strategy is to define needs as universal means which are necessary to humans for pursuing any ends at all, irrespective of the character of those ends (e.g. Doyal and Gough 1991: 54, 73, 79, 160; Ramsay 1992: 6, 13, 32, 37, 39, 70, 91, 111, 201); or as the necessary means to broad, generic ends such as species-normal functioning (Daniels 1985: 26,50,53,57) or flourishing or humans' aversion to misery (Wiggins 1985: 168–9, 154, 156–7, 191n14, 162); or as means to a generic end itself such as objectivation of the human essence (cf. Heller 1976: ch. 2). When this account of needs is not also taken as a special application or branch of a wider moral philosophy, it is presented as the preliminary or foundation of such a wider moral philosophy. Starting from a person's self-interest, their own ends whatever they happen to have, an account of needs is sublated into morals by appeal to reciprocal aid in needs meeting (an example is analysed in detail in Chapter 9). The point of the manoeuvre is to conflate claims about needs with moral judgements (e.g. Ramsay 1992: 17, 41).

The second main category of needs theories avoids this difficulty by taking a biological starting-point in empirical descriptions and analyses of human behaviour, and explaining needs in that context (evolutionary, biological, ethological, anthropological). This category too presents variants.

Biological conditions for individuals' survival or reproduction (or for the effective functioning of genes' human 'survival machines', as Dawkins puts it; Dawkins 1978: 52) are equated with needs in one variant. Among these one finds, unsurprisingly, writers whose primary interests are in genetics or physiology. However, the approach also has antecedents in evolutionary ethics in nineteenth-century Britain and Germany besides being found in the works of a scatter of heterodox philosophers such as Midgley and Timpanaro. These approaches start from putatively scientific accounts of the sources of human action, reconstructed from the findings of human biology, genetics and the more biologically or neurologically inclined psychological theories of motivation. Their biological orientation makes these accounts of needs pay greater heed than most philosophically oriented theorists to the idea that human needs are also intrinsically connected with what might be called the negative aspects of humans' lives: arbitrariness, contingency and tragedy, and illness and mortality (Timpanaro 1980: 45, 61). Such theories are directly relevant to the analysis of health needs and healthcare needs. They more or less explicitly regard the natural sciences as the paradigm of well-founded knowledge, including the bases for practical reason.

A psychological variant equates needs with drives, using a theory of motivation to specify human needs concretely. With obviously different practical implications, four main forms of this approach are as follows: classical Marxism (Marx and Engels 1975; Dietzgen 1906: 122–3, 137–8, 141); Taylorism and other managerial writers (e.g. Kast and Rosenzweig 1981); Mayo and subsequent 'humanist' psychologists such as Herzberg and Maslow; and psychoanalysis.

Humanist motivational theories have also produced taxonomies of needs. For instance, Alderfer differentiates needs for existence, relatedness and growth (Alderfer 1972: 6–21, 30–50); Herzberg, motivators and satisfiers (Herzberg 1959); and Maslow's hierarchy of needs is well known (Maslow 1954). Freudian theory is considerably more flexible and complex, classifying drives (and in that sense, needs) according to their origins and degree of consciousness (as pre-conscious, conscious or unconscious-repressed). Many adherents of the different psychological variants present the successful practical manipulation of drives and motives (whether in management, clinical practice, political activity, education or marketing, depending on the case) as practical evidence of the scientificity of their favoured theory.

Both variants generate developmental theories of how needs, in the sense of drives, are formed, and how and why they vary. Of course these developmental theories also differ, partly according to the general theory of motivation from which they spring. Better-known examples include behaviourism (e.g. Skinner 1973), expectancy theory (Vroom 1964), path–goal theory (Georgopoulous, Mahoney and Jones 1957), equity theory (Adams 1963) and the 'need–goal–action' model (cf. Armstrong 1988). Historical materialism also contains an embryonic theory of the development of needs as motives, laying heavy emphasis on the historicity of needs, their social formation and satisfaction, and the formative (and deforming) influences of ideology and of language (Voloshinov 1973; Dietzgen 1906).

Obviously the empirical element of these approaches is susceptible to scientific criticism. Maslow's theory has been criticised on pre-dictive grounds as inflexible, primitive and empirically implausible (Doyal and Gough 1991: 36; Hicks and Gullett 1981; Smith 1978: 135–7), and for ignoring some biologically based drives such a parental love (Smith 1978: 137). However, a logical criticism also arises. Previously (ch1§2) we noted four assertions which are typically implicit in a claim about needs: a claim about empirical characteristics of the person said to have needs; a claim that this gives that person a reason for action; the speaker agrees that that person ought to get what he needs; and a claim that the listener ought to agree with the latter assertion. Existing analyses of needs in general, and healthcare needs specifically, vary in how completely and successfully they cover all four elements and explain the connections between them. Taxonomic, biological or psychological theories of needs tend in effect to analyse the first two elements fairly thoroughly but run into difficulties explaining the other two. Some (e.g. Maslow and Dawkins, to name but two) move between the empirical to the other elements as though they were equivalent and this move were unproblematic. Of course, it is not unproblematic, taking its advocates across two well-known philosophical minefields.

Moore's criticism of the 'naturalistic fallacy' was that moral judgements (here, about needs) cannot logically be deduced from factual, even scientific, statements, including statements about drives and motives. Descriptions of what drives or motives humans have are simply statements of biological fact which do not of themselves compel moral assent (Moore 1929: ch. 7). One can always ask, 'I want X – but ought I to have it?' Some recent writers are willing to admit that claims about needs have some normative force; but although needs are a 'reason for action' they are just one such reason among many that the moral thinker can conscientiously accept, reject or countervail (e.g. Seedhouse 1988: 129, 132–3).

Anyone wishing to argue both that needs have a biological or psychological basis, and that one can accept the practical conclusions of the needs theory intellectually freely, on grounds of its truth or validity (or however one understands the counterpart of these in respect of practical reason), also confronts the classic philosophical problem of free will. To define 'needs' in biological terms suggests that, like the contents of our drives, motives and thoughts, our needs are 'externally' determined, inescapable and unchangeable. In that case, the standard presentation of the problem continues, both our needs and our ethical moral judgements about them are an effect of our genes or our social environment or both, having nothing to do with their truth or validity and not amenable to reasoned criticism. Dawkins, for instance, sometimes writes as though the only agents in human affairs were genes, treating the rest of the organism which literally personifies the gene as essentially the genes' 'survival machine' (Dawkins 1978: 21f). A very few writers, including Skinner, tackle the problem head-on by arguing that free will is only illusory (Skinner 1973: 14, 19, 37–8, 53, 58, 96).

Yet such theories of needs are defective, not because they are inconsistent with existing philosophical theories of free will, but empirically. It is a commonplace – but nevertheless true – that in fact people do sometimes change their opinions, moral positions, motives and (in that sense) needs by reasoning, by arguing with other people or by acquiring new knowledge. Radical behaviourism and the cruder forms of geneticist biology throw out the baby of these facts with the metaphysical bathwater of notions of the soul, of regarding the human mind as independent of the thinker's body, and of the fallacious assumption that any mental contents (including needs as motives) must be invalid simply because they are determined (as opposed to being invalid because they are determined in specific ways). Similarly, Moore's challenge to explain how factual assertions alone can ever imply moral conclusions demands an answer as much in respect of claims about needs as claims about right and wrong. More concretely, attempts to base a theory of needs on 'empirical' accounts of motives run a strong risk of uncritically justifying any *de facto* motivations as 'needs', taking a naively conservative and parochial view of human needs in doing so – for instance, by assuming that people intrinsically 'need' whatever consumer goods firms currently offer, as many marketing theorists do (Kotler and Clarke 1987: 5–6) or concentrating on identifying workers' needs which managers can harness using rewards and penalties (Rose 1989: 124).

At the opposite extreme another group of theories do show sensitivity to the philosophical problem of getting from empirical premises to moral conclusions; so much sensitivity, indeed, that they concentrate on analysing the two practical (the third and fourth) elements of claims of needs and simply deny any deduction of these from the first (empirical) element. These theories of needs tend to be strongly anti-naturalistic, denying the derivation of judgements about needs from statements about drives, motives, genes, evolution, society or any other purely empirical matter. Usually they analyse needs through the specialised application of a more general ethical theory. These general ethical theories are postulated on a priori grounds, often metaphysical or theological, for example an account of the 'human essence' or the 'human species', or human life as 'narrative'. One example is Hegelian Marxism (cp. Heller 1976 *passim*), which Wiggins rightly attacks for its

> philosophically debilitating refusal to say anything that will forejudge any part of the substance of the public criterion of need that it is supposed history will supply or to anticipate in any other way the needs that some future 'consciousness exceeding its bounds' will acknowledge as properly expressive of 'human essence'.
>
> (Wiggins 1985: 150–1)

Hegelian Marxism, however, is not the only account of needs that is debilitated in this way, nor the most debilitated. Neo-Aristotelian accounts of needs in terms of 'flourishing' or 'harm' (e.g. Seedhouse

17

1988: 9, 89, 129, 132, 151) are no less evacuated. This evacuation has the polemical advantage that one can fill out such terms as 'flourishing' and 'harm' with one's own substantive moral preferences and to that extent assimilate these writers' views on needs to one's own. It also makes it easy for these theories to be critical about whether particular social institutions or individuals' drives represent needs. However, the price is that no empirical grounds can be adduced in support of this criticism or for claims about needs (specifically, to ground the third and fourth elements in claims about needs). All that can be done is to appeal to 'our' intuitions about language, logic and morals, which are taken more or less on trust in the process.

An extreme position is methodologism; the attempt to justify a theory (in this case, on needs) purely by arguing that it reasons by sound methods, completely ignoring whether any factual evidence can be adduced for its substantive claims (Timpanaro 1980: 186–91). Rational choice accounts of needs, including contractarian accounts, are examples. Despite claiming to appeal to 'our' intuitions about logic, these theories introduce some strange, indeed bizarre decision rules (e.g. Rawls 1972: 17–22). The best-known example is the contractarian contrivance of starting one's reasoning about (*inter alia*) needs from a purely imaginary 'initial position' of a mentally healthy adult who is omniscient in some matters and utterly ignorant in others. Although the point can only be asserted here, these laboured decision rules themselves tacitly introduce substantive moral judgements and assumptions about political economy, formulated at a high level of generality, in order to guarantee further moral judgements about needs, equality, property and so on (MacPherson 1962: 19–29, 263–71; Sheaff 1979: ch. 3).

At least the third type of theory does address the question of how empirical claims about people relate to claims about what they need. This is done by analysing 'needs' as universal means, the means to whatever substantive goals a person happens to have (Doyal and Gough; Ramsay; and in a different way, Skinner). Empirical evidence can be cited to specify what these instrumental needs are (Doyal and Gough (1991: 4, 54, 155) and Ramsay (1992: 8, 111f) include health among them). To claim that these are means to any ends implies that the speaker of a claim about needs, his or her listener and the third party to whom the needs are attributed all have these needs in common. Then it is argued on grounds of consistency to argue that what the reader accepts that she needs, hence ought to get, the third party also ought to get.

Yet in doing so these theories elide various empirical and logical problems and insert various *non sequitur*s between the two empirical elements in claims about needs and the (third and fourth) practical elements (see Chapter 19). A problem with this approach is the fragility of the empirical claim that absolutely everyone, in all conditions, needs certain things (health, autonomy, etc.) as means to whatever ends they may have. Strictly speaking it only takes one counter-example to demolish each such claim and Freud alone provides several (e.g. Freud 1936: 36, 49). An obvious reply is that surely a generalisation about means would suffice, withstanding the exceptional counter-example but leaving the main argument substantially intact for practical purposes? This reveals the logical problem. Precisely because it admits exceptions, a generalisation would not *guarantee* that their readers have to accept the substantive recommendations about needs that these writers wish to make. Because defining something as a 'need' typically appears to give it the writer's endorsement (ch1§2), virtuous writers understandably want morally 'good' characteristics (such as autonomy, altruism and, of course, health) to count as 'real', 'human' needs and 'bad' characteristics such as competitiveness, egoism and invasiveness not to (Fitzgerald 1978: 200; Midgley 1980: 41). Their pursuit of guarantees and insistence that needs are universal reveal that these theorists are assuming that the only way to theorise the practical (third and fourth) elements in claims about needs is to theorise them as moral judgements; and their subsequent attempts to analyse moral judgements in terms of needs confirm this. Not only does this assumption remain to be proved, not least because there are non-moral absolute uses of 'needs' also to explain (ch1§2), but this approach to analysing moral judgements in terms of needs has problems of its own, as Chapter 9 explains. Lastly an analysis of needs in terms of universal means explains only the hypothetical use of 'needs', not the absolute use.

Existing theories of needs, then, founder on a dilemma. Either they sustain their preferred moral judgements about needs by evacuating the theory of needs of scientific content at best and by encrusting it with dubious metaphysical and pseudo-logical obfuscations at worst; or they elaborate an empirical, scientific content without any defensible means of generating the practical implications that give the concept of needs its relevance and importance for (among other things) health policy. These difficulties stem largely from a precipitate and question-begging assumption that claims about needs can only be moral judgements. Moral judgements are not deducible from claims

19

about the drives, motives, biology or genes of particular individuals; they apply universally and reciprocally to all humans. No wonder that such theories present needs in a literally disembodied way, as universal claims, not about particular individuals' needs but about needs common to all humankind (Wiggins 1985: 162, 164; and cp. Chapter 1); or that theories of needs that start from biology or psychology or social theories have difficulty in generating such abstract moral conclusions about needs.

§2 NEEDS AND NATURALISM

With 'needs' for 'healthcare', as with other concepts, a defensible theory must at least explore the logical and semantic relationships between, and the implications of, claims using the terms under analysis, explaining their sense, reference and 'adjacent concepts' in a way that is superior to other accounts (cf. Freeden on 'rights', 1991: 2, 10; Lamb on 'death', 1985: 12). Preceding arguments (ch2§1) have indicated what a complete explanation would cover.

It would, first, analyse the four claims typically combined in claims about needs, i.e. the claims that:

1 the relation between a person (or other subject) and a need-satisfier (a state of affairs or an action) satisfies the empirical criteria for attributing a need;
2 this person has reason to have the state of affairs in question (irrespective of whether anyone else also has reason to have it);
3 the speaker has reason to agree that that person get what he or she putatively needs;
4 the listener (or reader or ...) also has reason to agree that that person get what he or she putatively needs.

In respect of the first of these, a complete theory of needs would explain what the empirical criteria of needing are; to what characteristics of the person, the need-satisfier and relation between them the term 'need' implicitly refers. In consequence a complete analysis of 'needs' must explain why the relation between someone having a need and lacking what he or she needs only holds contingently and generally (as the word 'implicature' suggests) rather than necessarily (as 'implication' would suggest) (see ch1§2). In respect of the second element, it must also explain what kind of 'ought' is implied by the assertion that the person to whom the need is attributed (if not the listener or reader) has a reason for action to get the satisfier. The latter 'ought' might be a moral 'ought', a legal 'ought' or a prudential 'ought', or some other kind again. Similarly, what kind of 'ought' is involved when a speaker recommends that someone get what they need (element 3), and the grounds for this recommendation, are seldom transparent and demand analysis, as do the corresponding points in respect of the listener (element 4).

A rounded analysis of needs must cover all four of the above points, explaining coherently how they are logically related. To ascertain when it is valid to make the second claim on the strength of the first requires an analysis of what the empirical 'warrant' for attributing a need is, for example whether it is supervenience, reference, application of a logical rule or some other warrant. It also requires an analysis of what evidence is relevant, and the conditions under which that evidence can be claimed to be available. To know when the move from the second to the third claim is valid requires an analysis of the relations between the speaker's desires (or motives, purposes or 'values'; which of these terms applies requires analysis in itself) and the state of affairs in which the other person or group gets what they putatively need – healthcare, income support or whatever the case involves. Similarly, to know when it is valid to assert the claim requires an analysis of the relations between the speaker's desires (or motives, purposes or values) and those of his or her hearer(s).

To minimise question-begging, a theory of needs must rely as little as possible on substantive moral assumptions. It would certainly be question-begging not to demarcate clearly between 'our' conceptions of 'need', embodied in everyday discourse about needs (including policy documents) and whatever conception of need is actually consistent and valid. Moral or policy judgements must follow from the theory, not precede or ground it, if the theory is to give non-question-begging reasons for adopting substantive practical judgements about health and healthcare needs. We have seen (ch2§1) that many theories of needs place themselves either on a dubious empirical footing or none by prematurely conflating morality with practical reason *per se*. One thing to clarify here is just what types of practical reasoning are involved in making claims about needs. At a higher level of generality all this implies that a theory of needs must also, so far as possible, avoid prejudging wider metaethical debates on the characterisation of moral statements and their referents. In particular the term 'values' will be avoided as heavily theory-laden. As a generic term for both moral and non-moral practical judgements and for both judgements to do with needs and those that are not, the term 'practical judgements' will be used here. All these reasons caution against rushing precipitately into a moralised theory of needs until that becomes positively necessary because other types of practical reasoning (prudential, legal, etc.) have been exhausted. More positively, these considerations imply that a theory of need must incorporate among its foundations the relevant empirical findings of the biological, psychological and social sciences. To that extent, a theory of needs must be synoptic, tracing the relations between the contiguous parts of these disciplines and healthcare ethics.

For these reasons the present strategy will be to see how far we can ground practical judgements about health and healthcare needs naturalistically, from relevant findings of the biological, psychological and social sciences, before 'stepping up' from an empirical and prudential to a moral account of needs. Yet a theory of needs must eventually address the relation between needs and morality, for at least some uses of 'needs' seem moralised (see ch1§1), and this too must be analysed and explained (see Chapter 9). Other theorists' difficulties suggest that this task should only be approached after a thorough analysis of the empirical and pre-moral assumptions involved in claims about needs.

This approach also offers epistemological advantages. Many ethical theorists assume that the closer the epistemological parallels between an ethical theory (in this case, a theory of needs) and science, the surer the grounding of that ethical theory. This view is also accepted here, though only assumed rather than argued from first principles in the depth that it merits. To minimise earlier theories' difficulties a theory of needs must at least have a logically transparent structure (displaying its assumptions and qualifications explicitly) and, insofar as it is naturalistic, be predictive (verifiable or falsifiable), and hence corrigible. Yet as Timpanaro argues, to mimic the epistemological form of a science is insufficient to establish the scientificity of a theory. The theory must also be compatible with, or even incorporate, the substantive findings of the relevant empirical sciences. This is another reason to base it on a schema that summarises the relevant empirical findings in biology, social theory and the psychology of cognition and motivation. The biggest weakness of this book will be the impossibility of doing more than refer to a little of this material here.

One empirical observation especially must be accommodated: the experience, as most ethicists stress, that our desires are able to motivate or to restrain our actions, especially our moral desires and desires connected with practical reasoning, notwithstanding any scientific explanation of our actions. If actions are to be explained in terms of desires, if desires are to be accommodated within a motivational account of drives, and drives then explained scientifically (in biological and genetic terms) any empirically plausible theory of needs must nevertheless explain how desires, reasons, other 'contents of consciousness' (and processes of consciousness) contribute to human action and to the formation and identification of needs. A theory of needs must at some point address the questions of how needs, or beliefs about them, can motivate action through the medium of desires and reasoning. It must also explain how the concept of needs is used to criticise both desires and drives, and in what senses claims about needs are (ch1§1) at least partly rationally and publicly corrigible and criticisable (on grounds that require elucidation). The positive lesson to draw from the failure of scientifically based theories of needs to address philosophical problems that these requirements pose is that a defensible theory of needs must also explain when claims about needs are true (or at least valid) and why. To illuminate the substantive applied problems of healthcare ethics a theory of needs must also indicate grounds on which to criticise putative 'needs' and prioritise among genuine needs; criticise desires as reasons for action, in terms of needs; and elucidate grounds for deciding whether and whose needs should be satisfied. Then it would become possible to relate needs to the issues of healthcare practice, healthcare management and health system design from which we started (ch1§1).

§3 NEEDS AND DRIVES

A central task for a viable theory of needs is to theorise the interfaces between an empirical, scientific theory of human drives and human nature on the one hand, and, on the other, the logical parameters determining when the practical recommendations, both prudential and moral, involved in claims about needs are valid and why (ch2§1). Claims about needs typically recommend states of affairs, sometimes prudentially and sometimes morally. This is to recommend actions, whether actions by the person to whom a need is imputed or by whoever else would have to act (or deliberately do nothing) in order to realise the need (ch1§2). Thus the needed state of affairs must be a possible object of action by whoever ought to realise it. Any theory of needs therefore presupposes a theory of human action. That is the main interface at which the two major constituents of a theory of needs meet.

A state of affairs that is needed is one that someone has reason to bring about and in that sense ought to bring about (ch1§2). It must therefore be one that can be realised by human action (including negative actions – deliberately doing nothing) although not necessarily the action of the person to whom the need is attributed. The perimeter both of a general account of human action and of valid practical recommendations on grounds of needs must therefore be the range of contingently possible human motives, actions and their objectives (cp. MacLagan 1951: 183). So the logical parameter that most clearly and precisely relates to the scientific parameters noted above is the ' "ought" implies "can" ' dictum. This dictum restricts this range of needed states of affairs to those that are both logically conceivable and causally can exist as a result of human action. A state of affairs in which everyone lives to be 200 years old probably does not satisfy this condition. A state of affairs in which I can be immunised against smallpox does satisfy it; and a state of affairs in which everyone's healthcare needs are met is an unclear case. The action necessary to realise what we need must lie within someone's 'physical and psychological power to do' (Hare's formulation, 1972: 79, remains as lucid as any). It places factual constraints on the range of logically possible practical judgements, among them possible judgements about 'needs'. By virtue of its content the ' "ought" implies "can" ' dictum applies to all practical recommendations, whether they be moral, prudential, or any other kind. Whatever kind of practical assertions claims about needs involve, they will only be valid if they comply with the ' "ought" implies "can" ' dictum.

An ambiguity surfaces in speaking of what human motives 'can' do and of human 'powers' to act. To speak of 'our powers' or of what our nature 'permits' us to do might be thought to suggest the idea of a limit, within which human motives are completely undetermined by the body, and subject only to the influence of reason. This dualistic interpretation is widespread among philosophers. However, a second interpretation is available. This is the idea of motivation, 'allowing' us to act in a more positive sense: that what energises us to act at all, and in that sense enables us to act, is a set of drives that are, in a way yet to be explained, given by our biological, more specifically our genetic, nature. On this view, our biological nature not only limits the range of possible human actions, but is the positive source of our actions. The second, positive sense of what humans 'can' do, implies the first (although not vice versa). Although we owe all our actions to our drives, the range of actions that our drives stimulate is limited by the character of these drives. To say that our drives and hence our actions

24

are 'determined' is to say that they occur in specific ways and on specific occasions determined by our physiology. They are so constituted by our physiology as to be capable of occurring (i.e. acting) in some ways and not others. However, the converse does not hold; the negative understanding of what humans 'can' do does not imply any specific positive view of how human action occurs.

Only a positive theory of how human action occurs is tenable nowadays. It is as necessary for an account of action as for an account of non-conscious behaviour (reflexes, etc.). Inexorably the evidence continues to accumulate that human drives and motivation are physiological, bodily activities. (Good summaries of its current growth point are Jack Copeland and Patricia Churchland's contributions to the neurophilosophy debate – Copeland 1993; Churchland 1986.) There is, second, an ontological argument although here it can only be stated as a premiss. What exists, and can be known to exist, are the referents of evidentially and practically (experimentally) well-grounded science. On this view, claims about what type of entities exist are contingent, empirical claims. This implies that well-founded scientific claims give all, and the only, evidence for the existence of entities that is available. The results of modern sciences point much more strongly to drives being physiological entities (in this case, processes) than to their being the activity or mode of being of a non-physical, indeed metaphysical, 'free will' or 'soul'. Ethicists who want to assume or to analyse the fact of reasoned, conscious practical choice must articulate why this fact is compatible with, or even a corollary of, a scientific theory of drives. A theory that represents choice as a faculty of the residual, gradually decreasing part of human consciousness which cannot be explained in scientific, physiological terms is likely to share the fate of anti-evolutionist theory; and deservedly. What we 'can' do must therefore be theorised, not in the second way but in the first, naturalistically and scientifically. The previous section argued that, as far as possible, a theory of needs should have a factual, scientific foundation. Part of that foundation, it has been argued, is an account of human action and hence of drives. A scientifically based account of drives intrinsically furnishes the second, positive kind of account of what we 'can' do.

Such an account of human motivation traces some of the motivational contents of our consciousness back to drives entering our consciousness from other body systems. We are directly conscious of these drives both as immediate occurrent bodily stimuli (hunger, pain, etc.) and as a general state of motivational, practical energy, as our ability to will and to initiate action independently of immediately occurrent bodily stimuli. To argue that human biology furnishes the necessary consciousness and initial motivational contents of consciousness leaves open the possibility that further determinants of motivation – knowledge, intellectual and decision-making capacities – might be added through social relationships or generated as it were internally to consciousness by the thinking brain itself. Indeed the co-formation of motivation and behaviour through social contact, above all with parents, appears to be an evolutionary characteristic of many species of 'higher' animals (Midgley 1980: 53f, 307). Our evolution from other animals suggests that we are like them in this respect.

Yet we also know, as another 'contents of consciousness', that our conscious reasoning, decision and volition can influence, divert, delay or stop us from acting. At least some of our desires are, to that extent, products of our consciousness itself in addition to whatever the sources of drives external to consciousness initiate their formation. This presupposes that our desires, our reasoning, our reasons for acting and our biologically given motives are of an ontological, indeed of a causal, kind. This is so, notwithstanding the fact that they are all conscious; indeed, because of it. Only a compatibilist account of consciousness can accommodate both the facts about the physiological sources of much of our motivation, and the fact that we can consciously form and re-form our own motives. Our consciousness is a flow of simultaneously mental and physiological events. They are of three main kinds:

1 Contents of consciousness whose occurrence we cannot consciously control. In having these contents our consciousness is relatively passive. Sensations are one instance but certain types of motivation (hunger, thirst, tiredness) are another.
2 Those in which we spontaneously generate new mental products of our own making (including occasions when we use contents of consciousness resulting from the first, more passive processes as raw material): the processes of thinking, imagining, dreaming and the like.
3 Those in which we consciously initiate bodily action.

When it is anything more sophisticated than instant intuition our reasoning about actions in general, and specifically about actions to do with needs, is a process in which we derive reasons for action from anterior reasons by some process of conscious inference. This is so, irrespective of whether the inferences are logically valid or the

26

opposite. At one end of this chain of inferences is a volition that initiates action. At the other end, the regress to anterior contents of consciousness must stop somewhere. The foregoing implies that where it stops, so far as our consciousness is concerned, is at those drives that are given by our biology, much as sensations are. This account of conscious volition leaves open the possibility that the chain of inferences may be extremely convoluted, muddled, and influenced by several different drives at once. It leaves open the question of how far, and in what ways, learning, language, logic and knowledge contribute to, or even constitute, these inferential convolutions. Also it leaves open the possibility that different degrees and types of consciousness may be involved in different inferences or at different points in a long chain of inference. (Sometimes we concentrate hard on our practical thinking and in forming our desires and volitions; at other times we do so in ways that are little more than reflexive.)

This mode of explanation takes drives, consciousness in general and desires specifically, to be physical processes, the activity of the central nervous system and the other body systems. 'We' are conscious bodies. Nothing in this should surprise anyone with a nineteenth-century knowledge of physiology. The evidence is familiar and ever-accumulating that contents of consciousness and mental acts of many kinds (moods, perceptions, sensations, beliefs, neologisms) can be created and influenced by drugs, surgery and physical trauma (see Churchland 1986: 68–9, 82–3). These are one special case of manipulating the conscious body; another is by manipulating it cognitively through speech and other forms of communication (which implies through social contact). It is entirely conceivable that one day clinical and pharmacological interventions will become precise enough to be able to create specific, predetermined consciousness in a patient. Concomitantly, it is conceivable that a future neurophysiology will be able to specify what configuration of neurone activity constitutes each drive, desire, thought or inference. Informatics methods such as neural networking and parallel processing are gradually imitating more closely the information processing that we also carry out consciously, including the ability to learn through practical experience (Churchland 1986: 113, 127, 129, 137, 199; Ifeachor 1993). The culmination of the tendencies would be to discover exact correspondence of bodily activity with contents of consciousness, so that a description in terms of bodily activity would be translatable into a description of thought content and vice versa. The two discourses, the physiological discourse and subjective discourse (in terms of motives and other contents of consciousness) would practically become directly intertranslatable. At present rates of progress this convergence seems likely to occur one day and unlikely to occur suddenly or soon.

A compatibilist account of drives is therefore the point at which an empirical account of needs in terms of drives makes contact with the logical requirements that an account of needs as 'values' (for instance, as 'valued' states of affairs) must satisfy, if that account is to be logically tenable as a source of practical guidance. Factual and logical considerations converge in grounding a theory of needs in an account of drives. Indeed they meet at something like the premiss of Bentham's version of utilitarianism:

> Nature has placed mankind under the governance of two sovereign masters, *pain* and *pleasure*. It is for them alone to point out what we ought to do, as well as to determine what we shall do. On the one hand the standard of right and wrong, on the other chain of causes and effects, are fastened to their throne .... The *principle of utility* recognises this subjection.
>
> (Bentham 1948: §1, original emphasis)

Utilitarianism is often criticised for the error of 'deducing' substantive moral assertions too immediately from an empirical claim about motivation. Less often noticed is what makes Bentham's argument nevertheless so plausible. This is his assumption that one function of practical reason is to make us conscious of the motivation that we – not 'reason' or logic, morality or the law – already and inevitably supply to all our volitions and action. This part of Bentham's reasoning is valid; the main difficulty with classical utilitarianism lies not there but in its obsolete and falsely reductionist theory of motivation. As Thomson puts it – although he disagrees with analysing needs in terms of drives – a modern counterpart of the utilitarians' motivational 'sovereigns' is to conceive of needs as homeostatic lack initiating a drive (Thomson 1987: 13).

Claims about needs typically recommend some course of action, asserting that (ch1§2):

1 the relation between a person (or other subject) and state of affairs (or corresponding action) satisfies the empirical criteria for attributing a need;

2 the person in question thereby has a reason to have the state of affairs in question (irrespective of whether anyone else also has such a reason);

3 the utterer of the claim also has reason for that person to get (or do) what he or she putatively needs;

4 the audience of the claim also has reason for that person to get what he or she putatively needs.

All uses of 'need' imply that the person having the need has reasons to try to realise the state of affairs that he or she needs, irrespective of whether anyone else has reason to realise it too. Indeed some claims about instrumental needs assert just that (ch1§1). The needed state of affairs must be the possible object of action by whoever has reason to realise it. Assuming that all human action is motivated by drives (a point requiring further analysis – ch3§1), to call something a possible object for action is to say that it is the possible object of a human drive. In this case, the relevant drives are those of whoever ought to realise the putatively needed state of affairs. If 'needs' expresses a prudential reason or an instrumental need, the implied prudential 'ought' necessarily applies only to the person to whom the need is imputed. The allegedly needed state of affairs must therefore be a possible object of drives that he or she (biologically) can have. Here a claim about needs implicitly refers in this indirect way to the drives of the individual to whom the need is attributed. It necessarily involves the first two of the above elements although, depending on the circumstances, it might also involve the third and fourth elements, and more often does than does not. For instance, moral judgements formulated in terms of 'needs' imply that everybody ought to try to realise the needed state of affairs, if they can. The state of affairs to be created must then be a possible object of the drives of all these people, including the person to whom the need is attributed.

The common feature in all these uses of 'needs' is the implication that the needed state of affairs must be the object of a possible drive of at least the person to whom the need is imputed. On one hand, claims about needs imply that what is needed must be the objects of possible actions and hence of the corresponding possible drives. On the other, to speak of a need implies a reference to someone who has the need (ch1§2). This implies that the drives in question are those of the people who have the need under discussion. The surface grammar of the word 'need' also suggests this. These persons' possible drives must therefore be either a part of, or the whole, empirical criterion for attributing a need. Here, as previously, 'possible' means 'both logically and (more narrowly) causally possible'.

An analysis of needs in terms of drives is therefore as necessary a foundation for an explanation of when recommendations for action that are grounded on needs are valid and why, as it more obviously is for an account of needs in biological, psychological and social terms. Note that what is being proposed here is an account of needs *in terms of* drives, not an account of needs *as* drives. The latter is ruled out by the fact that the concept of 'need' can be used, *inter alia*, to criticise our drives. Analysing needs in terms of drives does not compel us to accept that all drives are needs, and thus all drives are in some sense (yet to be explained) defensible or valid or 'values' in terms of critical practical reason. One could, for instance, argue that not all drives count as needs although some do; or that some of the biologically possible drives to which 'needs' refers are counterfactual. These remain open questions at this stage in the argument. However, the above considerations do imply that the relationship between the person who needs and what they need, which is the empirical criterion of both prudential and moral judgements about needs (ch1§2), lies within the domain of drives and their satisfiers. Drives and their satisfiers are the referent of the first of the four assertions made in an expressive claim about drive.

Analysing needs in terms of drives is also likely to satisfy the preceding criteria (ch2§2) for a defensible theory of needs. The approach has a scientific basis free of substantive moral judgements and minimising theoretical presumptions about the nature and logic of moral thought. Its epistemological assumptions are only the lean ones that an empirical description of drives is possible with no more 'value-ladenness' than comes into any empirical description. It immediately identifies one empirical criterion for attributing a need to a person: that he or she has a certain type of a drive (of what type still requires analysis – ch3§3). Since drives are sometimes satisfied, this immediately explains why the connection between having a need and lacking something is only a contingent conversational implicature, not an implication. An explanation in terms of drives appears able to address all four elements of the claims of needs, although exactly how requires further explanation (ch3§4). Analysing needs in terms of drives also offers the prospect of explaining why needs are reasons for action. It can obviously explain the prudential uses of 'needs'. Whether it can also explain the moral uses is at this stage an open question. However, a scientific account of drives suggests that it is a misformulation to describe drives themselves as 'reasons for action'.

Whether and how a scientific account of drives can be reconciled with the fact of consciously reasoned human choices about actions, including actions in pursuit of needs, is obscure and controversial. This problem must be addressed at the outset of a theory of needs in terms of drives; indeed, next.

§4 NEWTON AND THE NEURON

Explanations of conscious voluntary action in terms of physiologically originating drives provoke old objections. A theory explaining needs in terms of actions and actions in terms of drives confronts both specific objections to analysing needs as in terms of drives and more general objections to regarding all human motivation, including drives, as physiological processes.

To regard drives as physiological processes seems 'overly' deterministic, say Doyal and Gough (1991: 35). It would imply that human action generally, and the pursuit of needs specifically, are caused; that every one of our practical decisions is fully determined by anterior events and fully predictable from them. If choice is a physiological process its outcomes could not have been other than they were, given the causal inputs to it. If we explain needs in terms of drives, and drives as physiological processes, our belief that we choose our actions is illusory. We do not, indeed cannot, really choose what to do. But as we know, our choices are not fully determined by our physiology (Doyal and Gough 1991: 39). We can override physiological drives and our needs. Our needs, says Thomson, do not compel us to act (Thomson 1987: 14, 23). They are not related directly to action even though they do tend to produce action once a person knows what he or she needs (Thomson 1987: 99). Thus, 'people can force themselves to do things on the basis of what they consider to be good reasons when their instincts, so to speak, are screaming the opposite' (Doyal and Gough 1991: 39). Humans, unlike animals, can modify, check, divert or frustrate their own needs (cf. Flew 1978: 45). These objectors agree that our behaviour sometimes has physiological causes, but only those behaviours whose origins bypass consciousness altogether – for example, reflexes. The argument that our action is not externally compelled is deployed against both a physiological account of drives and thus against an account of needs in terms of such drives.

If choice is really an illusion, the objections continue, we do not choose our beliefs, desires or reasons for acting any more than we choose our actions. We think what our circumstances and physiology cause us to think. A physiological account of choice thus requires us to give up speaking about 'intentions' or 'purposes', 'desires' or 'reasons' in any sense suggesting that these conscious motives decide our volition or action (cp. Flew 1978: 99f). Such concepts would be redundant if our central nervous system, our genes or some other biological process were really what initiates our actions. But then, continues the objection, we would also have to give up evaluating people's desires and motives. Explaining behaviour physiologically (for instance, in terms of drives) would make it logically impossible to criticise people's desires or motives or choices of action, or to evaluate their reasons for acting in terms of truth or validity (or morality). Anterior causes, not individuals' reasons or choices, would then be responsible for humans' actions and it is logically impossible to categorise causes as valid or invalid, as blameworthy or the opposite.

Intuitively, it does often seem that to explain an action is in some way to legitimate or justify it. This is perhaps why some people round upon attempts to 'explain' criminality or deviance as fostering a 'culture of excuses' (Riddell's account of the 1988 Conservative Party Central Council describes a classic example – Riddell 1989: 171). More sophisticated thinkers rarely advocate ignorance as plainly as that but they still insist on separating explanations of actions in terms of drives from the justification of action. Just as blaming people for physiologically caused actions would be futile, so trying to persuade them to act otherwise would be pointless, no matter how sound the reasons that were put to them (including reasons to do with needs). One way of summarising these points is to say that behaviours and drives are not equivalent to reasons for action (cf. Doyal and Gough 1991: 53).

More specifically, objectors argue that equating needs and drives makes it impossible to criticise drives on grounds of needs. But, they argue, such criticisms are possible so the terms 'drive' and 'need' are not equivalent:

> Drives primarily explain behaviour; needs primarily justify it: hunger and thirst must be distinguished from the need for food and water. The primary role of needs is to indicate what we ought to do in the name of self-interest: needs are justificatory reasons or values rather than explanatory reasons.
>
> (Thomson 1987: 13–14; and cp.
> Doyal and Gough 1991: 37–8)

Some drives, such as a drive for alcohol, are not needed and some needs (e.g. for exercise) have no corresponding drive (Doyal and Gough 1991: 36; Thomson 1987: 13). Explaining needs in terms of drives also, it is objected, fails to accommodate the idea of needs as (moral) values. It has been argued that what makes X desirable is some characteristic of X, in virtue of which it is desirable. Desirability is an attribute of X itself, not its relation to anything else, for instance my drives. It is always possible to compare actual human desires with what humans ought to desire. 'Need' explains actions by reference to a perception of value; this is not how drives explain (Thomson 1987: 13). Our drives are not inherently relevant to how a person ought to live (Thomson 1987: 14), but our needs are.

Distaste for relativism grounds another objection. If needs are defined in terms of drives, and drives are always the drives of particular individuals, it allegedly becomes impossible to speak of universal, or even common, 'needs'. This removes an avenue for the reaching of consensus about needs and even for resolution of disputes about needs by rational argument. It is also alleged that relativism is self-defeating; to dismiss your claims of needs as merely relative to your own drives implies that my claims about needs can be dismissed in a similar way, hence that no well-founded claims about needs can be made at all.

Various mistakes are made in objecting that a physiological explanation of drives denies the possibility of conscious human choice. One mistake is to suppose that the physiological character of drives implies the total determination of action by non-conscious forces, as if our 'physiology' were something completely external to our consciousness, forming and stimulating our otherwise inert, passive consciousness (drives included). Either this simply (and question-beggingly) assumes that our consciousness itself cannot count as one active physiological 'cause' in its own right, or it arbitrarily takes 'cause' to mean 'external cause'. Either way, the objection relies on a very specific model of causation. Misleadingly comprehensively, Flew and others call it 'physical determinism' or 'physical causation', 'contingent necessity' or even 'materialism' (Flew 1978: 177). They assume that, given a set of causes external to an object, the object can only react in one way, determined exclusively by those external factors in combination with the laws of nature. They then assume that an account of drives as physiological processes applies these general ontological assumptions about the nature of matter and causality to the material (here, physiological) substance of our conscious processes.

The account of causation which these critics perceive in a

physiological account of drives is least inadequate to Newtonian mechanics, to explaining the behaviour of billiard balls and other middle-sized solid inert objects. Even in that special Newtonian context of comparatively inert objects, however, it does not have quite the implications that the critics suppose. Newtonian mechanics assumes that a solid object receiving, say, an external mechanical impulse reacts as it predictably does partly because of the object's own internal characteristics and structure, which therefore also enter the list of causal factors. In other contexts there is no a priori reason to suppose that an object that responds to external causal stimuli, in this case the thinking brain, cannot also and simultaneously be a modifier or even an active causal originator, of physical events in its own right. Modern conceptions of matter and causation and both main versions of modern neurophilosophical accounts of the mind (e.g. Churchland 1986) suggest that consciousness can be understood in much this way, as the activity of a material thing (i.e. the human body); hence Churchland's use of the term 'mind-brain', which will be adopted here. Ability to choose beliefs and actions is itself a physiological capacity and physiologically determined, a faculty that we have innately whether we will it or no (as Flew agrees, for very different reasons – 1978: 117). To presume that 'physiological causes' must all be 'external' to consciousness simply begs the question. There is no a priori reason to think that a mental event cannot be both conscious and physiologically caused.

Yet anti-determinists rightly insist that an explanation of needs in terms of drives must accommodate the observation that we do choose many of our actions, a fact that they theorise as 'free will' (ch2§3). The concept of free will is an attempt to articulate that it is *we* who do the choosing. Yet this is entirely compatible with stating that the 'we' who choose are physiological entities and that our choosing is one of the physiological processes that constitute us. Neither is it necessary to suppose that all the work is done by 'genes' or the central nervous system or some other sub-structure or sub-system of the mind-brain. The mind-brain, and indirectly the whole set of physiological systems on which it physiologically depends, is the author of drives, choices and volition; and of the other contents of consciousness, including thinking in the medium of language. A physiological view of drives, and hence an account of needs in terms of drives, neither denies the fact of conscious practical choice nor explains it away as an illusion.

So the objection that if choice is a physiological process, its outcomes could not have been other than they were, given the causal inputs, is a harmless truism; harmless, because it only says that if all causal factors, including the agent's thinking, had been different, the outcomes would have differed. The outcomes of the agent's practical decision-making choice do not occur inevitably, despite his or her choices, but because of the way that he or she chooses. If this outcome is predictable, it is not predictable from causes external to his or her consciousness but because of the stability of that consciousness itself. If this was a person of very strong and stable desires, beliefs and, say, moral opinions, his or her choices would be predictable, even logically inevitable given the facts and his or her moral beliefs; but still choices.

The objectors have only considered two polar theories: either that all contents of human consciousness including human choice are completely externally determined; or that they are all completely undetermined. There are many other logical possibilities. Conscious processes, including the formation of desires as the consciousness of drives, might be externally determined in some respects, internally determined in others, underdetermined in others. Different processes of consciousness (perceptions, desires, beliefs, emotions, logical thought, etc.) might be determined to different degrees and in differing ways.

The objection that theorising drives in physiological terms makes subjective discourse – about desires, purposes, intentions and so on – redundant contains a grain of truth but one whose size is overstated. If consciousness is a physiological process, our having the various beliefs, desires, sensations, decisions, volitions, etc., that we do is a matter of different types of physiological process occurring. In principle a subtle physiological science could discriminate and localise the various contents and processes of a person's consciousness. As their common referents are eventually identified, propositions about what individuals are conscious of and the corresponding propositions about their physiology will become practically intertranslatable. Yet this does not imply that one discourse is dispensable, any more than the translatability between some concepts in physics and chemistry does. Although they have common referents, the two types of description are each adapted to different uses.

Intelligent aliens who could translate physiological propositions between their own language and, say, English could describe and understand human consciousness as a set of physiological processes. But they would not necessarily be able to learn and use all our experiential concepts about consciousness (such concepts as intentionality, desires, motives, purposes, etc.) as we do, because of their presumable difficulty in relating these to any experience that they have or in imagining what our experience of intentionality would be like (much as someone blind from birth might be able to understand a physiological account of vision but not colour descriptions). Unlike them, humans can in principle make translations between, say, measurements of the intensity of the neurochemical or neuro-electrical activity that pain is, and subjective statements about what sort of pain this person is feeling (although this is technically unattainable for the foreseeable future – see Noack and McQueen 1988: 73–8). Physiological descriptions and subjective ones are also adapted towards different types of practical interventions for altering other people's consciousness. Descriptions in terms of contents of consciousness, beliefs and reasons are practically oriented towards what might be called cognitive interventions: supplying new information, giving reasons for action, expressing emotions and so on. The former are oriented towards interventions that could (given the clinical techniques) produce exactly the same contents of consciousness pharmacologically, mechanically or surgically instead. There is this much validity in the claim (Flew 1978: 164) that concepts that presuppose the use of language cannot be logically reduced to physical terms.

Physiological analyses of the beliefs that a person has, and of the mental processes by which he or she came to think them, leave us as logically able as ever we were to judge whether the propositional contents of these beliefs be true or false, valid or invalid. We do not have to presume that the contents of consciousness are a priori true or false, valid or invalid, just for being physiological events. A physiological account of consciousness accommodates the fact people can choose what to do and what to think, and make these choices on grounds of truth, consistency and evidence, or not. What a physiology of consciousness could tell us, at most, is what contents of consciousness a person has, on a particular occasion; this is different information to information about how these beliefs logically relate to each other and to whatever they are beliefs about. Only the crudest versions of sociology of knowledge and psychoanalytic theory dismiss particular beliefs as false simply because those beliefs are 'determined'. Rather, it is specific types of determination that produce false belief and then it is not the determination itself that makes the falsity but the logical relations between, say, a belief and whatever it is a belief about.

Since a physiological account of desires, as of drives generally, does not displace all responsibility for action, beliefs, motives and choices from people onto outside 'forces', it also leaves scope for praising, blaming and judging actions, and for trying to influence these actions by reasoning. Whether it leaves as much scope or the same kind of scope as received 'common sense' does, remains an open question for now, to be returned to later. Philosophical conservatives have their reasons for wishing to conserve 'our' existing concepts of when and why to praise, blame and attribute personal responsibility but it is odd to see radical theorists such as Doyal and Gough demanding the same. But this demand does not permit us to disregard physiological explanations of human action because it might embarrass 'our' moral practices. In what ways and to what extent human action is physiologically determined is a question of scientific fact which the ethicist has no theoretical discretion to accept or refuse according to whether they are too 'overly deterministic' for received ethical opinion. We may only retain the concepts and practice of blaming, praising and judging at the mercy of the facts as to what it is in humans' power to do.

These general objections to explaining needs in terms of drives, and drives in physiological terms, might almost demolish an eighteenth-century physiological account of drives and consciousness. Pitched against more modern conceptions of drives, physiology, causation and matter they pass harmlessly and irrelevantly by. Yet there remain the more specific objections to analysing needs in terms of drives.

One is easily punctured. The implausibility of existing theories of needs in terms of drives tells against empirically or conceptually feeble theories, not against all possible theories of needs in terms of drives. A more serious objection emphasises the contrast between needs (a critical concept) and drives (an empirical concept). One point of a theory of needs, and *a fortiori* a theory of needs in terms of drives, must be to criticise our existing drives (including desires) on the grounds of need. So 'drives' could not completely be substituted for 'needs' in such a theory. Yet needs must, on the above arguments (ch2§3), be the objects of contingently possible drives. A formulation in terms of contingently possible drives does not imply that all drives count as needs, nor that all putative needs have a corresponding drive. If such a formulation could also generate some way of critically differentiating needs from at least some drives, critically differentiating drives that either were needs or were connected with needs from other drives, it would escape this objection.

As for the charge of relativism, it is true that analysing needs in terms of drives implies that all drives are drives of particular individuals. Yet this does not imply that critical appraisal of an individual's drives (including desires) in terms of needs is a priori impossible, although this demands further explanation (ch3§3). Neither does it imply a priori that there are no common, or even universal, objects for different individuals' drives or needs. It all depends on what substantive theory of drives, and hence of needs, is adopted. We will have to return to these possibilities later (ch3§4). They do not remove the charge of relativism entirely but they do take much of the sting out of it.

This leaves the objection that objects are desirable (or not) by virtue of their characteristics, and that the concept of 'need' explains actions by reference to perceptions of this characteristic while explanations in terms of drive do not. However, drives also explain actions by reference to a perception of a characteristic of their object. In these cases the relevant perception (or misperception) is that the object has causal characteristics that will satisfy the drive. If the object of the drive is a person, for example one's lover, these will be personal characteristics; physical characteristics in the case of hunger; and so on. In the case of desires, the relevant characteristics are purely empirical. It is a matter of theoretical preference whether one also classifies this empirical characteristic as a 'value' but if one does it is a prudential value, not a moral value. One way in which explanations in terms of needs do differ from explanations in terms of drives is in respect of who has this perception. In the case of a drive, it is the person who has the drive who perceives (or misperceives) that the object will, as a matter of fact, satisfy his or her drive. Whether he or she has this drive and belief is a brute fact. When something is described as a need, it is usually the person so describing it who perceives the 'value', irrespective of whether it is a 'value' to him or to someone else and irrespective of whether it is a moral, prudential or some other kind of value (ch1§2). A critical difference between a need and a drive is therefore that needs have, in some way that will have to be explored, withstood a considered, critical scrutiny to which drives, considered purely as drives, have not been exposed.

Granted, an analysis of needs in terms of drives cannot immediately explicate the concept of needs as moral values. The price we pay for starting with a comparatively non-question-begging account of needs in terms of drives is that at the outset we only can analyse a pre-moral, prudential concept of 'needs' that way. Without adding further assumptions a naturalistic, hence prudential, account of needs in terms of drives is not equivalent to a theory of morals. Neither does it immediately explain the senses in which needs can be theorised as 'values', moral or non-moral. Any remaining ways of criticising drives and desires exclude moral criticisms; but whether this excludes all possible types of criticism remains to be seen.

In summary, the strongest objections of analysing needs in terms of drives are weaker than they first seem and the rest are nugatory. The next task is therefore to elaborate a theory of drives as the basis and perimeter for a theory of needs (ch3§§1–2). Since 'needs' is a critical concept, it will then be necessary to review the ways in which drives, so theorised, might be susceptible to criticism (ch3§3). Then we will at last be in a position to relate needs, at least in this sense, to health and healthcare (Chapters 4–8).

3

NEEDS, NATURE AND SOCIETY

§1 DRIVES AND THEIR STRUCTURE

Needs for healthcare have, it transpires, to be analysed within a general theory of needs (ch2§1) and a general theory of needs has to be based upon a theory of drives (ch2§3). The next task is therefore to outline the requisite general theories of drives and of needs as preparation for analysing needs for health and healthcare. A defensible theory of drives, their structure and priority, would derive from the substantive discoveries of social theory, empirical psychology and biology (ch2§2). Mercifully the present task of linking a theory of drives with needs for healthcare does not compel us to complete that vast task in its entirety. However, it does demand a conceptual schema into which an empirical, scientific account of drives would fit (either verifying or falsifying it), in such a way as to relate drives to health, healthcare and needs.

By previous arguments the foundation of such a schema must be a biologically based analysis of drives, taking our drives as some of the physiological processes of which we are constituted (ch2§3). Yet at least some conscious drives (desires) are simultaneously also the products of our consciousness, of our thinking, associating, inferring, reasoning and so on, sometimes carried out in logically valid ways, sometimes not. For thinking is at once both a physiological process and one that is answerable to critical logical and epistemic standards (ch2§§2–3). This suggests two main classes of drive. One class is of those drives furnished to consciousness from other body systems as given contents of consciousness, much as our sensations are. Such drives are natural: innate and genetically determined, even if there is a degree of openness or plasticity in what satisfiers they take (Midgley 1980: 282, 311). The other class is the drives that we consciously make

40

from these raw materials, according to both circumstances and what we think and learn.

Natural drives, then, are 'essentially human' in the senses of being inescapable and biologically constitutive of our human nature. Here 'essentially human' does not necessarily mean, as it does in texts from the neo-Aristotelian tradition (e.g. Doyal and Gough's), 'distinctly' or 'uniquely' human in the sense of not being shared with other animals. Humans' natural drives are plural, complex and shared with other animals (Midgley 1980: 201–51). They are also 'basic' in the sense of being motivationally *sui generis*, being drives of which we become spontaneously conscious (e.g. as we do of hunger) and not the outcome of other conscious processes. Originating from a homeostatic lack in other, non-conscious body systems, natural drives are determined in the sense of occurring unbidden to our consciousness, as given conscious desires for types of objects and actions. They phenomenologically 'assail us' (Thomson 1987: 100). That they arise 'unbidden' does not imply that they are always irresistible, only inescapable (Thomson 1987: 24–5, 27, 88, 110–11, 123, 127). Being physiologically determined, they are also determinate in the sense of having determinate ranges of satisfiers, of being quelled in a determinate range of ways. Among our drives are our instincts (Midgley 1980: 311) which add specific behavioural dispositions to the motivational effect of a natural drive. An example would be the bonding through the physical contact between mother and new baby immediately after the birth. In some cases the disposition is negative, an instinctual inhibition rather than a drive (Midgley 1980: 26n1).

These biological drives are interculturally fairly stable but not universal. Evolutionary change has continued even during the historical timescale although (as Timpanaro observes) so much more slowly than social history as to make natural drives comparatively stable during a historical purview (Timpanaro 1980: 43). One's natural drives also depend upon one's sex, stage in the life cycle, environmental and disease experiences, possibly even on one's ethnicity. Certainly some can be acquired and lost during one's life cycle; sexual drives are one example, addictions another.

Natural drives are dispositional. Most of them are not continuously motivationally active, although they are normally activatable if an opportunity for satisfying them occurs. When they do occur we have varying degrees of consciousness of them and pursue them with varying degrees of conscious concentration. For example, we normally breathe inattentively, virtually reflexively until something causes us to suffer breathing difficulty or shortness of breath. These different degrees of consciousness are not surprising considering the physiological nature of natural drives. To speak of degrees of consciousness leaves open whether a theory of drives can or should take up the psychoanalytic belief in pre-conscious and unconscious-repressed natural drives (Freud 1972: 327–44). Ample historical evidence attests that while natural drives have a biologically determined range of physically possible satisfiers (Midgley 1980: 53; and cp. Thomson 1987: 64, 127) people learn to meet them with opportunistically available forms of satisfier: 'Hunger is hunger, but the hunger gratified by cooked meat eaten with a knife and fork is a different hunger from that which bolts down raw meat with the aid of hand, nail and tooth' (Marx 1973: 92; more fully, see Tannahill 1971 and 1976; von Paczensky and Dünnebier 1995). The range of physically possible satisfiers of a natural drive is determined by the satisfiers' causal characteristics (nutritive content, atmospheric content, etc.), which are intrinsic to the satisfier. This applies both to objects such as foods and to actions such as sexual activity. These characteristics are logically universal and claims about them depend upon the way the world is (Wiggins 1985: 152). Although finite, this range of satisfiers is nevertheless wider than the range that is practically available to people in most circumstances. Through habit, reinforcement and overdetermination our natural drives tend to focus upon quite specific kinds of satisfier, sometimes for particular individual satisfiers.

That we learn what satisfies our rather open natural drives has two implications. One is that the form of satisfier that people seek for their natural drives can be altered by their choices, decision and knowledge. Another is that although the object of a conscious natural drive (what a person desires in having the drive) usually lies within the wide range of physically possible satisfiers and within the narrower range of currently socially available satisfiers, this is not always the case. In this way drives are similar to what Thomson calls 'interests'; they 'explain' desires, but 'non-instrumentally', being the general reason(s) for a desire (Thomson 1987: 71–4).

One result of satisfying humans' natural drives tends to be our survival and reproduction (Midgley 1980: 26n1, 27n3) because of the rough evolutionary fit between human nature and its environment. The fact that these effects would cease if, say, the atmosphere suddenly changed to ammonia or a cocktail of car exhaust gases illustrates that our surviving and reproducing has only a contingent, empirical relation with our natural drives. When it occurs, the effect depends on our genetics, physiology, environment and indeed our own actions. There is a clear causal, and a logical, distance between the conscious objects of a natural drive and the usual effects of satisfying that drive. For example, the effect of eating is usually that we live a little longer. But not always; the food might be poisoned. However, the anticipated satisfier of our hunger, the thing that we are consciously motivated to do or to get is not survival (rarely consciously desired as such by most people) but whatever meal currently takes our fancy. What the natural drive is a drive to get is the satisfier itself, not the extraneous effects of getting it. We have neither a 'natural drive to survive' nor an 'instinct to propagate our genes' but drives for food, sex and so on whose satisfaction tends to have those effects.

Usually satisfaction of a natural drive has two effects. It neutralises or quells the drive itself, although only temporarily in almost every case. Gradually the drive reasserts itself, with an increasing degree of consciousness, after a point even becoming painful in the case of some natural drives (e.g. when the effects of the fourth pint of beer are becoming felt and the corridor-less train is nowhere near a station). Second, satisfaction of the drive usually contributes to the biological renewal of the agent, typically the agent himself but occasionally vicariously, in the form of a descendant who will usually outlive his or her parent. Natural drives can be categorised and prudentially ranked according to the effects of satisfying them.

An obvious first category is survival-related natural drives, so called because one dies if these are frustrated for long. These natural drives cannot be overridden at all – whether 'rationally' overridden or not (*pace* Thomson 1987: 103) – and the person survive. Survival-related natural drives are what Wiggins would call a 'basic' drive (he would say 'basic need' – Wiggins 1985: §8) because, given the laws of nature, fairly invariable environmental facts and the human constitution, they cannot be frustrated without physical harm to us. If a survival-related natural drive remains unsatisfied the physiological processes constituting the person who has it will start to break down after a determinate period of time. Usually the person will be painfully conscious of it before then unless he or she pre-empts these disagreeable effects by consuming more air, food or other satisfiers sooner (cf. Ramsay 1992: 79). How long the period is, depends on which natural drive is involved (a few minutes for oxygen, many days for some nutrients) and how old and strong the person is. We can label this time the 'period of urgency' of the drive. It is possible to rank survival-related natural drives by their period of urgency, and by the period of urgency remaining since the person having the drives last satisfied each of them.

Reproduction-related drives, which are centrally but not exclusively the sexual drives, are a second category. They have no period of urgency. Freud's view, for instance, seems to have been that when sexual frustration causes psychological harm this is not because sexual frustration is harmful in itself (although it is a misfortune to be avoided). The psychological harm came rather from repressing the sexual drive, by refusing to acknowledge to oneself that one even had it (e.g. Freud 1977a: 84–6, 156–62).

Acquired natural drives have already been mentioned. They can be acquired in two ways besides reaching such life-cycle events as weaning or puberty. In one case new natural drives are acquired as the result of some earlier action in pursuit of another natural drive. For example, a young mother acquires her natural drives for mother–infant bonding and to breastfeed as a result of sexual activity, itself naturally driven. Other more artificial drives are acquired through a person's own action but still count as natural drives because they occur spontaneously to consciousness without any conscious antecedents. Such are 'addictions' to tobacco, alcohol and some other drugs. Frustration of some of these natural drives causes short-term physical pain and derangement of bodily (including mental) processes, and so these drives have a definite period of urgency once the addiction is established, even though satisfying them now will cause more severe longer-term physiological destruction.

A residual category of natural drives remains. Because our natural drives and instincts are an evolutionary product there is no reason to expect exact correspondence between the activities necessary for human survival and reproduction on the one hand and the range of actions motivated by the totality of our natural drives on the other. It is reasonable to expect us, as animals who have evolved, to retain residues of natural drives (including instincts) which helped our remote ancestors to survive and reproduce but have become redundant for human survival and reproduction, persisting only because no evolutionary cause has 'selected them out'. Other natural drives apparently have an evolutionary value, but in an ancillary role to other drives rather than as direct contributors to survival and reproduction. Aversion to pain and to the causes of anxiety and fear are examples. Mary Midgley discusses the examples of animals' dislike of being stared at and of overcrowding (Midgley 1980: 9–13, 77); Dawkins discusses parenting (Dawkins 1978: 99–101) and humans' aversion to incest (Dawkins 1978: 107, 167). It seems unlikely that these drives have a period of urgency.

The risk in proposing this residual category of natural drives is that one creates a theoretical home for all sorts of dubious 'instincts' for whose existence there is scant evidence and whose real theoretical function is, allegedly, to legitimate reactionary social policies. A well-worn example is the debate about the alleged 'deprived child syndrome' (Bowlby 1965; Mitchell 1975: 228–9). However, one must not throw out the baby of recognising the full range of humans' natural drives and instincts with the bathwater of dubious socio-biological claims.

The other main category of drives are, on the above premises, those that we form consciously. We form this second category ourselves, by our own thinking, in a stronger sense than simply selecting, or becoming used to, a small part of the range of physically possible satisfiers. Suppose that reasons can sometimes motivate actions, and that desires can. To do so, they must be drives. Reasons and desires are essentially conscious. So on the view proposed here, they must be conscious forms of drives, i.e. motives. As we introspectively know, only a small proportion of them directly express natural drives. It has already been argued that the conscious thinking which forms this second category of drive is a physiological process (ch2§§3–4). Whatever the degree of consciousness, this working up is undertaken by the mind-brain, specifically the brain stem and probably with 'higher' brain involvement in some cases (Lamb 1985: 34). Any such process produces an output from raw material which it 'works up'. In this case the output is motivational. Some input to this 'working up' must therefore contribute the motivational element to the resulting drive. Its motivational element must therefore either be contained already in the original contents of consciousness from which this working up starts, or be added from some other motivational contents of consciousness, which already possess it during the working up. Either way the ultimate source of this motivational raw material must be the only motivational element present to consciousness and which predates the process of consciously 'working up' this secondary category of drive. This previous motivational element can only be the drives that occur spontaneously to consciousness, and which we have already analysed as natural drives.

Empirical theories of motivation rely heavily on such a concept of mental 'working up' which transfers motivational force from one content of consciousness to another. A main point of differentiation between the contending empirical psychologies is how they elaborate this concept and connect it to the debates about mind and body touched upon earlier (ch2§§3–4). It appears as 'association' in a psychological tradition that runs from Bentham to Skinner, as 'cathexis' in Freud and his intellectual descendants. These concepts explain non-natural drives by tracing their derivation from natural drives. 'Tracing the derivation' means mapping the process of 'working up' in the opposite direction to the way in which the working up actually occurred: from outcome to origins. Among philosophers writing about needs, Thomson also recognises the necessity to explain, structure and group our desires (e.g. Thomson 1987: 66–8, 74–6, 127, 134n12) and that this demands a substantive as well as a philosophical theory of motivation (Thomson 1987: 72).

Any remotely empirically plausible theory of such derivations must recognise the vast variety of ways in which, as we know introspectively, our drives and desires arise. For our motives are a complex product of feeling and reason (Midgley 1980: 259). Previous points suggest at least four axes of variation in how these derivations occur.

First, the degree of consciousness might vary for instances of 'working up', from reflexive through automatic to fully self-conscious levels. At this stage there is no reason to exclude such ways of 'working up' as the Freudian processes of repression, resulting in unconscious-repressed drives. So while the 'working up' will typically produce conscious drives (desires), this is not necessarily always the result. Whether a person who has them knows how her drives originated and have been formed, and how she articulates her drives, and among them her reasons and desires, will again depend on contingent factors: what language the agent speaks, what concepts this language has for articulating drives (as motives) and the agent's belief system (which might give strong reasons to deny having certain motives, for instance by including them among the seven deadly sins). 'Working up', which begins before language or belief are acquired, cannot then be articulated to oneself at all. The articulation of desires and reasons is most often through the medium of language, an 'edifice inhabited by ideology' (Voloshinov 1973: 13). There is no guarantee that the language of motivation that a person uses when he or she attributes a drive to someone will always, completely or accurately conceptualise the drives involved (Thomson 1987: 66, 71–2, 74).

Second, the length and complexity of the 'working up' can vary, with very many intervening mental operations between the natural drive and its derivative in some cases. (Not every case is so simple as that of wanting a box to climb on in order to reach the apple.) Because of these variations and extraneous physiological factors (e.g. how far one is into any period of urgency of the original natural drive) one would expect great variations in the strength of motivational force (cathexis) transmitted to different resulting drives. Sometimes the resulting drives might have as strong a motivational force as a natural drive, at other times a barely perceptible motivational force, resulting in drives with little more motivational force than, say, non-motivational imagination or conceptual thought. Indeed, even the activity of abstract thinking is motivated. This suggests that the contrast between cognition and motivation should be understood, not as a qualitative contrast but as opposite ends of a continuum of mental processes, all of which combine cognition and motivation in varying proportions. Lastly, the types of 'working up' can differ in epistemic and logical status, ranging from the most strictly deductive 'working up' using explicit logically universal, empirically sound causal principles, to the loosest, vaguest, most implicit, arbitrary, fallacious association. This last type of variation is very relevant to ethical analyses.

Epistemically one can distinguish two main types of 'association' here. One is instrumentality. Then mental 'working up' consists of working out (explicitly or implicitly) which objects give the extrinsic benefit of enabling either the direct satisfier of a natural drive or another extrinsic, instrumental drive satisfier to be obtained. (The box-and-apple case illustrates this sort of 'working up'.) This type of working up is logically answerable to such epistemic standards as truth and consistency. The other type is arbitrary association, for instance when a person comes to desire objects that are proxies for other satisfiers or simply coincide with other satisfactions (perhaps for causal reasons or by sheer coincidence). (One wants coffee at a pavement café not because one is thirsty but because that is all part of the pleasure of relaxing on holiday in Paris.) These drives originate instrumentally but their satisfaction is intrinsic, serving no further drive-satisfying purpose. One example is the relation of 'expression': 'The desire [to climb a mountain], as it were, expresses a need for excitement to achieve, to pit skills against the risk to life' (Thomson 1987: 64).

The resulting drives, and hence the actions that they motivate, can on this view be overdetermined, satisfying many other drives at once. Their 'working up' includes the concatenation of (real or imagined) instrumental relations. It too is dispositional and recurrent, not necessarily a once-for-all event. So the present view does not compel us to postulate, implausibly, a one-to-one correspondence between single drives and single actions (Thomson 1987: 55).

In motivation, causality and logic, all such drives are derivatives from natural drives. The total structure of individual drives is thus a logical hierarchy in the sense that 'higher', more 'worked-up' drives logically depend on 'lower' drives for their practical, motivational rationale, as well as being, contingently, produced by them. Nevertheless, this account differs from Maslow's (which uses 'needs' as we use 'drives') in two ways. The present theory limits the scope for a fixed, trans-historical hierarchy of drives to the natural drives and even then emphasises their plurality and mutual irreducibility (satisfying my thirst is irrelevant to my shortness of breath). Unlike the drive hierarchy that Maslow proposes, the hierarchy proposed here is not universal but individualised, historicised and strongly linked to a person's social place. Historical generalisations about individuals' historical drives are possible, but epistemically risky.

A person's drives are 'concrete': the 'summing up of many determinations' (Marx 1976a: 31), both genetic and biographical. This biography comprehends people's available and learnt satisfiers, their social role and generational experience and, not least, their own activities in manipulating their physical environment (hence learning what there is there to manipulate, and how) and managing their social relations. Their drives and the way in which they are structured are at the same time a social product, because the social relations that people encounter in their family, school or workplace, and through which they develop this structure of drives, are largely determined by wider social relations. The belief systems which also constitute these structures of drives are likewise largely a social product. Since all these social relations have a history of their own, a person's drive structure is simultaneously a biological and a personal, a social and a historical product. However, his or her natural drives are least, and his or her 'worked-up' drives the most, prone to develop through these non-biological mediations. So for short the 'worked-up' drives are called 'historical drives' in what follows.

All this suggests that we have structures of drives, becoming ever more complicated during our lives with multiple, convoluted inter-relations and connections back to the natural drives. There is no reason to suppose that this structure of drives is an orderly, consistent, harmonious whole. After all, it emerges in a rather haphazard way. This leaves open the possibility of all sorts of problematic relations such as repression and sublimation between different drives. Much of the large conceptual repertoire of psychoanalysis – to name but one empirically based theory of drives – catalogues the many possibilities for conflict, reinforcement and mutual frustration between different drives.

Drives occur diachronically. Not only do different survival-related natural drives have different periods of urgency. Because drives are dispositional, drives that are instrumental to, or arbitrarily associated with, satisfying other drives might occur at different times to the drives from which they derived. To illustrate this, consider the low-level instrumental historical drive for means to satisfy hunger. Hunger is a predictable, fairly stable natural drive but food production through horticulture requires (unlike hunting, gathering or pastor-alism) intense activity at certain seasons (seed-time, harvest) inter-spersed with rather inactive periods. In this case, one would empirically expect the drive for the means to satisfy hunger (seed, agricultural tools and doing horticultural work) to occur only seasonally although most people want food daily. At harvest-time it is usually necessary to resume working right after one's midday meal, illustrating how historical drives can 'outlive' the natural drives from which they derive, occurring even when the drive from which they derive and which they serve is, for the while, satisfied. Such drives can also persist after the circumstances that gave them an instrumental point have ceased to exist (Fromm 1942: 244).

This brings us to the question of how drives are satisfied: a necessary preliminary to explaining how health relates to drives and thus to needs.

§2 DRIVES, ACTIONS AND CAPACITIES

Two critical determinants of the drives that people actually have are the ways in which they can, and in which they think they can, satisfy them. The links between drive, action and the satisfaction (or frustration) and the reinforcement (or alteration) of the original drive can be presented as a cycle (Figure 3.1).

The relationship between each stage in the cycle is causal, complex, contingent and opportunistic. The cycle is initiated either by a homeostatic lack (in the case of some natural drives); or by internal mental processes ('working up', cathexis); or by the stimulus of an 'external' satisfier providing an opportunity or reminder to get the satisfier for a latent but predictable drive (on hearing a loud noise

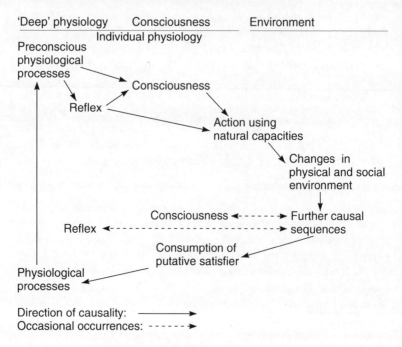

Figure 3.1 The cycle of drives and acting

outside I decide to renew my car insurance). The description of (some) needs as 'circumstantial' also applies to drives (Thomson 1987: 22). Three distinctions which Thomson analyses among the senses of 'needs' (Thomson 1987: 12, 21) also apply to 'drives' with just one verbal substitution. Thus we can distinguish 'drives' in the senses of the following:

1 dispositions, whether latent or occurrent;
2 occurrent drives, i.e. as unsatisfied and currently tending to motivate action (in the absence of counter-drives, uncertainty, external obstacles, etc.), whether natural or historical; preconscious, conscious or unconscious-repressed;
3 desires, i.e. conscious occurrent drives.

The right-hand side of Figure 3.1 represents the set of activities by which people manipulate their physical environment and interact with other people in attempting to satisfy their drives. This requires the natural capacities noted below. This interaction with the physical and social environment has many complex intermediate feedback

50

loops, sensory, cognitive and practically manipulative. Just how complex these are is shown by the difficulty in programming machines to complete actions such as walking or finding particular objects or places. The more complex a course of action, the more numerous the instrumental drives it is likely to generate in response to these feedbacks (for example, having discovered that a screwdriver will not shift the catch, one looks for a hammer). Because all action is motivated by drives, the agent's aim in it is to procure drive-satisfiers.

Success of course depends upon both non-human and human contingencies. (Will it stay dry for the harvest? Will the Deutschmark rise against the pound?) It is possible to contrast our consciousness of our desires and ability to act with our emotions, as our response to the ways in which others' actions affect us (cp. Sartre 1977: 296), or indeed to the way in which our own actions might frustrate each other (cf. Freud 1972: 64; and Freud 1936: 100). This suggests conceiving of our emotions as the passive counterpart of our drives, as our response to how our environment 'treats' us. In that case one would analyse the emotions as comprising three elements. There is a cognitive element, our perception of how events outside our control (including some that we have irretrievably brought about ourselves) will affect the satisfaction of our drives. An affective element consists of our instinctual, sometimes even reflexive, responses on perceiving these effects (for example, our reactions to evident great danger or to meeting an old friend). This is the way in which Freud, for instance, analyses anxiety (Freud 1936: 94, 105f). As with drives, evolution has resulted in a rough fit between experiencing emotions that are agreeable to the person having them and conditions or actions that do not hinder, and perhaps positively assist, our survival and reproduction. There are obvious evolutionary advantages in being able to learn from our experiences (Dawkins 1978: 60f). Linked with this, again often instinctively, are (third) motivational responses and a further cycle of action. An action that succeeds in satisfying the drive that motivated it therefore has a dual effect. It temporarily quells the drive itself but also strengthens ('reinforces') a person's confidence that a similar action will satisfy the drive when it recurs in similar circumstances.

On this view emotions correspond to drives in several ways. The more distant the derivation of a historical drive from the natural drives, the more weakly it is cathected and the weaker would be the affective and motivational effects of the emotions aroused by the prospect of satisfying or frustrating that drive. (One would also expect the affective and motivational effects to be stronger for unsatisfied than for satisfied drives.) Next, whereas natural drives originate in non-conscious physiological processes of which we become conscious, the reverse occurs with emotions (cp. Argyle 1978: 22–3). The cognition of an event that we believe affects the satisfaction of our drives produces, in some cases, non-conscious physiological effects such as blushing or stress. All these are further effects of our emotions, not their 'end' or 'purpose'. If emotions are the 'end' of anything, they would on this view be among the 'ends', or more accurately 'satisfiers', of our drives. Just as drives might tend to motivate in opposite practical ways, depending on the circumstances, so might different *faits accomplis* produce emotions that conflict with each and produce new drives conflicting with other drives that the person already has (again depending on the circumstances). This account of the emotions is the most conjectural part of the theory of drives and action outlined here. Nevertheless, a theory on these lines would explain why the structure of our emotions seems to a certain extent biologically given, indeed partly instinctual; why individuated through our personal experiences; and why so complex.

All this suggests that the motivational part of the cycle is renewed sometimes through feedback from our manipulations of our physical and social environments, sometimes through the emotional consequences of such actions and sometimes through the satisfaction of a natural drive 'wearing off'. Figure 3.1 should really show the cycle not as one circle but as many partly synchronised helixes of different sizes, starting and finishing points. Some natural drives (e.g. for food, air, pain removal) continue life-long. Others (e.g. sexual drives) have a more limited duration (Midgley 1980: 52). The structure of our drives literally develops life-long, nested within our biological life cycle and health 'career'. Pickin and St Leger describe its stages and chronology: prenatal, perinatal, early childhood, late childhood, adolescence, young adulthood, middle age, early old age, advanced old age (Pickin and St Leger 1993: 58f). All this has obvious implications for analysing health, health needs and healthcare needs.

The person acting upon the drive interacts with his or her environment and other people through the medium of his or her natural capacities. These are the bodily means of having the drive, acting upon it, obtaining (even producing) and consuming whatever satisfies it. The drive–action–satisfaction cycle necessitates the capacities for the following:

1 Having the drive itself, which involves not only the consciousness but the operation of many other body systems (hormonal, endocrine, reflexive, etc.), especially for natural drives.

2 Perceiving the state of one's drives (hunger, sexual desire, etc.); what satisfiers they are drives for; and whether they are currently satisfied.

3 'External' sensation and perception, orienting oneself towards potential drive-satisfiers in one's environment.

4 Practical problem-solving (Midgley 1980: 40), including remembering or imagining actions that will satisfy particular drives, and cognitive skills selecting which accounts of one's environment are likely to be true and consistent. These presuppose a life-long capacity to acquire, comprehend and retain knowledge about oneself and the environment.

5 Selecting what action to take, in the light of one's drives, the available satisfiers and means to obtain them, the circumstances, the likely results of one's actions, and any other relevant information.

6 Influencing other people, hence communicating with them; above all the capacity to acquire and use language, which is a medium for the cognitive capacities noted above besides communication.

7 Manipulating one's physical environment, necessitating a certain level of bodily mobility, dexterity, strength, sensation, etc. Exact specification of what these capacities are, at each life-cycle stage, is the province of occupational therapy and physiotherapy.

8 Mental and social capacities such as the assertiveness and concentration necessary for completing practical tasks.

9 Consuming satisfiers successfully. This capacity might be purely reflexive or instinctual (e.g. for the baby to suckle, swallow and smile; an adult's capacity for sexual pleasure, etc.). Here 'consume' is used for short, although the drive-satisfier is as often one's own action or another person as a physical thing. Nothing implying that this relationship is always one of only unilateral satisfaction should be read into the word 'consume'.

10 Capacity for emotional response, as outlined above.

All these capacities are an integral part of action (Thomson 1987: 41). The idea of an 'instinct' (as a combination of perception, drive and 'stereotyped' action) captures the point that, in reality, several capacities are sometimes bundled together.

Like our natural drives, our natural capacities are both biologically innate and capable of development, extension, learning and focusing. Some natural drives develop (and disappear) during specific life-cycle stages, and with them the corresponding natural capacities. The capacity to engage in sexual activity becomes needful once the sexual drives mature at puberty. Some natural capacities are sex-specific (e.g. to lactate). Over time certain natural capacities come to reflect one's physical environment, as when a person becomes acclimatised and then able to resume his normal activities in an extreme climate. Here too there is a rough evolutionary fit between the natural capacities we have and the types of action that are usually necessary for at least our natural drives. However, one cannot infer from that that the natural capacities have the 'purpose' of satisfying our drives.

Some natural capacities are flexible only in evolutionary and genetic terms (e.g. the range of our senses) but others are open to development and change within a person's lifetime. If, as ethological evidence suggests, motivation is necessary for the development and use of capacities (Midgley 1980: 250) the development of natural capacities into concrete skills itself occurs as part of the cycle noted above, realising the person's biologically given potential. The natural capacity is biologically given but the form in which it develops depends on the historical and geographic setting that the person (especially the child) finds herself in and upon what activities the person pursues. The change from one first language to another illustrates this. One must differentiate the natural capacity to, say, learn to read (i.e. recognise patterns of written signs, associate them with phonemes, etc.), from the actually acquired skill in its historical form of learning to read twentieth-century English (Midgley 1980: 297–8). What is innate ('natural') is the capacity, not the particular form in which it is realised. So the idea of a 'natural capacity' excludes the external conditions necessary for exercising that capacity. It also excludes whatever substantive practical choices a person makes about how to exercise his capacities. For instance, the natural capacity to walk is identifiable irrespective of one's destination, the purpose of the journey, or one's individual gait. Attribution of a natural capacity leaves open the questions of whether the skills, which possession of a capacity enables one to acquire and exercise, actually are acquired and exercised.

Since ethical theory makes much of the concept of 'choice' it is worth noting that on the present account, 'choice', like the faculty of 'reason', is actually a complex set of diverse capacities (Midgley

54

1980: 212): the natural capacities to decide factual questions; to select what action to take; and to articulate one's drives as (conscious) desires (thereby selecting a satisfier, since a drive is defined *inter alia* in terms of its satisfiers). The more weakly cathected a drive is, or the nicer the balance of cathexes between two or more drives which cannot all be satisfied, the bigger the influence that choosing is likely to have on the eventual action. Because drives can conflict, not all desires cause action, and because drives can have varying degrees of consciousness (pre-conscious drives, repressed drives, reflexes), not all action results from desires (Thomson 1987: 55–6). The present theory recognises wide scope for other conscious processes to disrupt the physiological sequence from pre-conscious process to drive to desire to action.

A person's environment critically determines what kinds of satisfiers satisfy his drives and which of these are available. In manipulating his environment a person uses the resources he finds there already: physical resources which embody given 'technologies' (above all, the comparatively simple ones of self-care, food preparation, shelter and so on), help from the other people whom he spontaneously meets (family, friends, workmates, fellow patients, officials, etc.), and the received knowledge, language and other components of local cultures and ideologies. Using these resources to meet one's own needs as fully as one can and as they allow, constitutes what therapists call the 'activities of daily life'. These activities are the concrete, practical manifestation of the cycle described above.

In principle this schema for a theory of drives and natural capacities becomes predictive at this point. To predict from it how an individual would be motivated and consequently act, it would be necessary to add knowledge of his particular drive structure (i.e. the substantive empirical data about the content of his drives and, where relevant, what remains of their periods of urgency), data about what satisfiers the agent perceives to be available, about what he perceives to be means for obtaining those satisfiers, and about his natural capacities. All this would imply what drives this person would 'work up' and which of these he would act upon.

If this schema is tenable it implies that all our actions are inherently (if not always successfully) instrumental, aiming to satisfy their motivating drives. Not that this means that all our drives are purely self-regarding; we have no theoretical reason yet to deny the possibility that individuals can have drives whose objects are much more important to other people than to the agent. Since our drives are embedded within our biological life cycle they can only comprehensively be explained and analysed with that process and timescale. Not exclusively nor fundamentally, but still to a substantial degree, our drives are the product of our own learning, thinking, reasoning and self-criticism. To that extent they are answerable to such epistemic requirements as consistency, truth and rationality. No explanation of them is complete which omits this feature. This brings us to the question of how to criticise these drives and thus to the connection between needs and drives.

§3 DRIVES, REASON AND NEEDS

A tenable theory of needs must show how an account of needs in terms of drives can also explain when needs are valid reasons for action and why (ch2§2). We have outlined a schema for an empirical theory of motives; of drives and desires (ch3§1). Yet 'needs' is also a critical concept, capable of being used to contrast needs with desires and to criticise desires. Claims about needs imply that a person to whom a need is imputed has a reason for action on account of that need; and perhaps other people do too. By referring to states of affairs and thus to the actions whose object they are (ch1§2), the term 'needs' also refers at one remove again to a person's possible drives (ch2§3), including desires as her consciousness of her drives (chs2§4, 3§1) and her actual drives. Her needs must therefore be, or be among, those of her causally possible drives that withstand critical scrutiny. But what kind of critical scrutiny? For the reasons outlined earlier (ch2§2) we cannot just begin adumbrating grounds of moral criticism before we have analysed the senses in which drives are amenable to publicly groundable, non-moral criticism.

Non-moral grounds are available for criticising drives because (ch3§1) drives are partly defined in terms of propositional beliefs about what satisfiers satisfy them. If the drive is not fully conscious (see chs2§3, 6§2), the proposition is implicit. In desires (conscious drives) these propositions are explicit in that a person is conscious of what he desires; indeed a desire is partly constituted by the proposition. When a person actively seeks some particular drive satisfier, his action can be described, *inter alia*, by propositions to the effect that what he is seeking to obtain is a putative satisfier of the drive that motivated the action. Either from the person's own account of his action, or by observing his action, descriptions of the drive and its putative satisfiers can be derived. ('The primitive sign of wanting is trying to get.') Without further analysing the relation between description and drive satisfier (which is the same as the relation between any other proposition and its referent), the following text speaks, for short, of the propositions 'corresponding to' a drive. Because drives can inherently be characterised in this way, five grounds are available for criticising the propositions about satisfiers which drives embody, and hence the drives themselves:

1 *Truth*. Statements about who has what drives have a truth value. A statement that an individual has a given drive is an empirical, theorised statement (as others in natural or social science). That it is very general, or involves a conceptual schema, or has a (partly) deductive structure does not imply that the theory is without empirical content (Flew 1978: ch. 1). It may be self-referential, hence expressive, and still have a truth value (e.g. 'I feel hungry'). The same arguments apply to desires. Of course people often attribute drives that they want other people to have to these other people. (Fraught father of tireless toddler: 'He looks as though he wants to go to bed.') They sometimes project their own drives onto others, for reasons that Freud, among others, analysed (Freud 1951: 23; 1961: 64, 92). Nevertheless attributions of drives are brute empirical statements.

2 *Relevance to the individual*. Instrumental historical drives have the intended effect of satisfying (other) historical or natural drives. So they provide valid reasons for actions for individuals who have these (other) historical or natural drives; but only for them (cp. Williams 1981: 103). Some satisfiers are simply irrelevant to particular people. To some historical drives will correspond true propositions, about how to obtain a given satisfier and about what effect the satisfier will produce; but the effect itself is simply not relevant to any drive that the agent has. For instance, a man might correctly assume that certain tablets relieve morning sickness, but he has no drive to which these are relevant, making it irrational for him to seek them for his own consumption.

3 *Epistemological transparency*. This applies to desires through which a person is conscious of his or her historical drives. The desires are transparent, if the person having them is aware of their derivation and rationale in terms of other drives. This necessitates a degree of accurate self-consciousness about one's biological nature and motivational biography (see ch3§1); and consciousness of what types of satisfier the drive has and their effects. Otherwise, the

person having the drive fails to perceive which further drives the satisfaction of the historical drive is relevant to and either under-specifies or over-specifies its satisfiers. Transparency is a precon-dition for endorsing instrumental drives in terms of means–end rationality, and all drives in terms of compatibility (see below). One consequence of desires being the consciousness of drives (see ch3§1) is that they may be a false consciousness.

4 *Means–end rationality* (cf. Williams 1981: 103). Here 'rationality' is used to refer to instrumental rationality, not in the sense of 'rationality in the choice of ends' (cp. Midgley 1980: 71). To criticise an instrumental drive in terms of means–end rationality is to ask the empirical questions of whether more drives (other drives besides this one) can be satisfied, or whether this drive can be more fully or often satisfied, by another satisfier. This basis for criticising drives is empirical and takes the satisfaction of the drive as a given. Hypothetical imperatives are propositions. In the case of instrumental drives this is unproblematic. However, a wrong choice of satisfier is also a wrong choice of means. For natural drives, we noted that only by evolutionary contingency does the effect of satisfying them coincide with the effect of reproducing the individual and species. Sometimes there is no coincidence. Then satisfaction of the drive is the criterion relevant to judging (prudentially) which effect to pursue. Natural drives do not have external purposes: for the person who has them, they are (among) his or her purposes in acting. To regard the evolu-tionary effects of satisfying the drive as its external 'purpose', or indeed to regard drives as having any external 'purpose' or 'reason' at all is erroneous. The only purpose that the drive intrinsically has is its own satisfaction.

Means–end rationality includes avoiding obstruction by other people pursuing their drives (Ramsay 1992: 40–1). This creates a presumption that individuals have an interest in cooperating. He has a prudential interest in enlisting others' active help or, as second best, preventing their interference in drive satisfaction. Whether this presumption applies, depends on the circumstances (so it does not provide a guaranteed foundation for morality; see Chapter 9). In some conditions (e.g. wars) individuals might obtain drive-satisfiers only invasively, by preventing someone else satisfying their drives. Means–end rationality also creates an assumption (also defeasible in some circumstances) against a person sacrificing some of his or her drives in pursuit of others, whenever that can be avoided.

5 *Mutual compatibility* of one's drives is thus another ground for criticising the totality of one's drive structure (Midgley 1980: 359). The compatibility in question is both logical and, more narrowly, causal. Drives conflict in the sense of having contingently incompatible satisfiers – for example, both sleeping and listening to a lecture (not that this stops some people from trying). This is one special case of a negative, instrumental relation between two drives. Another is when the effects of satisfying one drive indirectly make it harder to satisfy another (over-eating might make one less sexually attractive); or because circumstances prevent me from pursuing all my occurrent drives at once (I could use my free evening either for reading or for meeting friends but not both); or because pursuing one natural drive directly reduces one's natural capacities. Even the modest consumption of potentially addictive materials can have this effect (e.g. shall I drink myself senseless this evening?). So can background physical disease (e.g. if walking too far precipitates heart failure) and certain types of ('unhealthy') satisfiers (e.g. contracting HIV from a sexual partner). When drives are incompatible, the question arises: which drive's satisfiers is it least imprudent to sacrifice?

Many natural drives are life-long and the structure of drives develops throughout an individual's life (ch3§1). The drives subject to criticism on grounds on their mutual compatibility (or incompatibility) are therefore the whole of an individual's drive structure, including her desires and the corresponding possible actions, for the whole remainder of her life. To suggest this is obviously a counsel of critical perfection. Few people know how long they are likely to live or in what circumstances, still less how all their drives are likely to develop. Then all that is practically possible is critically to appraise a person's existing and foreseeable drives. Nevertheless, there are instances where the future state of a person's drives can be forecast with some confidence. Many of them are relevant to health, healthcare and health policy (see ch4§2). At least the drives for food, shelter and pain relief and many other natural drives continue life-long. When these forecasts are available, it is practicable (and prudent) to take a life-long view in criticising a person's drives on grounds of their mutual compatibility. On this basis, it is possible to criticise my (I suspect transient) desire for cakes because it is incompatible with my longer-term desire to avoid the pain and disability of heart disease and premature death from it.

Where drives conflict, the following methods are available for prudently minimising their incompatibility:

1 Remove the contingent causes of conflicts of drives, wherever possible, as this is the most effective satisfaction-maximising method. If it is not possible, a prioritising method becomes necessary.

2 Prioritise unsatisfied natural drives over unsatisfied historical drives, as the historical drives arise only as means to, or side effects of, satisfying the natural drives. (This is an application of the relevance criterion noted above.)

3 Prioritise among occurrent unsatisfied natural drives according to the remaining period of urgency; most urgent first.

4 Once the natural survival drives are satisfied there is time to take a longer view. A fundamental method of maximising the extent of drive satisfaction of both natural and historical drives is by maximising life expectancy.

5 Then prioritise among the unsatisfied historical drives so as to maximise the range of historical drives satisfied. To do this, prioritise among occurrent instrumental drives, according to which is most overdetermined (most highly determined first). Following this rule maximises the number of further drives that will be satisfied. If the present theory is correct, people will already tend to use the above rules, or approximations to them, in practice, thereby developing their mental capacity to do so (see chs4§1, 6§2). Here, however, they are presented more formally as logical requirements of prudential reasoning.

Drives can therefore be criticised when the propositions that they imply (or embody) about their satisfier(s) contravene one or more of the above requirements. Besides excluding moral criticism of drives at this stage, this theory limits the criticisability of drives in other ways.

Compatibility is a negative criticism, a 'filter device'; drives that are not incompatible with the other drives that a person has, survive it. Drives may also be underdetermined; many means may be available to satisfy a given drive. If, as a tie-breaking criterion, none of them are relevant to other drives or criticisable on other counts, there is nothing to choose between these means on prudential grounds. They are non-irrational rather than positively rational (cf. Gert 1990: 280–1).

The truth of statements about means of satisfying drives does not depend on implicit reference to any particular persons; neither do general statements about the causal or logical derivation of types of drive from one another. But since drives are always the drives of some particular person, empirical attributions of drives are always implicitly relative to some particular persons, on the above account of drives (ch3§1). Claims that drives withstand criticism (as above) therefore also implicitly refer to whoever has the drive. They do not necessarily apply to another person. (The aforementioned criterion of relevance makes this explicit.) Prudential, as opposed to moral, judgements are not logically defective just because they are person-relative. (They may be false, but that is a substantive, not a formal, defect.)

Practical reasoning must start somewhere, whether in a priori meta-reasons, or the faculty of choice conjuring desires *ex nihilo* (or *ex spirito*), or, as argued here, in *sui generis* natural drives. Natural drives do not have reasons; they are reasons both for action and for other historical drives. They are reasons for action because they can be articulated consciously and are the point at which prudential reasoning stops; its assumptions. Yet natural drives are, according to the criteria for criticism offered above, neither rational nor irrational. They are instead the premise for criteria of prudential rationality (cp. McDowell 1979: 346) although they have arisen through the arbitrary, aimless processes of evolution. They are also causes of action, motivating action irrespective of further reasons. They are the point at which it becomes both logically futile to seek further prudential reasons for action (because none are available) and practically pointless (because no such reasons could override the natural drive for a longer term than its period of urgency; and this is not a matter of choice). Natural drives, including conscious ones, are as brute empirical as sensations are. Thomson and others conclude that drives cannot have justificatory force; but another possible conclusion is that natural drives mark the limit of critical reasoning about actions. The ' "ought" implies "can" ' dictum entails that, since all a person can do is act on some drive or other, the ends of action are posed by drives, not by literally disembodied reasons. So the present account of drives and action implies a conception of rationality which is partly formal and partly substantive (cp. Gert 1990: 280). It is partly substantive in the sense of implying a list of non-irrational ends of human action; the list of natural drive satisfiers that survive the types of criticism outlined above. These patterns of criticism too are partly formal and, insofar as they invoke factual knowledge, partly substantive.

To explain how a drive arose (ch3§1) does not make it cease to exist. (Psychotherapy aims for the reformulation of the drive, not its abolition.) Neither does it determine, of itself, whether the drive withstands criticism by the criteria outlined above. Whether the explanation endorses a drive as rational or exposes its irrationality depends not upon the fact that the drive has been explained, but upon the substantive explanation and how the drive, as so explained, fares against the criteria noted above.

Many natural drives coexist, not reducible to each other. Neither are all historical drives reducible to each other. There is an arbitrary, irreducible plurality of drives (which is why the utilitarian belief that all drives reduce to a single entity is falsely reductionist – see ch2§3). A person's drives are the product of his biology, biography and environment (ch3§1). They are the product of the accidents of evolution, the genetic lottery; accidents of birth including the parents and society and social place into which he was born; his subsequent biography which offered some and withheld other satisfiers, opportunities and directions for developing his natural capacities; the belief systems (including ideologies) he encountered; and the inherent underdetermination of some drive satisfiers (see above). All these factors are both given and historically contingent, and in that sense arbitrary. But 'arbitrary' is not equivalent to 'irrational'. Arbitrarily formed drives may be non-rational (as are the natural drives) or prudentially rational (means, as it happens, to satisfy other drives). They may contingently also be irrational, on the above criteria, but are not inherently so.

Claims about 'needs' refer to the object of possible drives (ch2§3). An empirical account of drives describes what drives are contingently possible. Within that range, drives can be subjected to non-moral criticism in respect of the truth of the propositions that they implicitly embody, their mutual compatibility, relevance to the agent, transparency and the effectiveness with which action upon them will attain their satisfiers. Drives withstanding these criticisms are epistemically tenable; for short, 'rational' (cf. Sadurski 1983: 422). Of course the drives that a person actually has will usually differ from those that she would have, if her actual drives were modified to meet these criticisms. This critically modified set of drives has the critical, counterfactual character that 'needs' has, when it is contrasted with 'drives'. On this basis, we can construe the primary sense of 'a need' as 'a drive or an object of a drive, such that the proposition that the drive-object will satisfy the drive withstands criticism by the standards of truth, compatibility with the agent's other drives, means–end rationality, agent-relevance and transparency'. Here 'object of a drive' means 'that which the drive is a drive to do or get'. This account of needs combines the two indispensable elements of a theory of needs: scientific foundations and a means for criticising and deriving 'reasons for action'. It readily explains the relation of implicature between needs, drives and lacking. It obviously explains the prudential uses of 'needs'. This appears enough to explain why in some cases the occupants of all three roles implied by the utterance of claim about needs (ch1§2) have a reason to act on account of a need, and why in other cases only the person to whom the need is imputed has such a reason (see ch3§4). The account of needs proposed here may, on further analysis, also explain needs as moral values; at present that remains an open question. Certainly the needs corresponding to natural drives do not a priori serve any further purpose (*pace* McCloskey 1975: 2); for the person who has them, they are among his purposes in acting.

On this basis, a person's needs are the partly counterfactual structure of drives and satisfiers that satisfy the largest critically tenable range of his existing drives. The range of drives whose likelihood of satisfaction is maximised begins with the natural drives and continues up the hierarchy of his drives. It is a structure because it has the attributes of contingent compatibility among its constituent drives, explicit conditionalities and instrumental relations between them and, insofar as it embodies empirical knowledge of both the 'external' world and self-knowledge of the individual's own drives, logical relations with the agent's factual beliefs. In these ways it is analogous to the structure of drives (see ch3§1). Insofar as individuals' actual drives fall short of the critical standards noted above, claims about their needs will be counterfactual. What a person needs is therefore:

1 The totality of his desires, which are his consciousness of his drives. A person's desires can be found simply by asking (taking the usual precautions to remove any incentive for him to lie).
2 Minus: any desires embodying empirical errors about means and satisfiers.
3 Plus: any desires that would result from substituting valid, relevant knowledge of means and satisfiers.
4 Minus: those members of any pairs (or larger groups) of conflicting desires that are least urgent or further from the natural drives

in the hierarchy of drives (here 'conflicting' despite, and after, application of the decision rules noted above.)
5 Plus: desires that would result from substituting any alternative (compatible) means and satisfiers in the less urgent or remoter desires.
6 Plus: recognition of any pre-conscious or unconscious drives.

This yields a list rather than a structure of needs; it is not necessary completely to analyse the derivation of drives from each other. There is a prima-facie but corrigible presumption that desires express needs. Compatibility is a negative criticism; drives that are not incompatible, survive it, even if they are gratuitous in that satisfying them satisfies no further drive. When they are not positive means to satisfying further drives, these criticism-surviving drives are not irrational, at worst only arbitrary and non-rational. These non-instrumental, associated drives then also qualify as needs.

In this way needs are definable extensionally, in objective terms (Thomson 1987: 100), although partly counterfactually. The counterfactual elements share the logical characteristics of other counterfactual statements. Claims about needs are contestable empirically and logically, either as statements of fact about the existence of natural drives (hence without disputing any putative end that they serve), or about the validity (instrumental necessity) of historical drives. Changed beliefs alter desires (as Thomson 1987: 59), but only changed facts alter needs. 'False needs' (or *a fortiori* 'artificial needs' or 'repressive needs') (Marcuse 1968: 189, 193; Sartre 1977: 124) would then be a shorthand for 'drives that succumb to at least one of the above grounds for criticism and are therefore only spuriously "needs" '. Such a concept is entirely coherent, whether or not people actually have 'false needs'. However, false 'needs' (*qua* drives) cannot be fundamental (*pace* Thomson 1987: 31) because natural drives are not susceptible to the above forms of criticism; only their putative satisfiers are, at most.

A general theory of needs as rational drives yields only prudential, not moral, judgements. The logic of prudential judgements is in some ways simpler, and in others more complex, than the logic of moral judgements. Specifically, the account of needs proposed here looks rather relativist, and we have still to see whether it can explain all four of the claims that are involved in using 'needs' to recommend, say, a health policy (ch1§2). To complete the general account of needs and prepare the ground for analysing such notions as 'health', 'needs for healthcare' and 'clinical autonomy', we must examine these matters next.

§4   NEEDS AND RELATIVISM

Until we reach the threshold at which we cannot avoid moralising the concept of needs, our account of needs as rational drives is prudential and therefore relativist. Accepting Wiggins' claim that statements of need are relative in three ways, the present account adds a fourth, more disturbing to many ethical theorists.

Wiggins argues (Wiggins 1985: §7) that claims about needs are relative, first, to a 'parameter' of harm or flourishing. The present theory of needs interprets 'harm' differently and more specifically as the frustration of drives. What harm this does depends on what drive is frustrated. At one extreme, the harm in frustrating natural survival drives is physical injury or death, if they are frustrated for long enough. At the opposite pole, the only harm in frustrating non-instrumental (purely contingently associative) drives is a degree of discontent. Frustrating false needs will do no greater harm and in some circumstances actually help the person 'flourish' by removing an obstacle to the satisfaction of other drives and opening the way to a more effective satisfier. The present theory implies that these frustrations necessarily harm only the person whose drives they are.

Wiggins argues that this parameter of harm (as he understands it) is, second, relative to a culture and to people's conception of harm. Rather similarly the present theory explains non-natural needs, and the learnt satisfiers of many natural needs, partly as a product of social conditions and to that extent culturally relative. Insofar as it recognises that individuals often have a clear perception of their own needs (see chs3§2, 5§2), the present theory also takes Wiggins' point that the harm done by frustrating individuals' needs can be defined at least partly in terms of their own conception of harm, in respect of harm to themselves.

What counts as harm or flourishing is (third) also relative to the particular circumstances of the 'time or times ... associated with the need' in Wiggins' view. The present theory agrees that what people need is historically relative because of the historicity of the social relations through which drives are formed, because it is historically contingent what satisfiers are available, and because an individual's needs are situated in his own life cycle (ch3§1).

To these three comparatively anodyne types of relativism the present theory adds a fourth. Unless additional moral assumptions have been brought into play (see Chapter 9), claims about need are always implicitly claims about the needs of particular individuals. Claims that do not specify whose needs, whether explicitly or by implication or by conversational implicature, are either elliptical or logically incomplete, failing to identify the particular individual(s) to whom they implicitly refer as the person(s) having the needs in question. Nearly all ethical theorists challenge this fourth sort of relativism. A standard objection is that

> ethical relativism is untenable since it actually refutes itself. Ethical relativism claims that there should be fundamental differences in the moral standards of different communities or of different cultural groups. This is a normative claim which applies to all societies all of the time and which demands that normative claims do not apply to various societies all of the time.
>
> (Karhausen 1987: 27)

Thus, the relativist's own moral claims cannot bind anyone but himself, or at most members of his own social milieu. Even then, the objection goes, if his moral claims are simply the product of his social setting they cannot be 'objectively' valid (because objectively valid moral claims would be valid for everyone, everywhere); but this is tantamount to saying that they are not valid at all.

This last fallacy was exposed earlier on (ch2§4). Tenable objections to ethical relativism are objections to relativism as an account of morality. Moral thought, as opposed to transparently prudential thought, indeed cannot be plausibly represented as relativist. But here we are dealing first with a prudential concept of needs, not yet assuming that a prudential concept of needs is equivalent to a moral concept of needs. The standard – and valid – objection to relativist accounts of morality is irrelevant to prudential reason. There are no a priori grounds to think that everyone everywhere must have the same drive structures and satisfiers and the empirical evidence is patently against it.

Previously it was argued that a claim about what someone needs unpacks into at least two, and often four, claims (ch1§2):

1 The relation between some person and some state of affairs (or action) satisfies the empirical criteria for needing something.
2 The speaker endorses that this gives that person a reason for action.

3 The speaker also has reason for that person to get what she putatively needs.

4 The listener also has reason for that person to get what she putatively needs.

The foregoing discussions of drives and needs (ch3§§1–2) analysed the relations between the first and second elements. Now we can start to analyse how the third and fourth elements relate to the first two, reiterating the proviso that until we proceed to a moralised account of needs, the analysis is restricted to prudential claims about needs.

The analysis so far implies that prudential claims in the form 'A needs X' are (as critics say – ch2§1) ambiguous. They are ambiguous between:

1 a proposition about what A would desire if A's drives and desires were coherent, self-conscious and factually well informed (see ch3§2), irrespective of anyone else's drives and their rationality; and

2 claim 1 plus an elliptical expression of the speaker's own needs, equivalent to 'I need A to have X'. Whether this claim is true depends on whether A's having X is compatible with the satisfaction of the speaker's own needs, which depends in turn on the circumstances. Analogously the hearer is also being told that he too needs A to have X.

The second of these is the more obvious prima-facie interpretation of 'A needs X' as it is what the surface grammar of the expression suggests. Nevertheless only the first interpretation is the minimal core reference to a subject and a state of affairs involved in all attributions of needs (see ch2§3). As its truth does not depend on what the speaker needs, it can be labelled an 'anthropological', purely descriptive, attribution of needs. It uses only the first two elements involved in claims of needs. Because on the second interpretation 'A needs X' actually expresses what the speaker needs, irrespective of whether A in fact needs X too, it can be called an 'expressive' use of the word 'needs'. The second interpretation only applies in addition to the first, if two further conditions both obtain. One is that the speaker's needs and A's are in fact mutually compatible; the other is that 'needs' is being used in a moral sense, which guarantees compatibility a priori (see Chapter 9). Additionally the hearer must also need A to have X, implying (analogously) that the hearer's needs and A's are compatible, either contingently or because morality guarantees it.

How claims about healthcare needs are to be interpreted, and whether they are valid, depends in the prudential case upon what substantive satisfiers the various parties to the claim would desire; upon whether their desires are rational (in the senses explained above – ch3§3); and upon whether the different parties' satisfiers are compatible. The descriptive, 'anthropological' element in claims about healthcare needs is the premiss without which expressive judgements about healthcare needs, including moral judgements, cannot get started. To determine the validity of such claims we must analyse what substantive health and healthcare needs patients, doctors, healthy people and other participants in a health system have in these descriptive, 'anthropological' terms. Then we will be able to relate their needs in that sense to needs in the more expressive senses, the senses usually used in the health policy debates from which we started. At last we are ready to analyse the connections between health, healthcare and people's needs for these.

4

HEALTH NEEDS

§1 NEEDS AND HEALTH

Defining needs as rational drives implies a corresponding conception of health. Being a critical concept supporting (or subverting) practical judgements about healthcare practice and health policy, the concept of 'health' is as contested as the concept of 'needs'. Most accounts of 'needs' and 'health' link these concepts with both prudential and moral judgements. We, however, are so far limited to prudential, not moral, judgements, and these in what was called descriptive, 'anthropological' rather than 'expressive' form (ch3§4). However, any coherent definition of 'health' refers at least to individual humans' physical state, with their mental state as a special or an analogous case (cp. Fulford 1989: 13, 75, 145, 258). This points towards a prudential definition of 'health' as 'the bodily state which a person needs'. Having theorised mental activity as a special case of bodily activity (ch2§§3–4) the proposed definition can later be qualified to differentiate mental from non-mental health (ch6§3). Initially it is necessary to explain the general conception of health, defined in terms of needs, which underlies both the mental and the non-mental aspects of health and the corresponding healthcare needs (Ramsay 1992: 7, 102, 105).

At first sight it might seem that what satisfies a drive is the particular satisfier itself: the food, the novel, the lover or whatever. However, it is not the mere having of the satisfier that does so but the consumption of the satisfier; its active intellectual or physical appropriation by the person who seeks it. Although consumption presupposes that the satisfier is available, 'consuming' it is an activity. This is most evident in such natural drives as breathing or elimination but it also applies to historical needs such as the desire for cultural activities. Even the most passive 'intellectual appropriation' such as watching a film requires that a person be able to perceive, appreciate and take pleasure in the satisfier. Thus the object of a drive is the more or less active consumption of the satisfier, often (but certainly not always) preceded by its imaginary identification, a plan of action for getting it, acquiring the necessary practical and intellectual skills, and practically carrying out the plan (ch3§2).

All these are bodily activities consisting in the exercise of natural capacities (ch3§2). So all drives imply a need for the exercise of the relevant capacities, both those constituting the drive itself and those involved in consuming the satisfier. Adults possessing the full range of these capacities thereby possess the ability for self-care through the activities of daily life. Even in their finished form as learnt skills, natural capacities consist of congeries of functions of body systems and structures (including the mind-brain) although there is rarely a simple one-to-one mapping of body structures and functions onto the natural capacities, which usually draw on many such bodily functions. This is clearest in the case of the capacities for social interaction through which nearly all our drives are pursued. Among our natural capacities is the capacity to feel pains and the corresponding drives to escape them. ('Pains' in the plural because, *pace* utilitarianism, there are qualitatively distinct kinds.) Although, thanks to evolution, the usual effect of avoiding pain is that we prevent or remedy bodily damage, this effect is contingent, approximate and not totally reliable. Inconsequential injuries are sometimes painful (e.g. a blow to the humerus) and some severe, even fatal illnesses nearly painless (e.g. pneumonia). Nevertheless pain removal is both a natural need in its own right and a contingent symptom of an instrumental need to protect or remedy a bodily function.

Virtually all drives (and therefore needs) thus imply an instrumental need for the painless operation of the bodily functions and structures constituting the natural capacities involved in having and satisfying them. The activities of daily life through which we do this are more or less tailored to what people's natural capacities ordinarily allow them to do at this life-cycle stage, assuming no exceptionally severe disease, impairment or social isolation. This is the bodily state that people need. This implies a generic definition of 'health' in terms of needs: 'the painless exercise of a person's natural capacities in the ways necessary for her actively to use her physical and social environment to obtain and consume the satisfiers of her needs'. These natural capacities include those involved in social interaction, intellectual life, reproduction, childbirth and child-rearing besides

70

those involved in manipulating physical objects, controlling one's body and moving oneself about. 'Painlessness' includes palliating the pains incidental upon our biological life cycle, including those of birth, giving birth and death. Reliance on the notions of 'natural capacities' and 'needs' makes this a definition of 'health' in objective terms. For 'needs', in the descriptive, anthropological sense, is itself an objective, empirical concept (ch3§§3–4). An individual's beliefs about whether a person is healthy and about what natural capacities a person would have if they were healthy, are corrigible empirically. For that very reason such a concept of health is also (and in that sense) critical. The state of a person's actual natural capacities can be compared with those that are necessary for him actively to pursue his drives. In this sense the proposed definition of 'health' in terms of needs is partly counterfactual.

Like Daniels (1985: 32, 105), Doyal and Gough (1991: 50, 54) and Ramsay (1992: 6, 13, 32, 37, 70, 111, 201–12) we have defined health as a generic bodily means to many other ends. Unlike them, the present definition states the ends served specifically in terms of rational drives (ch3§3). It also takes health to comprise not only the bodily means of pursuing one's ends painlessly (as these authors do) but also having the natural drives themselves, the capacity to 'work them up' into historical drives, and the critical capacity to know and desire what one needs (ch3§§1–3).

Several factors determine what level and mixture of natural capacities a person needs, to satisfy his needs. People possess natural capacities in varying degrees, from the bare minimum necessary for life upwards and with varying degrees of restorability once their capacities are impaired. The present theory defines 'health' in terms of capacity for need satisfaction through the activities of daily life, and a person's needs are determined by a combination of biological, intellectual, social and biographical factors (ch3§1). This implies that there are three threshold levels of health.

A minimum level of natural capacities that a person needs is to be able to consume satisfiers of her natural survival-related drives without actively producing them or even engaging in much social interaction to get them. This minimal level of function includes a minimal level of resistance to the diseases to which consumption of air, water and food usually exposes a person. At this level of natural capacity, and thus of health, a person is just biologically viable. This threshold is important to healthcare ethics for many obvious reasons (see ch4§3).

Someone leading a routinised and stable life, but nevertheless meeting his natural survival drives and most other natural drives, illustrates a second threshold. (This might apply to the inhabitant of an asylum, monastery or other 'total institution' – Goffman 1984: 11, 43, 51, 279; or a poorly managed nursing home.) This person needs a wider, if still limited, range of natural capacities. Exactly what level of natural capacities this person needs, depends on the context of his everyday life. One can imagine a highly stable, routinised life requiring a limited range of some natural capacities but others to high level. (A high level of intellectual, but only a modest level of physical, agility seems necessary for functioning as lifetime residential academic head of an Oxford college; military life often seems to demand the opposite.) An older, more extreme example is that of people making a living as beggars (or in more genteel surroundings, invalids) out of their infirmities or mutilating their children for that purpose. We can call the level and range of natural capacities that are necessary and just sufficient to carry on these restricted, locally determined activities of daily life the 'local minimum level of "health"'. In most industrialised societies ('post-industrial' society being yet to come), for instance, he would usually need the capacities to wash, dress, toilet and feed himself, perhaps with some assistance, and to obtain further help when necessary. At this level a person can just sustain himself by independent self-care in his own home; the level necessary for 'care in the community' or 'normalisation' in the current policy euphemisms.

Most people, however, live less predictable and circumscribed lives. For their activities of daily life they need a level of natural capacities allowing them occasionally to develop new activities, new knowledge, skills and drives, and to respond to unexpected events. In industrial society this is an everyday state of affairs as both the social environment and individuals' roles in it change constantly. This necessitates a correspondingly higher level and range of natural capacities. The foregoing account of needs implies anyway that it is prudent for individuals to extend the hierarchy of needs which they have and can satisfy (ch3§3). For that, a person needs the mix and level of natural capacities, corresponding to the largest available scope for satisfying her (other) needs. Insofar as natural capacities depend on the functioning and structure of a person's body, these conditions imply a third threshold of health, that level necessary for exercising and developing her natural capacities to match the full range of her needs. To indicate its wide range, we can label this level of health 'full health'. It is what the word 'health' means when used without further qualification in the following chapters.

What the full level of health concretely is, can be discovered empirically in two ways. One might examine empirically what levels of natural capacity people in different historical and social circumstances have achieved, for instance their life expectancy or degree of mobility in old age. The top of this range demonstrates the feasibility of realising a certain level of health, but will tend, if anything, to risk underestimating the possibilities. Alternatively one might predict what level of natural capacities humans can theoretically achieve, from what is already known about human genetics, development and aging.

This conception of health implies a maximum besides a minimum limit to the fully healthy use of the natural capacities (and bodily functions constituting them). Our biological limits and life-cycle stage make an open-ended definition of health as the highest conceivable level of natural capacity absurd. The ' "ought" implies 'can" ' dictum excludes a definition of full health which stipulates that, say, 2- or 102-year-olds be capable of Olympic pole-vaulting. Yet placing the upper limit of fully healthy natural capacities at the upper limit of the individual's personal biological potential would in some cases place it too low, in others too high. Where someone's natural capacities are, say, too congenitally or genetically restricted for them to participate fully in the activities of daily life, and these limitations are incurable with present techniques, he might nevertheless reach his full personal biological potential in terms of using the natural capacities he still has. Defining health in terms of *individual* biological potential would prevent us from saying that this person could have better health if more effective therapies could be found. On the definition of health proposed here, he does not count as being in full health, but only as healthy in respect of his unimpaired natural capacities. Conversely, activities of daily life have been known to place such heavy demands on some people that they damage their natural capacities by over-use (e.g. in physical labour during early industrialisation). People have the biological potential for over-using their natural capacities, self-defeatingly in terms of maintaining, let alone developing, them. A definition of health in terms of natural capacities must instead be defined in terms of what an unimpaired human is capable of.

Daniels and others tackle this by defining 'health' as the biologically 'species-normal' level of natural capacity for humans (e.g. Daniels 1985: 28, 33; Ramsay 1992: 101, 105, 119). The word 'normal' has at least seven different possible senses in these contexts (Galen and Gambino 1988) but the one most relevant to this discussion takes normality as the minimum level of natural capacity that a person would have if his life cycle were unimpaired by disease or trauma. If 'normal', or any terms defining it, are taken to mean 'statistically normal', similar problems arise to those encountered by defining 'health' in terms of the individual's biological capacity. Some 'normal' levels of natural capacity can indeed be defined statistically as a modes (e.g. numbers of limbs) or qualitatively (e.g. 'can swallow' or 'fertile'). However, some can only be described quantitatively (e.g. body mass index, visual acuity). There the lower end of the 'normal range' (the lower threshold of 'health') can only be defined in a statistically arbitrary way; as within so many standard deviations from the arithmetical means of the quantitative measures used. But within how many standard deviations? One? Two? Three? Further, some biological states which are pandemic in some societies (Sedgwick mentions hookworm and dyschromatic spyrochetosis – 1982: 32) reduce natural capacities below the level demonstrably attainable elsewhere or cause pain or both. Indeed the whole species might be in similar straits (and probably is, for example, in respect of life expectancy). For each stage of a person's life cycle the normal range of natural capacity and bodily functioning is relatively stable during an individual's lifetime but on a longer perspective it is slowly changing because of changing nutrition, environmental deterioration and so on. Insofar as these changes cause an increase in their natural capacities, it represents an improvement in people's health. For purposes of defining 'health', 'species-normal' would have to be interpreted counterfactually in terms of unimpaired humans' generic theoretical biological potential in present conditions.

A definition of 'health' in terms of needs also implies upper limits to the consumption of the satisfiers of natural drives. An effect of actively satisfying one's drives through the activities of daily life is the reproduction of the individual person and, during young adulthood, her descendants (ch3§1). Where this middle-range consumption lies is evolutionarily determined and empirically ascertainable, as is the point beyond which further consumption yields no extra effect in maintaining the natural capacities. Levels of consumption of natural drive satisfiers outside this range (when that is physically possible; it is not where air and sex are concerned, for instance) actually impair bodily processes and thus disable the natural capacities which they constitute (either in extent or in longevity or both). This is also empirically established (e.g. West 1994 on obesity). For most people during most of human history, underconsumption and the resulting ill health has been widely prevalent. Overconsumption has been recorded among the rich in many societies (spectacularly in Gibbon n.d. i 39–40, 64–6, 611–12, ii 39–43, 572–4; Veblen 1994) but in developed capitalist countries it spread far down the social scale during the post-war boom. It incidentally also applies to addictions (acquired natural drives) in form of 'overdose'. As failures to satisfy the consumer's health needs, neither underconsumption nor overconsumption of natural drive satisfiers count as needs. Only the middle range of consumption does. Anticipating later discussions (ch8§2), this point can be illustrated graphically (see Figure 4.1).

Within the broad (but still specific) definitions noted above, the healthy range and type of natural capacities are particular to each individual. They depend on what his activities of daily life are, his biography, what other needs he has, including needs for learnt skills, and his life-cycle stage. For example, a concert pianist would only count as regaining even her 'locally defined minimum' level of health once she regained sufficient strength and precision of movement to

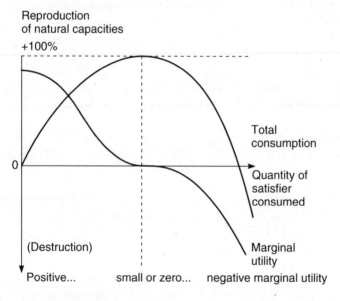

Figure 4.1 Natural survival drives: consumption, need satisfaction and 'marginal utility'

play at concert standard (requiring some natural capacities to an extent that most people neither have nor need). To that extent different substantive criteria of 'health' apply to each individual.

A person's activities of daily life are largely a complex of socially defined roles. We already noted how these affect drives and natural capacities (ch3§1). Some natural capacities are necessary for almost any conceivable pattern of daily life: communication, physical mobility, manual dexterity and so on. They are fixed by the natural world and the most general aspects of human society. Others depend upon the person's specific social place. A labourer needs a certain level of dexterity and physical strength, a train driver needs a given level of visual acuity. How many natural capacities a person needs, and which, also depend on how varied the social roles are that he occupies and how mobile he is between different social roles. The bigger these variations, prima facie the higher the necessary level of capacity. How large these variations are depends upon what type of society, and what social roles within it, a person inhabits. They are much larger for, say, a self-employed engineer in a capitalist society than for a herdsman in early feudal society.

In discussing mental health and illness Peter Sedgwick warned against 'the pitfalls of a biologistic approach towards the definition of health: an approach which, in attempting to eradicate social and personal value-judgements, may smuggle them back in through unexplored assumptions which are highly contentious' (Sedgwick 1982: 15). That also applies to the generic definition of 'health' proposed here. The natural capacities that a person needs in present society might well differ from those he would need in a society where he could more fully satisfy his needs. If health is defined in terms of capacity for 'valued' activity, the substantive criteria of health might well be different for the occupants of different social roles (Milio 1975: 51). Life in Utopia might be expected to demand greater natural capacities than present-day society does (Marx and Engels 1975: v 47): greater mental capacities (e.g. when liberal democracy supplants totalitarianism) as well as greater physical ones (e.g. when a rather sedentary person gets the novel opportunity to go rock-climbing). This is why a person needs more than the locally defined minimum level of health. Conversely, a more needs-satisfying social system might have the opposite effect on some natural capacities (e.g. by reducing the amount of heavy physical work that a person does). Does defining 'health' in terms of painless natural capacities necessary and sufficient for self-care and self-development through activities of daily life imply that existing activities of daily life, and by implication the social order in which the activities of daily life are embedded and which determines them, are defined as healthy too? Or that individuals' needs for healthcare amount to nothing more than a 'need' for them to adapt to their current roles in existing society?

To both questions we can answer 'no'. Many natural capacities (e.g. sensation, continence) are necessary in virtually all social roles and systems. Since the definition of 'health' proposed above comprehends these capacities, it does not discriminate in favour of any one social system. It has been defined in terms of natural capacities, abstracting from the specific social form ('skills') in which those capacities are developed and exercised. This defines 'health' more widely than as fitness for a specific role in a specific social system. Our account of needs implies that one thing a person needs is to inhabit whichever type of social system most fully meets his (other) needs. To recognise the fact that the existing activities of daily life and social roles are the current social media for trying to satisfy one's needs does not imply that the present social system is the most effective conceivable social system for that purpose; nor the opposite. The proposed definition of 'health' expressly assumes that individuals need sufficiently well-developed natural capacities to cope with new circumstances, new activities of daily life and new needs; and indeed to create these, for instance through political activity. It leaves open the logical possibility of saying that a given social system is ineffective at meeting its inhabitants' health needs, for instance by classifying Britain during the industrial revolution as an unhealthy society because of its inhabitants' short life expectancies, exposure to disease and industrial hazards.

Neither are we committed to believing that the healthcare activities aimed at delivering patients from the 'sickness role' necessarily support the harmonised functioning of the social order. Even if the Parsonian account of the sick role were true and complete, it does not directly consider patients' health, drives, capacities and needs. (Parsons was addressing different questions.) Depending on the circumstances, a patient may need to disrupt the social order rather than maintain it and a healthy patient has greater capacity to do this. Conversely, classifying a deviant as ill – even making her ill – may be more functional for preserving the social order than keeping her healthy – as has been alleged both of Soviet psychiatry (Szasz 1971: 216f) and of Western medicalisation of women's health (Ehrenreich and English 1979).

A person's 'need for health' is thus a combination of wide-spectrum instrumental need (for means to satisfy many further needs) and of natural needs (for painlessness). By focusing on our natural capacity to act, the present theory also suggests why health is (correctly) regarded as a 'basic' or important need. The World Health Organisation (WHO) view is well known: 'Health is a state of complete physical, mental and social well-being and not just the absence of disease and infirmity' (WHO 1946). This well conveys that physical, mental and social capacities are involved in having and actively satisfying one's drives (and *a fortiori* needs); and that the lack of disease or infirmity is necessary but not sufficient for this activity. A person's 'complete . . . well-being' depends on the external world (physical and social) besides her natural capacities functioning as necessary (ch3§1). Bringing these external conditions into a definition of 'health' is too expansive. What the external conditions for health are, is a separate empirical question not to be pre-empted by defining them into the concept of 'health'.

The prudential concept of health proposed here contrasts with most other ethical theories. They conceive of health either as a necessary means to all human 'aims' or 'ends', implicitly taken as moral ends; or as a moral end in itself. The present definition of health, and of individuals' rationale for seeking it, does not presuppose any moral position, only that people have drives. Being based on empirical concepts and prudential practical reasoning it is comparatively straightforward to operationalise. For obvious reasons many clinical indicators of health status focus on illness, not health (Bowling 1995: *passim*). But disease and impairment indicators are not necessarily direct indicators of incapacity or pain. There is no a priori reason that a general health status indicator should map directly onto clinical indicators for particular conditions or illnesses (*pace* Bowling 1991: 85) although the health impact of conditions and illness is definable by mapping them onto the range of capacities they disable and impair, and the pain they involve.

What is necessary for operationalising the proposed needs-based concept of health (and hence for health needs assessment at individual patient level) is translation between clinical indicators and the above concept of 'natural capacities'. This demands logical reduction without reductionism. The logical reduction is this: natural capacities are complexes of bodily activities. These in turn are complexes of biochemical processes, and these of subatomic processes. In principle, health indicators for each of these levels are reducible (translatable between levels). The translations between cognitive and physiological descriptions of mental processes involve a shift between 'internal' and 'external' standpoints towards our mental life (as ch2§4 explains). If the range of indicators at each level is complete, the translations can be done without loss of referential content; that is, without reductionism. This suggests that the concepts of 'natural capacity' and 'pain' stand at one end of a logical hierarchy of health status indicators. What we have previously called 'skills' (i.e. the concrete, socially specific form of natural capacities) appears to be the same concept that many clinicians, epidemiologists and psychologists express as 'function'.

A standard 'medical model' of health is sometimes criticised for limiting itself to non-mental intra-corporeal matters (Pickin and St Leger 1993: 54; Inglis 1983: 126–8). But a medical model is not inherently so weak or narrow. At its strongest it traces the micro-biological causes of ill health outside the body into the environment, including the social environment and the causes of ill health in consumer goods and the workplaces. Besides micro-organisms and chemical pathogens it also recognises cognitive causes of mental illness, and indirectly of some physical illnesses too (e.g. stress). Certainly a medical model is in an adverse sense 'reductionist' if it systematically ignores the large influence that social interaction and the external physical environment have on human health and needs. But that sort of medical model is simply scientifically, indeed empirically, defective. Similarly only an incomplete medical model ignores the relations between mind and body, instead of admitting the possibility of physical production of mental symptoms and mental production of physical signs.

Individuals' health is a product of their personal biology; of their experiences and of the physical and social environment that they inhabit; and of health services. We can now examine what this conceptualisation of 'health' implies about the need for healthcare.

§2 PERSONAL AND POPULATION HEALTH NEEDS

Now we can define what healthcare people need for sustaining their health, and thus what constitutes the under-use of healthcare, what constitutes health resource scarcity (ch7§2) and what constitutes over-use of healthcare relative to individuals' needs for health. A person's health consists in having the range and level of natural capacities necessary for satisfying his needs through his own activities of daily life, including social activities (ch4§1). The necessary natural capacities include consciousness of drives and the critical capacity to reformulate drives into needs (ch3§3). What makes a person need healthcare is, by implication, actual or prospective incapacity to carry out the activities of daily life that he needs. The cycle of drive, action and satisfaction (chs3§2, 4§1) fails in respect of one or more of the following natural capacities:

1 The drive itself (in the case of conscious natural drives its failure is experienced as a loss of desire for food, sex, etc.).
2 Sensation and perception.
3 Cognitive and practical skills including capacity to learn, concentration, decision-making, problem-solving and hence inability to articulate needs.
4 Communication, especially language.
5 Mobility, dexterity, strength.
6 Emotional response to success or failure in seeking drive satisfiers.
7 Active 'consumption' of satisfiers (e.g. inability to sleep or difficulty breathing).

To these failures must be added pains, including mental pains: anxiety, sadness and so on. The foregoing list covers failures of both mental and non-mental capacities. In due course we must consider how these two categories differ (ch6§1).

For the sufferer the practical significance of these failures is that they cause pains or reduce the sufferer's capacities to undertake the activities of daily life in pursuit of (further) needs or both. This is what the concept of 'illness' refers to. For different reasons Fulford, Sedgwick and others also hold that 'illness' and related concepts are significant for us because of their relation to human purposes (Sedgwick 1982: 30): in the present case, our needs. Two conditions are necessary to make human biological events count as an 'illness'. One is that the event seems to necessitate a corrective intervention. The foregoing definition of health in terms of needs (ch4§1) implies that the threshold at which a person needs healthcare is when pains or loss of natural capacity starts to disrupt her activities of daily life (cp. Stevens and Raftery 1994: i 16). This implies a failure gross or sustained enough to fall outside the (ill-defined) limits of accidental everyday variability in our natural capacities. Not every transient incapacity or pain represents a need for healthcare. Failures of capacity consist in an inability to do X even when one tries to, not the mere failure to have done X either because one did not try to or tried incompetently or was thwarted by some external obstacle.

Conceptualised in these terms, the concepts of 'health', 'illness' and 'natural capacity' are easy to relate to other familiar concepts, to which they are logically prior: 'disability' (long-term incapacity), 'dysfunction' (practically inadequate working of the body systems constituting the natural capacities) and 'impairment' (physical conditions causing body systems, including consciousness, to dysfunction). Attributions of illness involve both a (so-called) 'value judgement' and a reference that typically (but often indirectly) involves a causal explanation of the illness (Fulford 1989: 59–66; Sedgwick 1982: 32, 38). The family of related concepts can be understood as articulations of different aspects of these causal aspects of illness, either taking the 'value judgement' involved in attributing illness for granted or abstracting from it as irrelevant to causal (or other factual) analyses (Fulford 1989: 59, 73, 176, 183). However, all these related concepts are similar in placing the immediate cause of the breakdown literally within the sufferer himself (on the left of Figure 3.1), leaving open whether the precise cause be disease, aging, trauma or mental events (both 'physical' or 'mental' causes are physiological processes anyway on the present view – ch2§§3–4). Neither does it make any difference whether behind this immediate, intra-personal cause lie further, extra-personal causes such as bad housing or the death of someone close. This intra-personal causation is the second condition for a biological event counting as ill health.

Although some failures of natural capacity stem from a genetic or a congenital defect, such failures more often occur perinatally or later to a previously fully functioning, painless person: 'It is assumed that we are ill and made well, whereas it is nearer the truth to say that we are well and made ill' (McKeown 1976: 104).

This implies a hierarchy of healthcare needs, the second and each subsequent need coming into existence when its predecessor is frustrated. This agrees with Daniels in differentiating life-long healthcare needs from those that arise adventitiously (Daniels 1985: 26) through the onset of pain, impairment and disability. A fuller list of these types of healthcare is as follows:

1 Maintaining health through health promotion.
2 Self-treatment.
3 Curative healthcare.
4 Social care.
5 Palliative and terminal care.

It is more prudent for a person to maintain his health than to let it become damaged and then repair it. By maintaining health he loses neither the capacities nor the drive satisfactions which they are means of obtaining during ill health and its repair. Thereafter each type of healthcare is a fall-back from the next one up in the hierarchy. This is a prudential (not a moral) hierarchy in descending order of success in satisfying a person's health needs. The list extends the health economists' analysis of the demand for healthcare as a 'derived demand' from the demand for health and applies it to needs rather than demand (e.g. Mooney 1986: 24). In all categories different individuals have very different profiles of healthcare needs (Stevens and Raftery 1994: i 13). Nevertheless some general implications follow.

The largest pool of needs for healthcare are the needs of people who have not yet presented as patients to the health system (Stevens and Raftery 1994: i 6). The immediate healthcare need of people who are not already ill is for health maintenance ('health promotion') to prevent degenerative and environmentally caused illnesses. How people satisfy their drives, and especially their natural drives, has a direct effect on their health (ch4§1). Much research already exists about the determinants of health. Pickin and St Leger list the main 'health modifiers', relating them to the main stages of the human life cycle (Pickin and St Leger 1993: 56–172). They include water supplies, sanitation, employment, housing, transport, 'culture', social isolation and social status. Healthcare as traditionally understood (clinicians, hospitals, laboratories and other 'sickness services') is barely relevant to these. What is relevant is 'primary prevention' – measures to reduce the risks of ill health occurring at all: health promotion, health education and preventive healthcare, especially on an intersectoral basis (the 'new public health'). These include services for health-screening consumer goods and services, for environmental protection (air quality, town planning, use of agricultural chemicals, building design, 'environmental stress' – Commoner 1991: 217–22), family planning and occupational health services. Influencing policy outside the health sector (for instance, on income distribution – Wennemo 1993: 440, 443), both at national and increasingly at international levels, has still larger health impacts. One must distinguish health outcomes (of these policy interventions) from healthcare outcomes (of health services, which serve both health needs and other needs; see ch4§3), and both from the health outcomes of healthcare (Shanks and Frater 1993: 260).

Apart from services to influence public policy intersectorally, most of these needs for primary prevention can be addressed by primary healthcare (in Britain, by GPs), and the residual few at hospital level (mostly secondary and tertiary prevention, i.e. preventing risks being realised as illness and damage limitation respectively) (WHO 1978: 24–5, 53). The most important are vaccination and immunisation, contraception, preventive dental care and personal health education. Secondary prevention includes measures intended to prevent normal life-cycle events, especially reproductive ones, endangering health (e.g. antenatal care and in some cases contraception and abortion) and some less obviously preventive activities such as waiting-list management.

In 1993 Wythenshawe Hospital staff decided not to perform a coronary artery bypass graft (CABG) operation on Mr Harry Elphick because he was a smoker. Mr Elphick died before other treatment could be arranged. The decision was attacked as victim-blaming by some and defended by others for signalling that we are all responsible for helping to maintain our own health (Underwood and Bailey 1993; Grant et al. 1993; Dearn 1993). In effect the critics assimilated smoking-related disease to self-inflicted injury or to cases where a patient refuses to assist the doctor or comply with the treatment. (I have no reason to think that Mr Elphick himself was such a patient; and someone who started using such a heavily promoted, addictive product before its dangers were widely known is not the only person responsible for the resulting illness.) Does emphasising the need for health promotion and preventive healthcare lead to these inconsistent, need-denying conclusions?

If the purpose of health services is to provide healthcare on the basis of need (see ch1§1), the overriding criterion of eligibility for treatment is that the patient needs healthcare. Being seriously ill certainly meets the criterion of needing healthcare and it makes no difference to that fact how the need arose. Except when suicide is warranted (see ch5§2), a patient still needs healthcare even when she has injured herself, and even if she really is unlikely to comply with the treatment plan. Self-injury and non-compliance are failures of rationality on the patient's part, not evidence of an absence of need.

Although some health promotion activities are provided individually the most powerful, intersectoral activities work at whole-population level (see above). Ministers' edicts about these, and about healthcare resource scarcity (ch7§2) and healthcare management (ch7§1), tend to refer not only to the 'health' of individuals but to the health of communities or populations: 'The Secretary of State recently restated the key of objectives of the NHS as being . . . to lead the drive for improvement in the health of the nation' (Department of Health 1993: 5). More persuasively, some epidemiologists also refer to populations' health needs: 'a population based needs assessment is more than the sum of individual needs assessments. This is because the former must take into account future needs and also the needs for prevention and health promotion' (Pickin and St Leger 1993: 183). We already noted some intersectoral activities pursued at whole-population level. Certain less obvious influences on health also affect whole groups: herd immunity; eugenic policy; population policy; and some small-scale therapies, such as family therapy. Some clinical outcome indicators also apply to groups, not individuals.

Previous chapters, however, imply that the notion of 'a population's health needs' is logically misconceived. Only individual creatures have needs. To impute a need to a population is, strictly speaking, a category mistake. To say 'the population needs food' is like saying 'the population wants to go for a walk'. At best the claim that 'the population needs food' is a shorthand for saying 'each member of the population needs food'; at worst, it attributes to a group what logically can only be the attribute of its members taken singly. Needs logically attach to individuals just as their forenames do. Different individuals' needs logically cannot be added up to produce a 'population need' any more than their forenames can be combined to produce a 'population forename'. Indeed, it is equally nonsensical to speak of adding up even one individual's qualitatively different needs for different types of healthcare (or any other consumer good). Granted, it is logically conceivable that we could add up, say, the heights of every member of a population to produce an aggregate 'population' height although it is hard to imagine what practical or scientific purpose this would serve. This aggregation is logically possible because heights can be measured in common, cardinal units and because it would be physically possible to combine these individual heights (by the bizarre method of placing everyone end-to-end in a single continuous line). Nothing analogous can be said of drives, drive satisfiers, practical rationality and hence needs.

A simple way to prevent this logical problem is to propose clearer, tighter linguistic restrictions on how we use the word 'need'. But does this logical problem imply that the entire project of health promotion is vitiated because it addresses a non-existent entity, the health need of a population? One way to answer this doubt is to review what theoretical work the notion of 'population health needs' actually does, in the main areas of health policy to which it is applied.

Infectious diseases can be eradicated by preventing their transmission among a population. The minimum percentage of a population who must be immune (or immunised) to achieve this can be established empirically for particular diseases. A population achieving this minimum percentage is said to have 'herd immunity' (although not by McKeown, who denies that the concept has any practical relevance to public health – McKeown 1976: 76). Vaccination, among other factors, has already led to the world-wide eradication of smallpox. The WHO intends that diphtheria, polio, neonatal tetanus, measles, mumps and congenital rubella will follow (WHO 1979: 16/ target 5). Is this target an example of a population health need? Individual members of a population each have a health need to avoid being infected by other members, and each of them reciprocally needs (nearly) everyone else to be infection-free. Both the immunity and the need are the attributes of each of these individuals. In these contexts 'population health need' is just a shorthand for 'all these individuals being immune'.

Similarly, genetic disorders can only be eradicated at whole-population level (or nearly so). Until gene therapies are more developed, the only way to eradicate such genetic defects as cystic fibrosis or sickle-cell anaemia is to prevent them being inherited: a eugenic policy. It would be implemented through prenatal, or preferably pre-conception, genetic screening of potential parents, followed by aborting any foetuses shown, on further screening, to have inherited the genetic defect. (It is also possible to palliate some impairments resulting from genetic disorders such as phenylketo-nuria.) Such a eugenic policy is very different both in methods and scientific status from the spurious 'eugenic theories' advanced to justify the forced sterilisation, vivisection or medicalised killing of mentally handicapped people, non-whites and other victims of the Nazis, and even in some US states (Barker 1989). Nevertheless it has been criticised as another misuse of medicine for purposes of social control (Zola 1975: 180).

Eugenic policy differs from the eradication of infection in terms of what needs and whose are involved. For the sake of their own health everyone needs the eradication of infectious diseases. In contrast, a successful eugenic policy would meet health needs of the potential descendants of present sufferers; and needs of potential people are potential needs, not actual needs. A claim that existing people need such a eugenic policy must appeal to one of the following:

1 Whatever needs existing people have, not to have genetically defective children (perhaps future genetic research will, incidentally, make clearer whether or in what ways this is a natural need – see ch3§1).

2 More indirect needs, such as a putative need to reduce the cost of health or social care for people with genetic defects.

3 Future generations' needs. These are sometimes cited not only as a rationale for eugenic policy, but more often as the rationale for conserving natural resources and environments, or for a population policy. As they do not yet exist, future generations do not have any needs (in the sense outlined in ch3§3). Until they do exist, no policies can be justified on that ground. However, the needs of people alive today extend forward for their lifetimes, in many cases another one or two generations (ch3§1). By then the effects of a eugenic (or of a population or of an environmental policy) would begin to accrue. People alive today have need enough to consider and support these long-term policies, both on our own account and because of whatever needs we have or will have, to secure our children's welfare.

Nevertheless eugenic policy and anti-infection policy are alike in their status as putative health needs of populations. Freedom from genetic defects is a characteristic of individuals, as is the need to prevent genetic defects in one's children. To speak of a population-level health 'need' for genetic health is, at logical best, a shorthand for saying that nearly all of the individual members of this population would have to be free of a given genetic defect for that defect to be eradicated. Nothing beyond the (genetic) health of individuals is involved.

Many physical influences on individuals' health, such as air quality or the risk of being the victim of a road traffic accident or the availability of knowledge about health and healthcare, are indivisible. Legal and policy measures to promote health also apply indivisibly to a whole population in societies with 'rule of law'. Similarly many goods and services that influence consumers' health tend under industrial methods to be produced on so large a scale that large numbers of people consume rather standardised food, water, housing, transport and other consumer goods. Because the quality of these goods can be managed only at a collective level, this route to health promotion and disease prevention might seem to be a 'population health need' (cf. Pickin and St Leger 1993). But these items are common satisfiers for many individuals' healthcare needs. Again it is not another entity, 'the population', but millions of individuals who have these common needs. Similarly at micro-social level, irrespective of the therapeutic effectiveness of existing techniques, such methods as family therapy also address nothing more than the health needs of individuals. The difference with health promotion is that family therapy does so more through a common activity (or complex of activities) than through the consumption of a standardised good or service.

One aim of health promotion is to create a 'culture' or 'moral climate' that influences individuals' health behaviours and beliefs, for instance on the social acceptability of smoking in public or of specific types of diet. However, this provokes objections that moralising health promoters are over-extending a medicalised social control into ever further areas of everyday life, becoming 'health fascists' or the sort of person that the *Daily Telegraph* (revealing more about its own phobias than about health promotion) calls 'food-Leninists' (anon. 1994e). More intelligently:

> From sex to food, from aspirins to clothes, from driving your car to riding the surf, it seems that under certain conditions, or in combination with certain other substances or activities or if done too much or too little, virtually anything can lead to certain medical problems. In short, I at least have finally become convinced that living is injurious to health. This remark is not meant as facetiously as it may sound. But rather every aspect of our daily life has in it elements of risk to health.
>
> (Zola 1975: 180)

Although the labels 'fascism' and 'Leninism' are fatuous, the underlying objection to victim-blaming or unwarranted interference in the lives of more or less healthy people remains. Ivan Illich argued against cultural and social iatrogenesis, the over-medicalisation of every domain of life (Illich 1976: 26). Preventive care medicalises behaviour, initially increasing rather than reducing the consumption of healthcare (Bungener 1987: 125–6). However, the definition of health proposed here (ch4§1) does imply limits to the 'medicalisation' of everyday life. What limits the degree of medicalisation that healthy people need are the same empirical contingencies that warrant intersectoral health promotion in the first place. There are clear limits to which non-healthcare activities influence health. For example, most civil liberties questions, much of workplace organisation and most cultural activities do not have much direct influence upon people's health. Where factors outside the health sector evidently do influence health, the approach suggested here implies instead a partial demedicalisation of much of health policy and health service activity, in the sense of proportionately reducing the domination of health policy and health services by the interests and issues involved in providing clinical services.

Healthcare needs can be assessed at an individual level by comparing a person's actual health with full health, using the relevant health status indicators (chs3§3, 4§1). Here doubts about 'population health needs' raise more technical questions. Many health status indicators are probabilistic (e.g. five-year survival rates). They only apply to populations (even if comparatively small populations such as all the participants in a clinical trial). Using non-probabilistic health status indicators to assess the results of clinical trials still demands a comparison of the health status of groups of people. The prevalence of ill health in a population is (*pace* Stevens and Raftery 1994: i 14) a measure of how many of them currently need curative healthcare, and the concept of incidence can be used to predict how many will need it. Are these facts scientific reasons for retaining the concept of 'population health' and, correspondingly, of 'population healthcare needs'?

They are not. Non-probabilistic indicators characterise, quantify and analyse causal processes in abstract terms because the description of any causal process *per se* inevitably uses logically universal terms, abstracting from the particularity of the person or persons described. Standardised mortality ratios (SMRs) and other statistical population-level health status and outcome indicators (such as survival rates) summarise biological data about many individuals or formulate logical and mathematical relations between such summaries. In them populations are conceived as collections of individuals, without reference to any other bearer of health needs. Restricting the concepts of 'health', 'needs' and 'healthcare needs' to individuals does not prohibit the use of probabilistic, statistical or logically universal health status indicators. It is possible to conceptualise and quantify the health-determining relations between individual people without inventing another entity, a 'population', which also has health needs. Where prudential health and healthcare needs are concerned, the expression 'population health needs' serves, when it is not simply a logical muddle, as a shorthand for 'health needs of the individuals who …' (e.g. Stevens and Raftery 1994: i 5).

However, the expression has more sinister uses. Talk of needs presupposes some entity that has the needs (ch1§1). To speak of the community (or nation's) needs suggests that 'the community' is an entity with its own 'needs' (or other prudential or moral claims). In the absence of such an entity, a contrast between individuals' needs and 'society's needs' can only be an oblique reference to conflicts between the needs of different individuals. There are three main ideological uses to which the ideas of 'society's' or a 'population's health needs' can be turned.

One is to legitimate the incarceration and other invasive treatments of 'deviants'. Some patients do need involuntary treatment (ch6§3) but justifying it in terms of 'population' needs obfuscates both the valid reasons for it and some invalid ones. At times the reference to 'national' or 'population health needs' is, second, little more than a euphemism for the health policy interests of governments, health managers, businesses, the International Monetary Fund or World Bank (in many countries), religious groups or other bodies – policies whose relation to individuals' health needs is sometimes ambivalent to say the least (cp. Foster, Normand and Sheaff 1994: 175). Healthcare resource reallocations are (third) often predicated upon maximising the meeting of 'population health needs' (cp. ch1§1). Cost–benefit analysis to maximise the number of Quality-Adjusted Life Years (QALYs) purchased per pound is the best-known British approach (e.g. Kind and Gudex 1993: 94–108), with health economists busily trying to measure a non-existent attribute (the QALY total) of a single, non-existent subject (the population whose putative health need is being assessed). One purpose of doing so is to rationalise an inability (on the Health Authorities' part) or a reluctance (on the government's part) to purchase healthcare for people who apparently need it. Here the ideological point of speaking of 'population health needs' is that it 'counts as a gain what is really someone else's loss' (Russell 1986: 96). At these points, the notion of 'population health needs' becomes not just muddled but dangerous. It is more of a strength than a weakness of analysing needs as rational drives, and health in terms of natural needs and capacities (ch4§1), that it leaves no ontological status for a 'population' having needs for healthcare.

How, then, to explain the rationale for *Health For All 2000* and similar poulation-level health promotion policies? To say that a determinate population exists only as many individuals is not to deny that they share many 'social interests' or 'common goods': satisfiers that they all personally need. The earlier account of drives (ch3§1) implies many ways that can happen. Having common experiences, individuals acquire similar sets of drives and needs (to meet which, they might for example join societies of golfers, aeroplane enthusiasts or whatever). A health-related example is the need for clean, safe food preparation for people who eat out. Virtually everyone occupies a set of generic social roles, giving their occupants common satisfiers or means to get other satisfiers (for instance, through BMA activity). Again, individuals may be able to offer reciprocal satisfaction of each others' needs (e.g. at a rubber fetishists' club). Lastly some satisfiers are collective because indivisible, for example the construction of attractive townscapes or our need for clean air. Different health promotion programmes require different types of needs-based justification because a blanket appeal to the health need of a population is unavailable. But under the present theory such justifications are certainly available, and sound.

§3 NEEDS FOR HEALTHCARE

Although it makes by far the biggest contribution to individuals' health, health promotion activity cannot maintain everyone in full health. Descending the hierarchy of health services we reach the question of how to define what healthcare people need as illness sets in.

Self-care covers not only some aspects of health promotion (one's diet, exercise, etc.) but the self-administered healthcare for minor injuries or illness and a self-imposed triage when a person decides whether to seek organised healthcare – to become a patient. By its nature, individuals pursue their need for self-care outside health services. However, they need certain resources to do so, some of which the health system can provide. Knowledge of one's health and how to maintain it is one, which the education system and mass media also contribute to meeting (or fail to do so). 'Health behaviours' also demand physical resources: contraceptive supplies, means of occupational health and safety (protective clothing, machine guards, etc.), non-prescription drugs, dressings; and, for disabled people, adapted domestic appliances, access ramps, mobility aids and so on.

In the non-specialised activities of daily life, there is a (corrigible) presumption that a person's desires reflect his needs (ch5§2). Insofar as they do, his own activity rather than those of institutional staff are most likely to meet his needs when a person is mentally healthy (see ch6§2). Assuming that the natural capacities are maintained and developed by use, a partly disabled person needs to maximise the substitution of self-care for organised healthcare (for example, long-stay hospital patients who can prepare their own food and drink). This implies that people need 'normalised' self-care, 'independence' in their own homes, as soon as or for as long as they can. In terms of needs, what defines 'well-managed normalisation' is that it gives people in less than full health but still capable of some activities of daily life the means to meet for themselves those needs that they still can, which is likely to minimise the handicaps arising from disability. Obvious though these needs for self-care are, the present account of needs emphasises their importance, which is more than many health services do.

When self-care is impossible or insufficient, the onset of illness precipitates the need for acute, curative health services. (Writers and politicians tend to focus on these services as the most visible and expensive health services.) A definition of health as the painless use of natural capacities in the activities of daily life (ch4§1) also defines a patient's need for curative health services.

An explanation of consciousness as a special type of physiological process implies that curative health services have four types of treatment strategy available. Most obviously, they can intervene physically to remedy failures of non-mental body systems and structures, and use cognitive therapies (e.g. psychotherapy, behaviour modification) to remedy failures of mental functions. However, a compatibilist account of the mind-brain (ch2§§3–4) also implies the possibility in principle of using physical interventions to remedy cognitive failures, a controversial suggestion examined later (ch6§3). Conversely it also implies that psychosomatic cures are possible, producing physical results from cognitive therapies. The placebo effect is a familiar instance and one so practically significant that nowadays clinical trials are standardly designed, where feasible, as blind, double-blind or cross-over trials to eliminate its influence. Logically it is difficult to distinguish placebos from (other?) treatments (Gotzsche 1994: 925–6). Our account of health in terms of drives and needs leaves it an open, empirical question which treatments within each of these four categories actually are therapeutically effective (including so-called 'alternative therapies') or whether, in the two more controversial categories, any treatments are. In this way our theory avoids a standard criticism of 'Cartesian' models of health and healthcare (Inglis 1983: 261–3).

With an eye to economising on expensive healthcare some writers emphasise that a person does not need healthcare regardless of its ability to influence her health: 'Ineffective services are not needed; and effective services for which there are no potential takers are not needed'

(Stevens and Raftery 1994: i 6; also cp. Culyer and Wagstaff 1992). This much is unobjectionable but these truisms do not justify redefining 'need for healthcare' as 'ability to benefit' (Stevens and Raftery 1994). 'Able to benefit' is ambiguous. One sense is: 'able to have one's level of health improved by existing healthcare methods'. It is uncontroversial that people who are 'able to benefit' in this sense do need healthcare. The other sense refers to people who are equally ill but not able to benefit from existing services or therapies because these are technically underdeveloped. This ambiguity gives politicians and others an opportunity to define away the health needs of people whom present healthcare technologies cannot help, as not being 'real' healthcare needs. Obviously no one needs ineffective healthcare. But it does not follow that patients cease to need effective healthcare because the necessary techniques have not yet been discovered. What they do need is both the healthcare itself (once available) and (mean-time) for researchers to devise it. A need does not cease to exist because no one has the knowledge or resources to meet it. A person still needs his pain to be removed and his natural capacities to be restored irrespective of whether this is technically possible or probable. There could be few clearer illustrations of this than 'child B'; Jaymee Bowen. Suffering from leukaemia, she had a life expectancy of eight weeks without treatment costing £75,000 and only a 2.5 per cent probability of survival with treatment when her health authority decided not to purchase treatment for her (Weale 1995: 1). Yet if the choice is between a small chance of survival and none, the patient needs the small chance. Hence need for treatment is not equivalent to 'capacity to benefit' from existing services.

All that can currently be done for patients in this position is at most to substitute artificially for their lost capacities. These patients therefore need such resources as prostheses, appliances and domestic help to make good, albeit vicariously, the gaps in their natural capacities and hence need satisfactions. Modern medical and nursing techniques can increasingly substitute artificially for some reflexive or biological-system-level natural drives and capacities such as those for breathing and feeding. As the example of intravenous feeding shows, they can also partly substitute for the active consumption of satisfiers. The prudential rationale for doing so – the reason that the patient needs these substitutes – is to help him to satisfy as many needs as his condition allows (even with the risks and disappointments that this involves). Yet substitution becomes redundant, hence excessive, when it gets so extensive that no more drives (hence no more needs) of the patient's own remain (see ch5§2) or when it unnecessarily replaces self-care (see above). Managing social care in patients' own homes, residential care or hospitals through the residents' own participation in process democracy might be one way to prevent this problem (Saltman 1994: 220).

The last stage in this hierarchy of healthcare is reached when even substitution for some of the patient's natural capacities becomes impossible. Then what the patient needs is palliation of pain and of the effects of losing her natural capacities, and to minimise iatrogenesis (e.g. by preventing bedsores or wasting in an immobile patient). Everyone who does not die suddenly will need terminal healthcare. The gradual unravelling of natural capacities pushes a person's capacity for drive satisfaction further and further down the hierarchy until not even the most urgent natural drives can be satisfied. For practical purposes, in terms of needs, death has come when the cycle, however residual, of having drives, acting and satisfying them has irretrievably broken down. This implies that what terminally ill patients need is for as many of their needs to be satisfied until the last possible moment, not the protracted maintenance of low-level biological functions after the capacity to have needs is irretrievably lost (see ch5§2).

Hospitals and doctors are far from irrelevant to all these needs for healthcare, but considering the full range of a person's healthcare needs, the doctor's and the hospital's contributions are more circumscribed than first appears, and circumscribed in two ways.

Health service planning on the basis of needs would put promotion, prevention, primary care and self-care in the central place, giving hospitals and kindred institutions a residual function of remedying failures in those services and giving social and terminal care services the tertiary role of dealing with the hospitals' failures. On this view Virchow and the early social democrats were correct in arguing that what people need is a health system that makes most healthcare redundant (Labisch 1987: 281, 289). By analogy with Engels' predictions about the state in socialist society (Engels 1976: 363) they argued for the eventual withering away of hospital healthcare. Yet healthcare could not totally wither away. People would always need an irreducible minimum of primary healthcare for health promotion, initiating curative response to whatever ill health and accidents nevertheless occur, and responding to course-of-life needs (birth, reproduction, death) besides whatever wider political and social measures are necessary to maximise their self-care in the activities of daily life.

Comparing existing health systems with these implications of a needs-based theory of health reveals a second limitation in the role of doctors and hospitals. It is not at all obvious how many of their activities, particularly in research and development, actually relate to people's needs for health. Specialised activities such as forensic medicine obviously raise this doubt but so, on the face of it, do more mainstream activities such as contraceptive services, for the latter seem to have more to do with thwarting a natural capacity than maintaining it. If individuals' needs for health prudentially justify providing a spectrum of healthcare that in one respect is wider than is usually supposed, they seem in other ways to justify only a much narrower range of healthcare than people are often thought to need. This raises a further question: if people do not need those activities for maintaining their health, do they need them at all?

§4 NEEDLESS HEALTHCARE?

To suggest that many health services do little to meet health needs might seem a plausible view of iatrogenic or incompetent healthcare. However, the preceding account of what health services people need for maintaining their health did not mention many of the currently available forms of healthcare. It did not, for instance, mention the treatment of people with dangerously 'diminished responsibility'; genetics; contraception; abortion; or most of the new reproductive medical techniques. Influential critics have dismissed much modern healthcare as being of unproven value (Cochrane 1972: 31, 70) or even 'malignant' (Reiser 1978; Taylor 1979; Illich 1976). This poses two obvious questions: which kinds of healthcare do people not need as a means to health? And do any of these kinds of healthcare meet any other needs?

Answers are obvious where healthcare is clinically iatrogenic, causing greater impairment to body systems and structures than it remedies. The clearest form of iatrogenesis is the military and police use of healthcare technologies or workers in weapons development and in more 'clinical' experiments such as exposing terminally ill cancer patients to large doses of radiation in order to research the simulated effects of nuclear fallout (Zola 1975: 183). Medical participation in torture, physical punishment, executions and weapons development is obviously indefensible in terms of victims' health needs. Conceivably some of these, and some civil defence, political or criminological uses of healthcare resources, might meet third parties' needs and a favourite occupation of moral philosophers is to analyse imaginary cases where they do (e.g. Glover 1977: 262). Yet the abundance of imaginary cases contrasts with the rarity of real ones. If these uses of healthcare count as 'possibly meeting non-healthcare needs' at all, it is only on a philosophical technicality.

Those are extreme cases. Illich, however, argues that most main-stream healthcare is clinically iatrogenic, and more temperate critics agree that much of it is so even when administered competently, let alone negligently or incompetently or to patients to whose health needs it is irrelevant (Cochrane 1972: 31–2). The present conceptua-lisation of 'health' implies a distinction between two levels of iatrogenesis. At a strictly clinical level 'iatrogenesis' would be defined as 'healthcare causing any damage to physiological (including mental) processes or body structures'. Even effective healthcare usually has some adverse ('side') effects and there is a practical point in concep-tually distinguishing these necessary means to a net improvement in a patient's health from treatments having the opposite effect. Our definition of 'health' implies that healthcare only reduces a patient's health when its adverse effects are enough to reduce the painless use of his natural capacities. This is the threshold for iatrogenesis in terms of their needs for health. For short it can be labelled the 'practical iatrogenesis'. So the conception of 'health' outlined above places a slightly heavier burden of proof on those who argue that modern healthcare is to an important extent iatrogenic.

Some healthcare is not practically iatrogenic but equally has no practical effect in extending the patient's painless use of his natural capacities. In that sense, it is 'trivial'. A standard example is surgical treatment of a painless, non-function-impairing condition (e.g. liposuction, breast enlargement). Triviality is not an argument against all cosmetic surgery; only for distinguishing its trivial from its non-trivial uses. Cosmetic surgery that improves an individual's capacity for social interaction by removing an obvious disfigurement or removes severe emotional distress counts as non-trivial because it meets a natural need or restores a natural capacity (for social contact, say)(Glassner 1995: 160, 172). In a needs-based health system one role of the clinical 'gate-keepers' to healthcare (GPs, in Britain) might be to distinguish non-trivial healthcare from a medically oriented 'taste for luxuries', preventing consumers from seeking healthcare as the result of ignorance or desperation, for example where a patient clutches at the straw of a new 'miracle cure'. Doctors' 'taste for luxuries' includes experimental treatment which, when it augments scientific knowledge at all, does nothing to augment the patient's health (Pappworth 1967: 3–4, 9, 12–26, 76, 87, 101–47).

Many policy documents that justify NHS reform in the name of needs (ch1§1) also justify reform as a means to improving the quality of healthcare. Previous chapters imply that needs for healthcare are often overdetermined. In addressing patients' needs for improved health, healthcare simultaneously creates further needs: for information and reassurance, for satisfactory hospital 'hotel' services, for minimising disruption to daily life and so on. 'Quality' is often defined in terms of patients' needs in both policy documents and the more substantial literature (Ovretveit 1992; Sheaff 1991: 45) although without necessarily interpreting the concept of 'need' as proposed here. Nevertheless their work indicates that even the paradigm of healthcare, the acute hospital episode, addresses many other needs besides the need for health (when it does actually address the latter).

Some patients do not need healthcare (except palliatively) because they are now too ill to become viable. To paraphrase John Harris's questions (because we are still using 'need' in a pre-moral, 'anthropological' way – ch3§4), the critical questions about healthcare at the ends of life are not 'when does life begin or end?' nor 'what makes a body human?' (Harris 1985: 14f) but 'what characteristics justify using healthcare to conserve a person's life (or not)?' Harris answers: the capacity to value one's own life (Harris 1985: 17). In terms of needs for health the answer must be the prospect of sustaining one's cycle of drive, action and satisfaction (chs3§1, 4§1). To say that people need healthcare as a means to health implies that they need a narrower range of healthcare than they would if they needed healthcare as a means to preserving their lives.

'Viability' has been explained as 'the ability to sustain the cycle of drive – action – satisfaction with respect to the natural survival drives'. Not 'sustain unaided', note. Nearly all drives are in practice satisfied by enlisting others' help (ch3§1), including healthcare help. This definition of 'viability' therefore makes the threshold of viability depend on current healthcare techniques. Nowadays medical technologies (e.g. ventilation, intravenous feeding, catheterisation of urine) can substitute not only for some natural capacities and for the patient's own action but for the drive too. However, a patient needs this only because all her natural survival drives must be satisfied for her to survive. She needs these substitutions to complete her set of natural survival drives. This need for substitution presupposes the spontaneous operation of at least one natural survival drive. (Here 'drives' includes both conscious and non-conscious drives – chs2§3, 3§1.) The occurrence of a single natural survival drive indicates that a person is still trying to live and could, although only metaphorically, still be said to 'value their own life'. If no natural survival drives remained unaided, not even reflexive ones, she would no longer have any natural survival drives nor, *a fortiori*, needs. Our compatibilist account of drives (chs2§§3–4, 3§§1–2) implies that the organ whose irretrievable cessation of function marks the end of all drives and therefore needs is the brainstem. This supports David Lamb's definition, and the clinical operationalisation, of the concept of 'death' as brainstem death (Lamb 1985: 5–8, 14, 28–40).

People start (or cease) to need healthcare when they start (or irretrievably stop) having natural survival drives, and *a fortiori* other drives and therefore needs (ch3§2). Beyond this point, a person becomes viable at the point where healthcare can effectively substitute for missing elements in the cycle of natural survival drive, action and satisfaction. The foregoing analyses therefore imply that a person is viable when all three of the following conditions hold:

1 One or more natural survival drives occur spontaneously.
2 With the full range of currently technically feasible healthcare substitution for natural survival drives that are not operating spontaneously, all the person's natural survival drives would operate.
3 With the full range of currently technically feasible healthcare substitution for the relevant natural capacities that are not operating spontaneously, all the natural capacities that are necessary for obtaining and consuming natural survival drive satisfiers would function.

A definition of viability in terms of needs applies symmetrically to the beginning and the end of life. Where a person has not even one natural survival drive, he does not need healthcare for maintaining what remains of the drive–action–satisfaction cycle, whether at the start or the finish of the life cycle. When this point is reached is a matter of clinical judgement.

Some writers object to using the concept of 'viability' to demarcate the boundaries of a person's life for medical–ethical purposes. They object that at the start of life viability is (as noted above) a technologically shifting boundary. If it becomes possible to produce children outside the womb, viability will begin at conception, making the concept of viability redundant in the sphere of reproductive medicine (Glover 1977: 125; Harris 1985: 256n7). Also:

> With improved medical technology, we might be able to plug into other people for periods of the day to make use of organs we lacked. If an old woman were kept alive only by being dependent of her husband in this way, she would not be 'viable'.
>
> (Glover 1977: 124)

The concept of viability proposed here avoids these problems because it is not defined in terms of physical independence (as Glover assumes that the idea of viability must be) but as the availability of the physical processes (including consciousness) that constitute the natural survival drives. Physical independence presupposes viability but the two are not equivalent. The old lady whom Glover describes is evidently viable in terms of spontaneously having natural survival drives. Similarly a foetus conceived and brought to term entirely *in vitro* would become viable during that gestation. Whether the womb be artificial or human, the same criteria of viability and hence of the need for healthcare apply (More 1992: 427).

New healthcare technologies can already extend a few of our natural capacities synthetically. This is clearest in respect of assisted reproduction although inventions such as Prozac, with its alleged ability to reduce our susceptibility to depression, pose the same question: do we have a health need to extend our natural capacities? Helping a woman who has passed puberty but not the menopause to reproduce remedies or partly substitutes for her own natural capacity to reproduce. That counts as meeting a health need by our earlier definitions. She needs her natural capacity to reproduce, either to satisfy her natural drives to bear children (if there be any such natural drive) or to satisfy whatever historical drives she has to bear children 'normally'. If a woman of that age instigated it and brought up the child afterwards, complete *in vitro* gestation of a child would (if feasible) also meet these health needs. But equally, by this reasoning, enabling a post-menopausal woman to bear children is not meeting her health needs but (at most) her non-health needs. The same applies to enabling a widow to bear what are genetically her partner's children after his death.

If we do need to indulge the 'superman syndrome' – using healthcare technologies to extend our natural capacities – it is as a means to satisfy our non-health needs. This becomes evident if instead of new reproductive technologies we consider what would happen if a cheap, safe healthcare technology were invented that reliably doubled a person's IQ or longevity. The most plausible doubts that we need to do so arise because we suspect unforeseen snags. (How would one cope with being 160 years old?) 'Superman' technologies do not meet specifically health needs but the same sort of needs that cranes or trains meet. They artificially extend (rather than maintain) our natural capacities to satisfy our drives.

Other reproductive technologies are intended to impede the working of our natural capacities. Does this mean that, for instance, contraception is not a health need? Here we must distinguish the satisfaction of our sexual drives from their reproductive effects, and both of these from whatever drives we have to reproduce. If contraception is necessary for preserving the health of a prospective mother, she has a health need for it. If the health of her dependants is likely to suffer if she becomes pregnant, they have a health need for her to use contraception. Irrespective of that, barrier contraception meets another health need through its side effect of preventing the spread of sexually transmitted disease. Any kind of contraception would serve a health need insofar as it relieved women of health-damaging levels of anxiety or stress about sexual activity causing pregnancy. The alternatives of abortion and even childbirth pose much greater risks to health. However, it is likely that most people who use contraception do so for non-health purposes, wishing to avoid pregnancy because it would frustrate their other drives (e.g. to continue their education, pursue a career, or to rear a few children well rather than many children less well). If these drives withstood the critical scrutiny noted earlier (ch3§2) they would be needs but not health needs – although (as feminists point out) no less important for that.

Considered solely as a means of preventing births, abortion satisfies the same needs as contraception, although in a more clinically iatrogenic, risky and (typically) distressing way. However, abortion is also said to destroy an 'unborn child'. Moral arguments both ways have been thoroughly rehearsed elsewhere (e.g. Glover 1977; Tooley 1972; Thomson 1971). Here it is only necessary to note that the argument from potential is as irrelevant to needs as it is ineffectual against other objections to allowing abortion of pre-viable foetuses (Harris 1985: 134). Potential people have potential needs, not actual needs. Only actual needs give anyone a reason for action, and then only to actual individuals who have the relevant drives. As Mary Midgley says, 'Potentiality only matters because of what will happen when it is actualized' (Midgley 1980: 91) – or if it is actualised. However, this does raise the question of whether embryos (up to two months) and foetuses (two months to term) actually have needs. If not, is abortion legitimate up to the moment of birth?

The answer to both questions is 'no' if the decision whether to abort is made according to the criteria of viability outlined here. By birth the body processes constituting the foetus's natural survival needs and natural capacities are sufficiently developed for the drive–action–satisfaction cycle to begin. The spontaneous occurrence of its natural survival drives depends on the foetus having developed sufficiently. That occurs some while before the end of a normal-term gestation but only then is there a viable human that can at any moment start to have a child's natural survival drives and hence need healthcare or anything else. Objections to abortion on grounds of the unborn child's needs apply from when the foetus is viable but not before. Discoveries in foetal neurology will one day enable us to know when a foetus first develops the natural need to avoid pain (ch2§4). More has placed this as early as six and a half weeks after conception, reminding us that whatever claims that embryos have (in the present case, to be viable and to have needs) on development grounds apply irrespective of whether the embryo or foetus be *in utero* or *in vitro* (More 1992: 42, 45, 427). When a foetus becomes viable depends on the changing state of healthcare technology. If legal controls on abortion were based on the above notion of viability, and were intended to prohibit killing a foetus on the threshold of viability, no abortion would be legal after the earliest time from conception at which a child has been born and survived. Children of 500g birthweight and 23 weeks from conception now often survive to a healthy life. It is no argument against using this (or any other) criterion of viability, that the stage at which a foetus becomes viable becomes ever earlier as healthcare technologies develop. Defining viability in terms of the earliest occurrence of natural survival drives places that practical limit on how early this threshold of viability could ever be pushed.

Malthus expressed the best known of many subsequent alarms that world population will eventually exceed the size that available resources for food (and, we nowadays add, energy) production can sustain (Malthus 1992). There must be a theoretical limit to the population that the world's natural resources can sustain, although it is not clear which resources (water, land, energy, etc.) are the practically limiting factor, nor how long world population growth will take to reach this limit, nor whether world population growth will ever reach it before stopping for other reasons. However, the limit

looks close enough to prompt some governments to adopt a population policy, where one has not been adopted already for economic or
military reasons (e.g. in the former USSR – Sorlin 1969: 137–8). From
1982, for instance, Chinese policy allowed only one child per couple in
Kuangjo and other cities. Besides having a health rationale, these
policies have been implemented partly through health-system provision of contraception, abortions and sterilisation (sometimes by
subjecting pregnant women to financial or social pressures). Population policies offer the health benefits of preventing environmental
degradation and falling living standards, which are correlated with
deteriorating health status. What the population of a given country
will be in, say, 2050 is a matter already within the life expectancy of
many people now alive, hence directly relevant to their needs; but not
only, or even primarily, to their health needs.

Population policy is one example of what might be called the
political use of healthcare. Health needs that people clearly do have are
used to legitimate moral interference and control by health services
quite beyond those needs, for instance in the medical regulation of
prostitution in nineteenth-century Britain and Germany (Davenport-
Hines 1992). Many health services have refused to provide abortions
on religious (e.g. Ireland) or population policy grounds (e.g. Romania
until 1992). Whatever other justifications there may be for such
policies, health needs are not among them.

Behaviour modification has also come in for ethical criticism:
'serious ethical problems arise when behaviour modification methods
are imposed on captive populations (prisoners, the institutionalised
mentally ill or retarded, elderly patients in nursing homes and the
like)' (Eisenberg 1987: 109). The essence of behaviour modification
is that

> if it's in our power to create any of the situations which a person
> likes or to remove any situation he doesn't like, we can control
> his behaviour. When he behaves as we want him to behave, we
> simply create a situation he likes, or remove one he doesn't like.
> As a result, the probability that he will behave that way again
> goes up, which is what we want.
>
> (Skinner 1976: 244)

Paraphrasing in terms of drives, the behavioural therapist first
discovers what drive satisfiers the 'patient' already wants, then
constructs an artificial means–end association between the satisfaction
of one or more of these satisfiers and the 'behaviour' which the

therapist wants to 'reinforce'. Learning that the new 'behaviour' obtains the satisfier, the patient acquires what we have called an instrumental, historical drive for the new 'behaviour'. He has then learnt (not just 'reinforced') a fully fledged action (not just a 'behaviour'), motivated by acquiring a new, more or less conscious drive. Recent programmes advocating similar methods for therapy, education and social engineering can be traced back from Skinner (who was evidently familiar with William Morris's work – Skinner 1976: 147, 165) to Owen and the utopian socialists. Nevertheless such principles have been criticised as a basis for healthcare treatments, as being 'manipulative' or worse (e.g. Brown 1974: 155, 163).

A behavioural therapist's task is artificially to supply the relevant incentives. However, a therapist can do this either, as behaviourist jargon suggests, by strengthening ('reinforcing') existing incentives or by creating a new drive that completely countervails or replaces spontaneously existing incentives. To ask whether this is 'manipulative' is uninformative. Of course it is manipulative. Nearly all social contact involves getting others to do what we want (and having perforce to reciprocate in kind). A more incisive question is: does this kind of 'manipulation' increase or reduce the patient's natural capacity to satisfy his needs? Is he learning new needs or only new drives? A relativist view of needs implies that this depends on whether the action that the behaviour modifier is teaching is one that the patient needs. That depends on what effects acting on the new drives will have once the drives are (so to speak) carried over from therapy into other activities of daily life. In some contexts, behaviour modification would not be harmfully manipulative (e.g. teaching somebody with learning difficulties how to dress himself). In others, it would (e.g. 'curing' homosexuality by aversion therapy).

All these concern living patients. What of the dead? Having no drives the dead have, on the present theory, no needs, whether for their body parts or to be spared postmortem dissection for research or teaching purposes, or even for honouring the promises made to them when they lived. It is their surviving relatives and friends who have such desires as to honour promises to the dead; and sometimes these will be genuine needs, but they will be their needs, not the needs of the dead.

Needs for health and needs for healthcare are not equivalent. The means of producing healthcare, including the scientific knowledge, have wider uses than meeting needs for health and needs for health are met by other means besides healthcare. Individuals' health needs prudentially justify healthcare that includes not only preventive healthcare (vaccination and immunisation programmes, screening, etc.), acute healthcare, social care and terminal care but also activities that interfere in the provision of goods and services quite outside what is normally thought of as the healthcare sector: food and water, education, transport, leisure facilities and policy towards crime.

We also identified three main types of needless healthcare: when a person cannot be made viable; when healthcare only has a trivial impact on their health; and when the healthcare addresses somebody else's needs (whether or not health needs) rather than the patient's. Does this imply that health systems such as the NHS which purport to provide healthcare on the basis of needs are actually providing too much healthcare? The lack of a rationale for the above health services in terms of individuals' health needs does not imply that they have no rationale in terms of individuals' non-health needs. Neither does it imply that they lack justification in terms of non-health reasons (such as population or research policy) which are not transparently formulated in terms of needs. Nevertheless they count as 'health services' only by technical association with healthcare for health needs. The concept of 'health gain' (Department of Health 1993: viii) does not fully articulate why people need healthcare. People have other needs besides their needs for health (ch3§§2–3) and healthcare can address them too. Before dismissing this as obvious, one should recall that it is a conclusion in which British policy documents (ch1§1) show little interest.

Following chapters reconsider some types of healthcare which these conclusions call into question, including medicalised responses to deviancy (see ch6§2), euthanasia (ch5§§2–3) and clinical research (ch5§2). Since these types of healthcare are mostly provided through clinical practice we must consider that next.

5

DOES DOCTOR KNOW BEST?

§1 DOCTORS AND PATIENTS

Doctors are a mainstay of preventive healthcare for individuals, of curative services and other kinds of healthcare. When a patient can actively contribute to it at all, the doctor–patient relation is perforce a collaboration (Hart 1988: 284). It involves a complex of communications between doctor, patient and third parties. Patient and doctor each supply knowledge. Each makes decisions: when to approach the doctor; whether to accept the patient; what diagnostic tests and treatments to initiate; how far to comply with the doctor's advice; and so on. Then these decisions are implemented: the doctor 'treats', the patient 'complies'. Property relations come into play in the form of referral rights, freedom to prescribe, admitting the patient to hospital and payment. Both actors bring their pre-existing motives, beliefs and interests to the doctor–patient relationship.

It is not surprising, therefore, that studies tend to confirm that doctor–patient relations sometimes involve conflicts of interest and the exercise of sheer power. This has been examined from many angles: that of the physically ill patient (Illich 1976; Tuckett, Boulton, Olson and Williams 1985); feminist analyses of how male doctors treat women patients (Oakley 1976: 21, 54–7; Ehrenreich and English 1979; Foster 1995); the medicalisation of social deviancy (Foucault 1965; Szasz 1971); and that of the mental patient (see ch6§1). A relativist account of needs (ch3§4) suggests the possibility that not only do doctors and patients bring different motives and beliefs to their meetings (as might be expected) but different needs too. Besides his needs to carry out good clinical practice the doctor might bring, depending on the case, his business interests, professional interests, a role as representative of the state (e.g. by involuntarily treating patients) or his political interests (e.g. his eugenic enthusiasms – Barker 1989: 363–74). Thus medical judgements are practically inseparable from ethical judgements (Kennedy 1981: 83) including judgements about the patient's needs for there is no a priori guarantee that the doctor's needs will be fully compatible with the patient's needs. Neither is there any guarantee that what the patient demands will reflect the patient's own needs.

Some uses of the word 'need' actually obscure this fact. We already noted (ch1§2) that prudential statements in the short form 'A needs X' (without further qualification) are sometimes ambiguous about whose needs they really refer to: in this case, whether they tacitly refer to the doctor's, the patient's or somebody else's needs, yours, mine or some combination. Doctors have many occasions to pronounce upon needs because they are typically giving technical advice, hypothetical imperatives predicated upon the prudential end of restoring A's health. Sometimes either or both parties see this as a moral imperative too. For busy doctors whose most pressing interest is not logical analysis, the ambiguity of 'need' statements readily obscures the difference between the doctor's needs and the patient's, making it easy to confuse the former with the latter. There is this much truth in the claim that the idea of 'needs' can become a means of foisting professionals' judgements – or misjudgements – about what is best for a patient onto the patient or his relatives (ch2§1). It has been alleged that some putatively clinical decisions are of this kind, for instance when doctors decide the relative urgency of treating particular patients partly in light of whether patients are of 'interest' for teaching or research purposes.

A critical analysis of what patients and doctors actually need in the doctor–patient relationship is therefore central to a theory of needs for healthcare. The above considerations raise the following question: insofar as the conduct and nature of the doctor–patient relationship is legitimated in terms of the patient's needs, which decisions and judgements is it necessary for the patient to control, and which for the doctor to control? In the English-speaking world doctors appeal to the notion of 'clinical autonomy' to support their claims as to how the doctor–patient relationship ought to be structured and managed. Patient advocates have tended to invoke patients' rights to certain types of informed choice. This raises the question of whether clinical autonomy is defensible in terms of patients' (and doctors') needs, and if so, to what extent.

These questions can be analysed by applying the general model of the cycle of drive, action and satisfaction (ch3§1) to the specific case of seeking and receiving medical care. A first step is the formation of the patient's healthcare desires ('demands') and needs. As the second step the prospective patient selects means to obtain these corresponding healthcare satisfiers and as the third, having become a patient, actually obtains and consumes them. Previously we defined needs as the drives that a person would have if her drives were self-conscious, compatible, transparent, agent relevant and factually well informed (ch3§2). Whether and when medical paternalism is justified in terms of patients' (prudential) needs is therefore, above all, an epistemic issue. What scope for clinical autonomy a patient needs her doctor to have depends upon which of them has the fuller, more accurate or even privileged knowledge of each aspect of the patient's healthcare needs and of how to satisfy them. This is what we must focus on in retracing how the drive–action–satisfaction cycle takes place through the doctor–patient relationship (ch5§2). Since there is no guarantee that the doctors' needs and the patient's will coincide, it will be necessary to analyse the doctor's side of the doctor–patient relationship too, in a similar way (ch5§3). The patient's needs, however, are the starting point.

§2 PATIENTS' NEEDS

We pursue our needs for healthcare through the cycle of drive, action and satisfaction (ch3§2). However, a person's health itself consists of his capacity to undertake this cycle painlessly and without unusually large amounts of help (ch4§1). By following this sequence we can analyse what a patient needs of his doctor, what role these needs imply for the doctor's role and thus what degree of clinical autonomy patients need their doctors to have.

Besides suggesting what patients do need from healthcare, and in particular from doctors, this approach also reveals what patients do not need. Patients do not need, indeed need *not* to have, healthcare that they can undertake for themselves (see ch4§2). In particular, a patient needs the doctor not to act for her, when the patient can still make healthcare decisions and carry them out for herself, for instance in taking medicine or exercise, diagnosing and remedying small health defects, managing stable chronic disease (such as diabetes or, more controversially, drug addiction) and carrying out the activities of daily life. Even when patients cannot do this for themselves, they still need health services not to intervene where such needs can more effectively be met by third parties. For needs outside the domain of the 'expert' being consulted, expert and patient are on an equal footing. This would seem obvious but for the evidence of over-use of many kinds of healthcare in many health systems, resulting in the avoidable institutionalisation of patients (Goffman 1984: 121, 319; Martin 1983: ch. 1). Then patients need doctors to forebear. One thing that the mentally healthy patient prima facie does not need, indeed needs not to have, is moralising medical meddling (even when the law demands that the doctor meddle; legalities are a separate question). A standard example would be telling an under-16-year-old girl's parents that she was seeking contraceptive advice. It has been alleged (Young 1994: 9–10) that another is when doctors insist that heroin addicts be maintained on methadone, not heroin solely, because methadone does not give the pleasurable effects of heroin and has more pronounced side effects (methadone only prevents withdrawal symptoms).

Preceding analyses imply that even when patients do need medical intervention they are likely to know better than other people – even the doctor – what certain of their own needs are. In the following matters patients prima facie do not need the doctor to tell them what they need, although this presumption is only prima facie; criticisable and corrigible, as all presumptions about needs are (ch3§3).

To begin with, a mentally healthy patient has privileged knowledge of his physical pains and their mental equivalents (anxiety, grief, etc.) – 'privileged' in that only he knows immediately whether pain is occurring, in what intensity and forms. He also has privileged knowledge of his own occurrent desires, and his conscious thoughts, beliefs, memories, learnt satisfiers and overdetermination of desire satisfiers, and where the range of his desire satisfiers is underdetermined. (Our account of drives has left open the possibility that there are unconscious drives, and the possibility that unconscious drives are involved in the origins of mental ill health – see chs3§1, 4§1, 6§2.) Significantly for medical practice, his privileged knowledge includes knowledge of his degree of risk acceptance or risk aversion. The patient also has privileged knowledge of how his desire for healthcare is overdetermined: what combination of occurrent desires for health and for non-health satisfiers (convenience, self-image, material costs, etc.) different treatments are likely to satisfy. He has privileged knowledge as to whether information about his health and healthcare is intelligible to him, and how relevant it is to his drives, activities of daily life and conflicts of drives. If they withstand the critical tests outlined previously (ch3§2) all these occurrent desires are also his currently unsatisfied needs. Outside the areas of clinical expertise defined below, a mentally healthy patient is more or less as competent as the doctor to assess whether these drives are needs. This is relevant to the doctor–patient relationship because so much healthcare actually serves other needs than the patient's need for health (ch4§3). Where the patient has privileged knowledge, the claim that this knowledge is corrigible by the doctor or any other expert is weakest.

About certain other healthcare needs one can still claim that, prima facie, the patient usually knows best but the likelihood that a well-informed observer can correct the claim is somewhat greater. When it comes to knowledge of the patient's needs in the activities of daily life and the non-technical aspects of medical care, doctor and patient are on a more or less equal footing. By different means (examination and introspection respectively) both can assess, for instance, whether the patient's survival drives are grossly unsatisfied. However, a patient from a very different social background to the doctor's (e.g. is much richer or poorer, or of different ethnic origin or religion) is likely to know considerably more about its social and cultural requirements than the doctor does (Milio 1975: 56–8). A mentally healthy patient is as likely as anyone else to know how adequate his natural capacities are for the activities of daily life (occupational, practical, domestic and social functioning). Similarly the patient is probably best placed to judge the relative importance to himself of conflicting desires, for instance weighing the inconvenience of being treated at an awkward time or place against the inconvenience of the untreated condition (cf. Frankel and West 1993: 48). The same holds of what information he needs to know about the availability and effects of different treatment plans.

These are reasons for thinking that the patient prima facie knows best what he needs, in terms of the broad outcome and the management of the treatment programme. A mentally healthy patient is best equipped to decide these matters on the basis of his own knowledge supplemented by any more technical knowledge that he needs the doctor to add (see below). The patient needs the doctor to let him decide and accept his decision in these matters.

Only outside these areas does the mentally healthy patient need the doctor's knowledge, decisions and action. Even there, in his clinical capacity, the doctor has no technical knowledge that is not also available to the patient in principle: publicly verifiable or corrigible scientific knowledge. Insofar as medicine is a science, most of this knowledge is not only publicly verifiable but publicly verified (or falsified, in the case of discredited medical theories and methods of treatment).

Clinical practice can contribute to meeting patients' health maintenance needs by providing the patient with knowledge about her personal health status and of how to maintain her own health; and by providing preventive treatments such as immunisation and contraception. Patients also need healthcare as a means to the other needs that healthcare meets (ch4§4). Such events often stimulate patients to seek healthcare but the more common cause is a breakdown of their natural capacities or the onset of pain. When a patient needs her doctor, she needs the doctor to substitute for her own incapacity in getting and consuming healthcare.

Initially the patient may be incapable of knowing that she needs healthcare, whether through the recent deterioration of health itself or through longer-standing mental incapacity, or of knowing that this particular pain or incapacity indicates her need for healthcare (rather than being, say, effects of overwork or aging). Although the patient needs this knowledge, it is not enough to secure her healthcare. Even knowing, she may be unable to decide to seek healthcare or, having decided, be physically unable to act upon her decision. Then the patient needs someone to make good these deficits, as her proxy. Almost anyone can, say, call the doctor for her but the doctor's specific role is, as it were, the instrument filling these practical deficits of the patient in respect of technical expertise specific to the medical profession and its *de facto* prerogative of access to other healthcare resources. On this assumption we can define what the patient then needs from the doctor in the cases of the patient lacking knowledge, being unable to decide what to do, and being unable to do it.

Setting aside mental incapacity (until ch6§1), the first unsatisfied need of the patient would usually (depending on the circumstances) be for knowledge. Not only might he be too young or inexperienced to know that he needs healthcare, or simply unconscious; most people experience ill health unexpectedly, suddenly starting to need knowledge that they never acquired before because they never needed to. There are three main kinds of knowledge that the patient might need from the doctor.

One is knowledge of the fact that his health has deteriorated, to what extent and in what ways. Losses of natural capacity are often imperceptible to their sufferer, either because they set in gradually or are asymptomatic or because what has deteriorated is the very (cognitive) capacity for assessing one's own natural capacities accurately. Then the patient needs the doctor to assess the existence, extent and type of his healthcare needs for him; that is, critically to compare the patient's current health status with that of a fully healthy person of that age and sex. By definition, this deficit of knowledge which the patient needs the doctor to make good, occurs only in an ill patient.

Both the ill patient and the one using healthcare to meet non-health needs need to select the treatment whose net benefits are most relevant to their needs. A conscious, mentally healthy patient will already have most of the necessary knowledge of his various needs and activities of daily life (see above). Unless he already has this knowledge too (e.g. being a doctor or some other expert himself) he lacks and needs the specialised remainder. In part this remainder concerns his diagnosis and prognosis. This he needs the doctor to supply so that he can decide which treatments are relevant to his own needs. Of course the doctor is better placed to know about the patient's physiological processes, the interpretation of signs including those physically unobservable to patient and the significance of other health data. Although the patient has privileged knowledge of his own symptoms (including pains), the doctor is usually better placed to interpret their health significance. The doctor is 'better placed' not only because of his expertise but as an analyst without the patient's understandable susceptibility to cognitive dissonance or self-deception (Festinger 1962). Because the patient needs this knowledge, he also needs the doctor to help him overcome any cognitive dissonance in face of bad news about his health.

His training alone makes it likely that the doctor will know of more possible treatments than the patient does, and what other healthcare resources are available. Only one active treatment plan may be available but there is always at least the one alternative of doing nothing, 'letting nature take its course', and often a third option of doing little, of 'not striving officiously' (e.g. 'maintenance only', 'nursing care only' or 'pain relief only'). Because all treatment is potentially iatrogenic it is prudent from the patient's standpoint to put the onus of proving that he needs treatment on the clinician who proposes it. To decide prudently the patient also needs to know how alternative treatments differ in their probable effects on his pains, on restoring his natural capacities, on his activities of daily life and on the many other needs that healthcare also meets and about which the patient probably knows as much as the doctor (ch4§4 and above). Since the 'do nothing' and 'do little' options are available, he also needs to know his prognoses in these events. 'Side' (i.e. iatrogenic) effects of treatment are often of great practical importance to patients, as are the risks of each treatment option. (However, it is still prudent to take the risk if the alternative is to face a still bigger risk – Dawkins 1978: 183.) The considerations above suggest that the patient knows best what he needs in regard to risks, side effects and impact on non-health needs. In practice patients often desire reassurance on all these matters, and giving information about them sometimes meets that need too. All this information might have to be paraphrased or simplified for some patients to understand but essentially it is scientific knowledge of means.

Clinical practice is used to meet the needs of many other parties besides patient (see ch4§3) and doctor (see ch5§3). One merit of a relativistic account of needs is in making us consider whether these other parties' needs coincide with the patient's needs (see ch3§4). The patient needs to have good reason to trust the doctor not only in terms of technical competence but also in having well-grounded confidence that the doctor has chosen what treatment to offer him solely grounds of the patient's needs, not other conflicting interests. Among the latter might be the doctor's commercial or financial interests (for instance, income from private practice or for referring to a particular hospital or clinic); or professional or academic interests such as clinical trials with their risk of exposing the patient to an untried treatment or none. Creating safeguards that patients' needs will not be compromised in these ways is a task for healthcare managers, health policy-makers (see Chapters 7–8), jurists and the authors of substantive professional ethical codes, especially in regard to clinical autonomy (ch5§3).

When, and only when, the above information has been given, can a conscious, mentally healthy patient understand and select the treatment most relevant to her needs. In terms of needs this is what 'knowing what consent involves' is (cp. Faulder 1985: 33). Since a mentally healthy patient's desires are prima-facie (but corrigible) evidence of his needs (ch3§2), the prudential justification of informed consent is that it is necessary as a means for a patient to pursue her need for healthcare.

In providing this information the doctor is, according to earlier arguments (ch3§1), altering the patient's desires in direction of the patient's needs by making the patient aware of what her instrumental needs are. If the patient understands and accepts this information it becomes cathected and she comes to desire the treatment indicated, as means to the further satisfiers that she desired in seeking healthcare. When the doctor's knowledge of such matters is so much greater than the patient's, imparting it will virtually construct the patient's decision, the patient being largely passive. To represent this as a patient's 'consent' to the doctor's suggestions is barely an exaggeration. This explanation of informed consent in terms of needs shows why the informational element is central to informed consent and why it is often virtually inevitable that patients will be rather passive in the consultation. It is virtually inevitable simply because the patient lacks but needs knowledge about her diagnosis, prognosis, treatments and outcomes; and depends on a human expert, the doctor, for it (and for clinical care itself) (*pace* Sedgwick 1982: 138–9). (This might change as the medical 'expert' information systems which are already being developed come into use.) Nevertheless there remains a clear distinction between the benign 'construction of consent' (fully and truthfully communicating to the patient what will serve her needs) and contriving the patient's agreement, to meet the doctor's needs. However minimally, it is still the patient who consents in the informed consent scenario.

So it would be mistaken to conclude that fully informed consent would require the patient to have as much clinical knowledge as the doctor. What is relevant to the patient's needs are the likely effect of different treatments on her natural capacities, pains and activities of daily life. Only lay, not expert medical, knowledge is necessary for understanding that. For these purposes the patient does not need to know every conceivable risk remotely relevant to the proposed treatment, but only those that will affect the satisfaction of her needs for healthcare; and of those, only the most likely to occur. A degree of arbitrariness is unavoidable in defining 'most likely'. An obvious suggestion is for doctors to use the same levels of probability as they accept in clinical trials as indicating the significant probability that the treatment produced the benefits reported (e.g. the standardly accepted significance levels $p \leq 0.05$, $p \leq 0.01$ or $p \leq 0.001$).

Faulder (1985: 35) criticises 'therapeutic privilege': the practice of concealing from a patient that he has been entered into a blind or double-blind randomised control trial (RCT). This is a clear-cut conflict of interest. The doctor might need the privilege but not the patient. For the reasons noted above, the patient entering such a trial needs to know what treatment options and risks he confronts and, after the trial, what treatment he actually had. In a bona fide, well-conducted RCT he has a 50 per cent chance of having a treatment whose effectiveness, compared to the control, nobody knows. Giving the best standard treatment to the control group in an RCT does not negate – still less satisfy – the patient's need to be informed. For the patient, entering a well-conducted RCT is a lottery. Although it may be prudent to take that risk, the risk itself is necessary, even from the clinicians' standpoint, if the RCT is necessary for the production of new knowledge (Pappworth 1967: 28, 34, 43).

Sometimes a patient is forbidden to decide what healthcare he may receive, an occurrence less rare than first appears because many health systems (including the British) place control of access to 'secondary' services in the hands of doctors and other 'gate-keepers' who alone have powers to make the necessary referrals, authorisations, admissions, permissions or prescriptions. Patient and doctor each have part of the information necessary to determine what treatment the patient needs. Then a doctor can do what the patient needs, by taking the same decision that the patient would have made under conditions of informed consent, had the health system allowed it.

Where a patient abdicates his decision in selecting treatment the case is similar. The only difference relevant to their needs for healthcare is that in one case the patient makes no decision because the law forbids it and in the other because the patient himself is too diffident, for instance wishing to abdicate (what he sees as) unpleasant or difficult treatment decisions to the doctor; or is too ill to decide. Then the patient no longer needs to know his diagnosis or prognosis for that purpose, nor for his consent to be as fully informed as described above. Instead he needs the doctor as a substitute decision-maker, to 'do the thinking for him' as it were. Since theories of needs are often accused of warranting medical paternalism, this scenario demands an explanation of what conditions actually warrant doctors deciding treatments vicariously, in the patient's stead and on grounds of the patient's needs. The principles are the same as in cases where the patient is simply too ill to decide, because unconscious or experiencing only an intermittent or 'twilight' consciousness: the classic prima-facie case for non-voluntary treatment. Although there are no prima-facie reasons to think that he would oppose being treated, the patient cannot indicate what he does want. These circumstances pose the question of what would be admissible surrogates for the patient's informed consent (cf. Strasser, Jeanneret and Raymond 1987: 187).

An obvious answer is that the admissible surrogate is confirmation that the proposed treatment is treatment that the patient needs, treatment to which he would give informed consent if he could. Ascertaining what treatment this is requires information about the patient's diagnosis, treatment options and their prognoses, risks and outcomes. The doctor has that. But it also requires information about those needs of the patient, about which the doctor has no expert or privileged knowledge (see above). This raises the question of who is to give informed consent in light of these needs of the patient, when he cannot. In these rather complicated conditions it appears that a patient needs non-voluntary care when, but only when, all the following seven conditions apply:

1 The patient actually needs healthcare; he is not in full health (ch4§1).
2 The patient needs the proposed treatment. The conditions for this are the same as for voluntary care: that the proposed treatment offers fuller or more probable relief of pain or restoration of natural capacities or both than any practicable alternative, including the 'do nothing' or 'do little' options (ch4§1). The larger the potential damage to the patient's natural capacities, the easier it becomes to show that these conditions apply, with irretrievable loss of natural capacities (e.g. blindness or paralysis) as the clearest case.
3 The proposed treatment is actually available and offers a non-negligible probability of restoring the natural capacities, or of relieving pain (although the non-voluntary patient is typically unconscious).
4 To succeed the treatment must start before the patient gains or regains his capacity to chose (otherwise the patient does not need the doctor to do his deciding for him).
5 The treatment's effectiveness does not depend on the patient's active, voluntary compliance. Non-voluntary resuscitation is technically possible. Non-voluntary psychotherapy or physical exercise are not.
6 We have assumed that the purpose of the non-voluntary treatment is to restore to the patient as full health as is possible, *a fortiori* to life. This presupposes that the patient does not need non-voluntary euthanasia, nor a 'do not resuscitate' or equivalent order, nor assisted suicide. But does a patient ever need to die? Unless one accepts the late Freudian belief in Thanatos (the death instinct), there is evidently no such natural drive and even Freud regarded it only as a theoretical postulate (and on grounds of philosophical not scientific theory, Freud 1939: 101–2). Neither does death satisfy any natural drive except pain avoidance. For suicide to be a prudentially better prospect than life, that pain must be permanent, intractable and unendurable to the patient. Physical pains of this kind are all too well known but it is less clear what emotional distress (the mental counterpart of physical pain)

might correspond. (Perhaps extreme guilt and regret; one thinks of accounts of fathers forced to choose which of their children would be shot as a reprisal during the Nazi occupation of Greece.) As to whether he has pain, and its severity, and hence whether he needs to escape it, the patient has privileged knowledge. Even then only the circumstances make suicide a necessary means of escaping pain. What he actually needs is pain control. Suicide is only a desperate means to that.

There might, among the residual category of natural drives (ch3§1), be some whose satisfaction might only be secured by suicide, although only in rare and odd circumstances (e.g. a drive to protect one's children, if such a drive were shown to exist). This seems a theoretical possibility at most. Many people have committed suicide to satisfy what we called 'historical drives' (see ch3§1): for revenge; to protect colleagues; as self-punishment; to make a moral point; and for artistic and ritual purposes (Campbell and Collinson 1988: 1–20). Conceivably choosing the time, place or manner of one's death might bring other benefits (e.g. to avoid trial, disgrace, reprisals against one's family, etc.). Yet this can rarely, if ever, count as a prudent action. At root our historical drives are means to satisfying the natural drives (ch3§1) or side effects of doing so, so suicide motivated by any of these historical drives would fail the tests of instrumental rationality and compatibility with other drives, and perhaps also of transparency (ch3§3). Apart from pain avoidance, the only case in which non-voluntary euthanasia would not violate the patient's own needs would be to finish off the process of dying once the point of no return to viability had been passed (as in the Tony Bland and Karen Quinlan cases), although it is unclear whether this counts as 'euthanasia' at all.

So only pain avoidance offers a clear-cut need, and irreversibly passing the viability threshold a clear-cut occasion, for non-voluntary euthanasia. However, the fact that a patient is in severe pain implies that he is conscious and therefore (or at least, usually) able to decide, so that only rarely will a patient need non-voluntary euthanasia (as opposed to assisted suicide) even for escaping pain.

A patient needs non-voluntary treatment only until he regains the capacity to choose, i.e. the capacity for informed consent described above, when the doctor's decision-making becomes, at best, redundant. For mentally healthy adults, regaining consciousness normally suffices.

If these conditions are met, the next question is: who is best placed to give informed consent to non-voluntary treatment on the patient's behalf? In most health systems the doctor is legally responsible for treatment and, irrespective of law, has the expert knowledge necessary for informed consent (but not sufficient; see above). To decide competently on the patient's behalf one must know both the patient's health needs and his other needs for healthcare. Depending on circumstances, a close friend (or relative, neighbour, workmate, lover or colleague) will often know more about the patient's non-health needs than the doctor does; but each can, by consulting the other, acquire the two pieces of knowledge that the patient would need for informed consent. The relativism of our account of needs (ch3§4) highlights the patient's need to ensure that neither the doctor nor the friend is pursuing needs of their own, incompatible with the patient's needs for healthcare, in deciding on the patient's behalf (e.g. that the doctor does not want to experiment with a new treatment – Papp-worth 1967: 31–78 – or the son to be rid of a troublesome parent).

A patient who can understand the treatment options and choose which one he needs may nevertheless be unable to initiate the necessary action. A dramatic though rare instance is when anaesthesia fails during surgery, leaving a patient paralysed and unable to signal consent but still conscious of pain, and having very definitely decided what he needs to happen. More usually, patients are physically unable to treat themselves (although there have been rare cases of surgeons operating on themselves under local anaesthesia – Hoffenberg 1987: 50–1) besides lacking the requisite clinical knowledge. Here the patient of course needs the doctor and other health workers to implement the treatment plan for him; but as health workers often remark, the patient also needs to comply with their instructions for making his own practical contribution to treatment, and for relatives and other carers to comply too.

Again the question of whether patients ever need assisted suicide arises as the extreme instance. The narrowly defined circumstances in which a patient might need to die were noted above. He needs assistance if and only if that condition unequivocally holds and he cannot accomplish the deed. Some well-known cases in which patients have applied for court rulings to permit doctors to assist them in suicide do not satisfy the criteria of pain relief or irretrievable non-viability noted above: for instance, those of Ramon Sanpedro, crippled from the neck down since 1968 and of Sue Rodriguez, dying of incurable amyotrophic lateral sclerosis (anon. 1994b: 21–3). The present account of when patients need non-voluntary euthanasia and assisted suicide excludes nearly all conscious but severely disabled people. In the case of emotional 'pain', of which the patient has privileged knowledge, it is harder to define 'inescapable', 'intractable' and 'unbearable' severity. Perhaps the most feasible solution is indeed on the lines of the Netherlands legal stipulation that the patient's wish to die must be considered and lasting (Sharkey 1995: 21). Although this account of healthcare needs has rather conservative implications about when a patient needs assistance in suicide, its relativism highlights the obvious and difficult health policy question of how to construct safeguards to ensure that a patient can obtain assisted suicide if he needs to but protecting patients in all other circumstances. One safeguard lies in the aforementioned decision role placing the onus of proof on those who propose a treatment. However, it is conceivable that in some cases assisted suicide is the only means of escaping permanent, unbearable, intractable pain.

Assisting suicide can range from deliberately not pressing the nurse call button to giving advice, through supplying drugs to actually injecting the patient (as Dr Cox did for a patient in extreme pain – anon. 1992: 3); from actively killing to 'letting die'. The present account of healthcare needs excludes the doctrine of double effect in respect of acts and omissions, agreeing with John Harris that 'what matters is how our acts and decisions and actions affect the world and other people, not whether our responsibility for that effect is positive or negative' (Harris 1985: 47). This holds for direct and indirect effects alike (Harris 1985: 4–5). The relevant effects for us are the effects on individuals' needs, understood in prudential, not moral, terms. Active and passive euthanasia have indistinguishable effects on the patient's needs, as have all the intermediate degrees of activity between these two poles (cf. McMahan 1993: 273–4). The difference is one of means, and perhaps in type of motive of those who help to cause the patient's death and their scope for (perhaps emotionally necessary) self-deception. This consequentialist implication of our account of needs rules out as spurious the supposed safeguard of stipulating 'let die when necessary, but never actively kill'.

By signing a 'living will', prospective patients try to obviate their last incapacity to decide or to act. The foregoing implies that a living will would be justifiable in terms of a patient's needs if at least one of three conditions held (although two of these conditions are somewhat far-fetched). One is, that the living will anticipated when the patient would never regain viability and requested doctors actively to complete the process of dying then. A second would be, if the living will stipulated in advance what level of pain would warrant suicide. It is hard to see how a patient could stipulate this in practice, and then the living will would be rather shaky evidence of her needs, of practical relevance only if she was unable to decide for herself to commit suicide at the time. The third, equally unlikely, possibility is that the patient could predict a set of circumstances such that, given her fairly stable desires, the patient knew that she would take her own life if she could to avoid extreme emotional 'pain'. The onus-of-proof condition implies that the patient would need assisted suicide only if these conditions were clearly defined, were unambiguously and irreversibly satisfied, and (again) that she were not conscious enough to request assisted suicide at the time (e.g. 'Do not resuscitate me if there is any prospect that the Nazis will use me as a hostage').

In summary the kind of clinical relationship that a patient needs with her doctor is the so-called 'holist' relationship because in it the doctor recognises the relevance of the patient's mind, physical and social setting, as well as her body, to determine what healthcare the patient need. By implication, this is a participative relationship. To place the medical expertise that the patient needs at the patient's disposal, the doctor conversely needs the patient to comply in certain ways. He needs the patient to supply complete and accurate information as necessary to diagnose her illness and its causes. Similarly it is necessary for the patient to express her preferences regarding those needs about which, prima facie, the patient knows best. The doctor needs to obtain patient consent to the proposed tests and treatment, and the patient's practical compliance in the treatment (taking medicine, stopping smoking before general anaesthesia, exercising, etc.). Often the doctor will also need informal carers to comply (e.g. in treating children, frail people or people with learning disability). In some circumstances the doctor may also need the patient to provide physical resources or money. In Russia, for example, during the collapse of the Soviet system and at the time of writing (1994–5) it was necessary for patients who could to supply their own disposables (dressings, needles, etc.) and for all patients to supply their own drugs. All these are the converse of the patient needs examined previously (ch5§2). If we were using moral discourse we might designate them patients' reciprocal 'obligations' to the doctor. But as we are not, we can only classify them as historical needs of the doctor, assuming that he needs to meet his patient's needs for healthcare.

Only if the patient is incapable of participation does she need, as the next most prudent thing, the so-called 'expert' model of doctor–patient relationship. However, there is no practical guarantee that doctor–patient relations actually are 'holist' or 'mutually participative'. A relativist account of needs implies that a harmonious coincidence of doctor's and patient's needs is not preordained but has to be contrived by those who make and implement health policy; and indeed by doctors themselves. This implies a rather specific theory of clinical autonomy.

§3 CLINICAL AUTONOMY

From analysing what patients need from doctors, we turn to the doctor's needs. In developed capitalist societies, including Britain, doctors pursue their needs primarily through a set of professionally controlled institutions and working practices, at once referred to and legitimated as 'clinical autonomy'. A fundamental defence of clinical autonomy is that the doctor needs a degree of autonomy in making and carrying out clinical decisions (i.e. decisions on diagnosis, treatment, referrals and research) in patients' interests:

> In essence the concept implies: I will do my best for the patients or clients referred to me. The decisions I take will be mine and will always be in the best interests of the patient. I will use procedures, equipment or drugs to this end, regardless of cost.
> (Downie and Calman 1987: 225)

For present purposes the phrase 'in the best interests of the patient' can be construed as 'what the patient needs'. Taking the justification of clinical autonomy to be that it is necessary for, or at least assists, doctors to meet patients' healthcare needs, patients need clinicians to have autonomy to chose and administer healthcare that the patient would provide for himself if he knew how and could physically examine and treat himself (ch5§2). As a means to meet patients' needs for healthcare, clinical autonomy would be a vicarious autonomy exercised on the patient's behalf while the patient was unable to do so. The doctor would act as the 'patient's friend' in exercising clinical knowledge and skill.

A negative implication is that patients need doctors not to be autonomous to do anything incompatible with the tasks outlined in the previous section (ch5§2) (cf. Hoffenburg 1987: 4), and to be autonomous not to do anything incompatible with those tasks when third parties try to get him to do so. Where there is no scope for clinical activity, the only remaining scope for clinical autonomy is for the doctor to be free not to interfere where he has nothing to add to the patient's self-care. In a negative way, the doctor needs at least to be autonomous of institutional pressures to engage in the various kinds of iatrogenic healthcare noted previously (ch4§3). Torture and execution are the rare, extreme cases; the more everyday and pressing questions concern research and whether involving doctors in healthcare management, and especially in the allocation of scarce resources, compromises and abuses their clinical autonomy (Hoffenburg 1987: 28; and see below). In Britain at least, a central element of the notion of 'clinical autonomy' is that the doctor can and should work largely autonomously of health service managers (Tolliday 1978: 33, 37–8).

For obvious technical reasons the doctor needs intellectual autonomy to decide the patient's diagnosis and what treatment the patient therefore needs in light of the facts (Hoffenburg 1987: 17) including autonomy to refer the patient to third parties who, in the doctor's technical judgement, are competent to carry out treatments which the doctor himself cannot (Tolliday 1978: 48–9). For self-care the patient needs the doctor to be free to order whatever aids and appliances and make whatever administrative authorisations the patient needs for self-care. The patient needs his doctor to be autonomous to pursue the diagnosis and treatment indicated, unconstrained by third parties such as managers or payers wishing to avoid expensive treatments (e.g. courses for AZT), governments wishing to exercise political control (e.g. the Soviet regime concealing nuclear pollution by deleting parts of the medical notes of patients sent from Chernobyl for treatment in other provinces of the former USSR), firms not wanting to admit that their asbestos caused the patient's mesothelioma, and so on. The patient also needs the doctor to have autonomy to challenge fallacious clinical orthodoxies and public opinion (e.g. on providing contraception to schoolgirls) (WHO 1979: 56/target 38). As a practical corollary the doctor also needs to be autonomous of pressures to disclose information about the patient to third parties who might use it to interfere with the doctor's ability to meet the patient's healthcare needs. It is a familiar argument that any risk of disclosure might reduce a patient's confidence in using health services if the patient feared that the police, an employer, family or anyone else with power to harm him could learn about his health status from his doctor or how he came by a particular injury or disease. So there is a simple needs-based argument in support of this much clinical autonomy and this much confidentiality in the doctor–patient relationship. What complicates the picture, for the doctor, are the needs of third parties which the doctor may also need to serve. For example, other health workers have a health need of their own to know whether a particular patient is infective or violent.

All the above take 'clinical autonomy' to mean 'autonomy of third parties' extraneous influence on the doctor–patient relationship in clinical practice'. However, doctors also need a degree of autonomy of the patient too in order to protect the patient from himself, and not only when the patient is mentally incapacitated (ch6§3). Mentally healthy patients also need this protection sometimes. For example, they may misinterpret their case notes. Recently a patient read the diagnosis of leukaemia in his medical record, began to neglect himself and died as a result although his form of the disease was unlikely to be fatal (Alexander 1994: 9). Such patients need the doctor to decide autonomously when and how to explain their illness, for the doctor to have the autonomy to override the patient's desires for treatment that the patient does not need, especially iatrogenic treatment, and for the doctor to be autonomous enough ('detached' – Hoffenburg 1987: 72) to confront the patient's own cognitive dissonance towards a bad prognosis. Only rarely will this amount to autonomy to avoid explaining at all. Because the patient needs to be informed about his health in order do decide what to do about it (ch5§2), the onus lies with the doctor to prove that he needs not to be told. However, this proof might sometimes be available because the patient's desire not to be told is another prima-facie but corrigible indication of what the patient needs in this matter; although in this sort of matter a person is likely to know his own non-technical needs best (see ch5§2).

Doctors also exercise social control roles on behalf of the state, employers and other third parties: whether to admit a person to the sick role (excusing him conscription, or even punishment in the case of mental illness); whether to accredit him fit for employment; and whether to subject him to involuntary or non-voluntary healthcare in his own interests or those of others (see ch6§3). Now identifying and characterising a patient's signs and symptoms, assessing their scale, effects and prognosis, and attributing a cause is evidently a matter for technical clinical judgement. Whether they count as unhealthy, hence as illness, is not. That depends on what pain these signs and symptoms involve, and what effect they have on the patient's natural capacities (ch4§1). Granted, the doctor is likely to be practised in assessing and predicting what effect the signs and symptoms have on the natural capacities in everyday life – another clinical judgement. But whether they stop a person from actively and painlessly satisfying his drives is a non-clinical judgement – so, therefore, is the judgement of what sets of effects are in that sense unhealthy. For the epistemic reasons noted above, doctors therefore need intellectual autonomy in determining which signs and symptoms have which biological causes and what practical effects. In deciding which of these count as ill health, they need as much intellectual autonomy as anyone else but in their capacity as persons, not their capacity as doctors.

Whether a doctor is autonomous in these ways depends on the organisation and resourcing of the health system in which he works (see Chapter 7). This is 'autonomy' in an institutional sense. In another, epistemic sense the doctor becomes less autonomous as the scientificity of clinical practice increases. What diagnoses apply and what treatment a patient needs become more clearly determined as scientific knowledge accumulates, gradually moving towards protocol-based 'cookbook' medicine. This applies as much at population level (in intersectoral activity) as at individual patient level (clinical activity). This development appears to limit a doctor's clinical freedom (for instance, by the use of clinical guidelines), although in a way that can be justified on grounds of patients' needs. If it can be called 'autonomy' or 'freedom' at all, it is in a rather heterodox sense:

> Freedom does not consist in an imaginary independence of natural laws, but in the knowledge of these laws and in the possibility which is thus given of systematically making them work towards given ends. This holds good in relation both to the laws of external nature and those which govern the bodily and mental existence of men themselves ... the *freer* a man's judgement in relation to a definite point in question, the greater the *necessity* with which the content of this judgement will be determined.

> (Engels 1976: 144, original emphases)

Until scientific knowledge is exhaustive, however, a diminishing residual sphere remains where doctors have to exercise their discretion: 'clinical autonomy' in an epistemic sense. It has been argued that there is an irreducible minimum of practical trial and error in all clinical practice (Pappworth 1967: 9) and an irreducible epistemic risk. Because each patient's physiology and needs are individual and extremely complex, it is practically impossible to anticipate every clinical eventuality or decision. Where clinically important facts about the patient's history are unknown, the doctor can only make the best guess in the circumstances. Even when the facts are known and the patient clearly needs one specific treatment, many healthcare procedures run unavoidable practical risks to the patient, especially when the patient's health is already severely compromised. Clinical practice cannot occur without clinicians taking diagnostic and treatment decisions empirically and opportunistically as care progresses. If the patient is to receive healthcare at all, the doctor needs autonomy to treat to some extent opportunistically and on the basis of incomplete information, risking making what with hindsight might transpire to be errors of clinical judgement.

On other occasions, the patient may know her needs, expressing them accurately and fully, giving fully informed consent; but still the circumstances leave the choice of treatment underdefined. (For her there might be little practical difference between, say, two methods of cataract removal.) Paradoxically a treatment plan may be underdefined in the opposite case where the patient needs many tests and treatments more or less simultaneously (and the different tests and treatments are not incompatible, nor is the order in which different components of the treatment plan must be carried out inflexible). Both circumstances leave the doctor some discretion in how he proceeds. This is the so-called 'indeterminacy of complex cases' (Jamous and Pelouille 1970). When a patient needs healthcare she also needs the doctor to be able to decide and execute treatment with all these risks and uncertainties; hence for the doctor to have autonomy to make that much clinical trial and error, in good faith, without exposure to punishment.

Yet the patient also needs not to suffer from practically avoidable carelessness, ignorance or incompetence on the doctor's part, and to be spared probably ineffective treatments. The 1990 National Confidential Enquiry into Perioperative Deaths (NCEPOD) report comments:

> It would seem inappropriate to operate on moribund patients with a very poor chance of survival in those cases where there is known widespread malignancy (sometimes called the 'noble risk'). Nevertheless such cases continue to be reported .... At least 40 cases ... had taken place [that year] within the specialty of general surgery.
>
> (Campling, Devlin, Hoile and Lunn 1990: 192)

For instance:

> An 82-year-old lady weighing 42kg was known to have a poorly
> differentiated carcinoma of the lower oesophagus and a malignant
> lymphoma. She was graded as ASA 4. Nevertheless a five hour
> oesophagogastrectomy was done; at the operation it was noted that there
> was involvement of the spleen and lymph nodes. The patient died with
> respiratory failure.
>
> (Campling et al. 1990: 192, original emphasis)

('ASA 4' means 'Severe systemic disorders that are already life
threatening, not always correctable by operation' – Campling et al.
1990: 359. Operations have been performed on ASA 5 patients, 'in
desperation' – Campling et al. 1990: 211.)

Together the patient's needs and the doctor's needs provide reasons
to distinguish negligent errors and overzealousness to treat from non-
negligent errors (which are bound to occur in treating illnesses about
which medical knowledge is still deficient), and both from fallibility
(chance misfortunes which result in medical error, for instance where
one sign or symptom masks another). This implies that doctors need a
domain of autonomous clinical decision, in which their non-negligent
errors and fallibility are forgiven, escaping censure or penalty, while
cases of the kind just described do incur professional censure or other
penalty.

In these strictly clinical fields doctors can claim to need clinical
autonomy as a practical corollary of having to identify and meet those
patient needs of which the doctor usually has superior knowledge
(ch5§2). This does not show that doctors need, for putatively clinical
reasons, autonomy to decide about those patient needs about which
the patient's knowledge, although corrigible, is probably fuller (see
ch5§2). Yet there are circumstances in which the doctor will need to
anticipate these patient needs too. Sometimes a patient will express
her needs only vaguely or not at all, or express incompatible wishes
(e.g. the incoherent, semi-conscious patient) or be incapable of
informed consent (ch5§2). Often the doctor will be unable to ascertain
these needs soon enough for timely clinical intervention (e.g. for the
brain-damaged patient). In these circumstances, and when the patient
needs non-voluntary (ch5§2) or involuntary (ch6§3) healthcare, the
doctor needs discretion to anticipate what the patient needs in order to
start treatment at all. So doctors also need a domain of autonomy, to
decide in the interests of the patient's non-clinical needs, where the
patient cannot do so personally.

Two other defences of clinical autonomy in terms of patient needs appeal to more optimistic assumptions. For practical reasons a patient has sometimes to trust the doctor to exercise discretion. Even when the patient can give it, informed consent concerns the effects of treatment on pain, natural capacities and everyday life. Unless he is especially cautious or curious the patient does not need to know the minutiae of the clinical science and techniques applied to him. Provided the effects are what he needs for his health and other healthcare needs, such details can be left to the doctor to manage autonomously.

It might also be argued that clinical autonomy safeguards the patient because it makes the doctor personally responsible for the planning, outcome, quality and execution of treatment. Only if one allows the doctor autonomy to make and implement his own clinical decisions can one hold him responsible for the results. Both patient and doctor need the doctor to face this incentive in order to give of his best in serving the patients' interests. Some empirical assumptions have been made here. One is that attributing personal responsibility for the quality of technical work will motivate that person to work conscientiously and effectively. Expectancy theory, the organisationally oriented theory of motivation closest to the theory of drives presupposed here (ch3§1), tends to support this view but only if three conditions apply. The attribution of responsibility must be linked to incentives (material or 'moral'; see ch8§3); the incentives must be something that the recipient wants; and he must have good grounds for thinking that the quality of his work will actually determine whether he gets the incentive (Handy 1986: 38–43). This suggests that clinical autonomy is likely to have its claimed incentive effects only in specific institutional settings.

These add up to quite strong grounds for thinking that patients do need doctors to have clinical autonomy in the matters outlined above. However, a coincidence of doctors' with patients' needs cannot simply be assumed (ch3§4). This brings us to considering how the institutions embodying clinical autonomy, and the legitimations offered for them, compare with the above outline of what patients need by way of doctors' clinical autonomy. A historical account of how these institutions originated and persisted gives clues as to whose desires (if not needs) they satisfy, what desires, and how. Any differences between the institutions and patients' needs for clinical autonomy might, of course, simply be historical mischances. Nevertheless institutional clinical autonomy is largely the doctors' own collective creation. It is reasonable to assume that any gross and persistent differences arise at least partly from differences between doctors' needs and patients'. These differences largely spring in turn from the wider institutional . settings in which doctors and patients meet.

Collective professional autonomy emerged not only for reasons to do with patients' health or needs but for reasons connected with nineteenth- and early twentieth-century doctors' rather precarious respectability and social status which, as largely self-employed professionals, they needed to consolidate (Watkins 1987: 16–23). In private practice, both before and after 1947, collective professional autonomy was also a means to ensure exclusivity and hence a monopoly in providing the most skilled healthcare (Watkins 1987: 212–24). The negotiations establishing the NHS further illustrated the political and economic value of collective professional autonomy in maintaining UK hospital doctors' privileged occupational role, securing them merit awards, entrenched influence over NHS management and retention of private practice (Pater 1981). The institution of clinical autonomy has also sustained their 'power relations' over other health workers. As a territorial demarcation, the institutions of professional autonomy keep both managers and substitute carers out of the doctors' occupational domain, enabling the profession to limit the responsibility and development of what Etzioni calls the 'semi-professions' while delegating to them the less skilled, more menial and less rewarding clinical tasks (Etzioni 1969). While preserving doctors' occupational role and professional cohesion against outside (political or market) forces, the institutions embodying professional autonomy also conserve existing power relations within the medical profession (Watkins 1987: 20).

The outcomes of this history are that the medical profession collectively and autonomously decides the criteria for entry to profession and exit from it; medical school curricula; and what knowledge, skills and experience an aspiring clinician must have before he may practise autonomously. Professional bodies decide autonomously which types of alternative medicine and new technologies are to be recognised as therapeutically valuable, and which dismissed as 'charlatanry'; and which types of activity, research and development to reward (through 'merit awards' and other professional recognition). The profession also manages its own internal ethics and discipline, especially moral discipline. Until 1967 British medical professional discipline paid special attention to penalising doctors who practised the 'five 'A's': abortion, addiction, adultery, advertising and association (i.e. clinical practice jointly with someone not

126

qualified by the profession). Only since the early 1980s has this orientation been extensively supplemented or reviewed. The concomitant of professional self-regulation (i.e. collective clinical autonomy) is non-regulation by outsiders. This privileged organisational position has survived several NHS reorganisations although in many respects these institutional characteristics of clinical autonomy reflect the increasingly obsolete model of individual professional private practice (Tolliday 1978: 35, 43–4). In this sense clinical autonomy can be understood not as a need (nor, to moralise the point, a right) of the individual doctor as a clinician but as a member of a professional group whose members also wished to strengthen their bargaining position both in the healthcare market and in managerial and political negotiations.

A central justification for 'collective clinical autonomy' is that it maintains the quality of doctoring, for only doctors can knowledgably assess other doctors' work. Outsiders such as patients, managers and government cannot. This argument is odd enough to look spurious. Although doctors have obvious educational and practical advantages in accessing and applying clinical and medical scientific knowledge, an essential characteristic of scientific knowledge is that it is publicly available, testable and criticisable (notwithstanding the epistemological debates about what these terms mean). This implies that nobody can claim sole, or even privileged, access to it. Similarly, previous arguments imply that 'health', 'needs' and the derived concepts are publicly scrutinisable in much the same ways (ch4§1). Indeed the publicly visible benefits of professional practice are what legitimate and sustain professional institutions in the first place (Friedson 1970: 16).

Nevertheless, critics continue, the appeal to privileged knowledge is less spurious than it looks. Doctors also know better than non-doctors the incompleteness of medical knowledge and the failures of medical practice. The concept of 'clinical autonomy' screens ineffective medical practice from criticisms by tacitly assimilating medical errors to minor lapses in other domains where individuals are allowed autonomy (for instance, in aesthetics). At best, the notion of 'clinical autonomy' screens medical uncertainty, limited scientific knowledge, non-negligent errors and fallibility from non-doctors. At worst, it also screens treatments without supporting diagnoses; ultra-defensive medicine; massively invasive, futile attempts to keep moribund patients alive (for example, President Tito's gradual surgical dismemberment); reckless experiments; and doctors who, 'vain of their skills', over-reach themselves. Judgement by peers facing similar uncertainties is likely to be 'knowledgable' in the senses of 'empathetic', 'understanding' and 'forgiving' (Watkins 1987: 170).

Far from making doctors personally responsible for quality of care, the screening of all except gross incompetence from outside scrutiny suggests, say critics of clinical autonomy, that peer control is a mechanism more for enforcing normative than technical conformity. Screening non-blameworthy shortcomings of medicine suggests that collective clinical autonomy is intended more to shield medicine as a whole from demystification than to expose areas where further medical research, or *a fortiori* non-medicalised approaches to health-care, might be more effective. Clinical autonomy can result in the quality of clinical practice not being actively monitored (cf. Friedson 1970: 189f), unless a failure occurs which is either so obvious as to be scandalous or breaches either the formally codified or the informal 'custom and practice' ethics of the profession. An important element of the latter, in the British case, is the written and informal ethical rules restricting doctors' competition with one another and their collaboration with non-doctors wishing to offer 'medical' care (BMA 1981: 54–7). Doctors are also inherently more likely than non-doctors to 'know' the value of this.

One area of civil autonomy in which some doctors are interested is payment for private practice, for which they need autonomy in selecting which patients to treat. It is easy to imagine how an intelligent but commercially minded doctor could 'justify' financial selection of patients on clinical pretexts. Yet there are also reasons on grounds of patients' clinical needs for doctors to have autonomy in deciding who to treat (ch5§2). Doctors might also argue that they need autonomy to take on work that cannot be justified by patients' needs for healthcare (e.g. some kinds of forensic medicine, weapons development – ch4§3) but which the doctor pursues for research or political or financial reasons. At an opposite pole some doctors also need autonomy to follow their consciences in matters of non-scientific belief, for example moral or religious objections to providing birth control or abortion.

Even when personal gain is involved, it is not only financial gain that is at issue. Doctors also stand to exercise authority and receive deference, at least at the level of their social interaction with patients in the course of clinical work (Goffman 1984: 51–3, 90, 108, 287f, 335; Watkin 1987: 161). Clinical autonomy is commonly charged with over-empowering doctors in their relations with patients. If the doctor may choose what treatment will be proposed, say the critics, the patient is in a weak position to challenge. This applies as much to the conceptualisation of 'what is wrong' with the patient as to the choice of treatment; the mysteries of the profession disable the patient. 'If patients are allowed their own explanation, they can make claims to the steering of future treatment regimes' (Richman 1987: 95). Another, more prosaic explanation is that it makes the doctor's working life easier (Watkin 1987: 160). Some patients are simply more pleasant to deal with than others.

Some of the aforementioned characteristics and preoccupations are so tangential to patients' needs as outlined above and others so irrelevant as to make it difficult not to conclude that in institutional terms 'clinical autonomy' is primarily the legitimation of, the means to and the reward for an occupational monopoly. Just as populations do not have health needs (ch4§1), whatever putative needs there are for doctors to have collective clinical autonomy are the putative needs of individual doctors. Among these are autonomy to use clinical practice as the venue for meeting the doctor's personal needs for income, intellectual stimulation, social contact, status and all the other needs that work satisfies. These individuals happen to pursue them through working as doctors instead of, say, architects. Doctors need clinical autonomy in this collective sense for much the same reasons as members of any skilled occupational group need its trades union or professional association. This, however, is an application of general civil rights and freedoms to the medical sphere. Although patients may also benefit, and in many ways do (cf. ch7§1), there is nothing uniquely clinical about it.

The conclusion that doctors and patients need clinical autonomy for different reasons does not imply that the two parties' needs must a priori conflict any more that it implies that they must a priori coincide. Doctors' intellectual autonomy and practical discretion in exercising their clinical expertise are practically inseparable from clinical care. Insofar as patients need clinical care, they need those forms of clinical autonomy. Paradoxically this is because the doctor has in some ways too much, and in others too little, scientific knowledge about how to meet the patient's needs for health and for healthcare. As clinical knowledge accumulates, the justification on grounds of too much knowledge becomes stronger and the justification on grounds of too little gets weaker. However, an appeal to scientific authority also implies that clinical autonomy at the level of the doctor–patient relationship has determinate limits and is amenable to public demystification, defeasability and review. A conclusion that patients need this sort of clinical autonomy cannot coherently be extended, under cover of the multiply ambiguous phrase 'clinical autonomy', to show that patients also need the professional bodies and working practices that address the (supposed) organisational and political needs of doctors. Different arguments are required for that because in these matters doctors exercise civil autonomy in their clinical occupations, not clinical autonomy in clinical decision-making. These are political arguments. Some are available, for example when doctors and patients have a common interest in opposing healthcare cuts or organisational reforms of doubtful benefit to either party (ch7§1); or because professional bodies and the doctrine of clinical autonomy weaken some commercial pressures in healthcare. The patient also needs the doctor to exercise non-clinical 'civil autonomy' when the patient cannot, but here as a confidante and 'friend' on behalf of the patient's non-clinical needs, not as a salesperson or an agent of management or payer, the patient's employer or the state.

Other health professions could do this too. They also have clinical expertise, differing from doctors', which their patients need (Campbell 1987: 17). This implies that patients do not need clinical autonomy to be limited to doctors, nor even to individuals. A patient who needs a range of expertise necessitating care by a team of professionals rather than by one doctor by that token needs clinical autonomy to be exercised collectively by the team members, perhaps on the lines of the French *équipes de confiance* (Manciaux and Sand 1987: 165). To argue that patients need doctors to monopolise clinical autonomy would therefore be spurious. Doctors perhaps need that monopoly, for perfectly intelligible (and sometimes legitimate) economic and political reasons, but it is an obfuscation to cite 'clinical' reasons in defence of it.

Clinical autonomy in individual patient care is one thing; to legitimate professional bodies by using a namesake concept is another. Patients need the former. Whether they also need the latter, and why, depends on the wider context of health policy, health system design and healthcare management. To these matters we shall come, after confronting the outstanding question of when or whether patients ever need involuntary healthcare because of mental ill health.

6

NEEDS AND NORMALITY

§1 MEDICAL MODELS OF MINDS

Having argued (ch2§4) that mental activity is a special type of bodily process, the present theory of health needs seems driven towards a 'medical model' of mental ill health (i.e. mental illness or learning difficulties) as something that the patient suffers, which 'possesses' the patient, due to biological or social causes outside his control. Many a person in these circumstances has been alleged to need involuntary treatment, with confinement when necessary (Szasz 1971: 41, 43), to prevent him posing 'a danger to himself or others' (e.g. under the 1959 Mental Health Act and subsequent legislation). Any objections that he may have to being treated are allegedly vitiated when, and because, he lacks the mental capacity validly to decide for himself whether to have treatment. His refusal to accept treatment might itself be taken as further evidence of his mental incapacity. The present theory seems able to accommodate this standard 'medical model' and its justification for involuntary treatment quite easily; perhaps too easily?

Many critics of the 'medical model' theorise 'functional' mental illness as a motivated complex of actions for which the 'sufferer' is partly responsible and to whose treatment he can actively contribute. Laing came close to arguing that there is no such illness as schizophrenia. Rather, schizophrenics behave as they do, and have the emotions that they do, in response to family 'double-binds', so called because their victim suffers distress or retribution whichever way he acts towards other family members (Laing 1965). Objections to this characterisation of schizophrenia (e.g. Edwards and Bouchier 1991) miss this aetiological point. Laing's claims about the social origins of some functional mental illnesses stand (or fall) independently of whether those illnesses are sufficiently similar to paradigm

131

cases of schizophrenia to be classified as schizophrenia too. A psychiatric tradition extending back to Freud argues that many functional mental illnesses (e.g. the 'escape' into catatonia – Brown 1974: 35) are the patient's response to intolerable social, especially family, relationships (Brown 1981: 535; Freud 1959: 185, 203–4). Medical models, say the critics, focus on physiological, genetic and physical environment causes of mental disorder, overlooking social and especially family causes. Indeed, Szasz adds, the notion of 'mental illness' is often used to explain these conflicts away (Szasz 1971: 205). In fact so-called mentally ill people either suffer from neurological lesions or behave badly. But 'behaving badly' reflects their 'problems in living'. It is not a bodily disease (Szasz 1971: 124), not even a disease of the mind-brain. 'Mental illness' misdescribes what is actually a form of social deviancy (Szasz 1971: 27; also Foucault 1965: 245f). A notorious example is the classification of homosexuality as disease in the American Psychiatric Association's *Diagnostic and Statistical Manual of Mental Disorders II* (DSM II). The condition 'ego-dystonic' homosexuality (i.e. homosexual tendencies distressing to patient) was deleted only in 1987 (Stevens and Hall 1991: 299–300).

In these circumstances, says Szasz, treatment is little more than a punitive means of suppressing behaviour that doctors will not tolerate (Szasz 1971: 157n). For instance, 'Therapeutic response to aberrant same-sex behaviour was idealised [in the nineteenth century] as a more effective way to restore normality where punitive legal and moral attempts at social control had failed' (Stevens and Hall 1991: 294). So, Szasz argues, forcible 'treatment' of patients amounts to a punishment. Mentally unhealthy people are presumed to be unable to know their own interests (Szasz 1971: 157) and during their treatment suffer both force and fraud (Szasz 1971: 33–4, 93, 271). One way to put this (not Szasz's) is to say that health professionals are inconsistent, using the medical model to legitimate involuntary 'treatment' of the 'mentally ill' but not taking it so seriously as to develop non-punitive forms of treatment. All this, Szasz argues, makes involuntary treatment objectionably inconsistent with other liberal beliefs. When involuntary treatment is available as a background threat there are no genuinely voluntary mental patients (Szasz 1986). Other critics agree the facts but object for opposite reasons: that involuntary treatment of mentally unhealthy people is in practice all too consistent with liberalism. In US psychiatry 'normalisation' is taken, writes Brown, as conformity with the 'protestant ethic'. The patient is treated individually in isolation from society and held responsible for his own fate (Brown 1981: 524). Even in terms of health needs, say critics, involuntary treatment is counterproductive because it is generally iatrogenic (Szasz 1971: 191n), involving the invention of spurious categories of mental 'disorder' and treatments that physically harm and distress the patient.

Given its insistence on the physical character of mental activity, is the present theory of healthcare needs also susceptible to these criticisms? To escape them it has to differentiate distinctively mental from non-mental ill health but also show how mental ill health is nevertheless a special case of the general theory of physical health outlined earlier (ch4§1); and explain whether, and if so, when and why, involuntary treatment is warranted on grounds of the patient's needs.

By definition, the word 'mental' in the phrase 'mental ill health' must refer to the effects that ill health has upon a person's consciousness, to a failure of strictly mental activities rather than their preconscious antecedents or non-mental effects. Previous chapters situated a person's mental capacities among the range of natural capacities involved in having and actively satisfying drives (Chapters 2–3), identifying three main types:

1 Motivation: the occurrence of natural drives and of cathexis, through the working up of historical from natural drives to the point where volition occurs.
2 Cognition.
3 Emotion: the affective and motivational responses to the effects that an event or action will have upon the satisfaction of drives (ch3§1).

These are not mutually exclusive categories. That a process is cognitive, for example, does not imply that it has no emotional or motivational concomitants or effects. Each stage in the cycle involves a complex interaction of the different natural capacities and the disorders listed above mostly concatenate all three. A failure in any of these capacities might occur not just as non-occurrence but equally as 'mis-occurrence'. A person's mental processes do operate, but in unexpected ways resisting transparent explanation in terms of the patient's drives, beliefs and circumstances; and this can occur in differing degrees (Zola 1975: 173). The following list of more common instances is condensed from a standard textbook for medical students (Edwards and Bouchier 1991) and from *The International Classification of Diseases (9th revision)* (NHSME n.d.), which claims to be an exhaustive list of (what doctors regard as) mentally unhealthy conditions. Here they are grouped by the stages of the cycle of drive, action and satisfaction (ch3§2):

1 Disorders of natural drives, especially of survival and reproduction (sleep loss, frigidity, etc.).

2 Disorders in 'working up' natural drives, resulting in mis-recognition of one's own occurrent drives and of physically possible satisfiers (ch3§1), for example in some motivational 'personality disorders' such as those displayed by schizoids and histrionics, inescapable drives (compulsions) and self-injury. 'Self-injury' covers both intentionally self-destructive acts (e.g. self-mutilation, parasuicide, suicide) and intended effects of sado-masochistic sexual activity among other instances. Among the main forms of unintended self-injury are the effects of habitually using addictive drugs or alcohol and of certain types of sexual activity (e.g. the MP who strangled himself during a sexual experiment).

3 Cognitive disorders, such as abnormal sensations and perceptions such as depersonalisation (when the patient perceives his own body as lifeless or unreal); visual, olfactory, gustatory, tactile and auditory hallucinations; perceiving objects as larger than normal (macropsia) or smaller (micropsia); boundary loss; delirium; illusory pains and twilight states; paranoia. Schizophrenia arguably falls partly into this category, as does having inescapable, unwanted perceptions or ideas (obsessions). Delusions, for instance during paranoia, are usually defined as beliefs at abnormally great variance with the range of beliefs that are plausible either on the publicly available evidence or on the evidence available to the thinker. (Fulford extends the definition to include mis-formation of intentions. The foregoing account of drives – ch.3§1 – implies that delusions purely about facts will alter a person's historical drives – Fulford 1989: 151.) Among abnormal beliefs are continual, over-emphatic or recurrent thoughts which the thinker finds disturbing, painful or unwanted. Loss of cognitive functions such as concentration, memory, consciousness, orientation, ability to register new information or to understand other people (Argyle 1978: 220) occur in virtually all psychoses. Sometimes self-injury results form perceptual delusions (for example, a patient cutting her face to remove the imaginary white lumps that she 'sees' there).

4 Inability to initiate, inhibit or redirect one's actions. 'Action' covers both acting for oneself and enlisting others' help. Supposing that there are such things as human instincts, failures of the behavioural constituent of instincts would also fall under this heading (for instance, childhood catatonia). Other instances of inability to act or inhibit include unwanted, self-damaging behaviours such as obsessive rituals and factitious disorders such as hypochondria and von Munchhausen's syndrome. Even compulsive shopping has been mooted as an instance of mental illness (anon.: 1994c). More subtle practical disorders include neologisms and parapraxes. Inability to act in specific ways occurs in, say, infantile autism or during conversion in hysteria. Extremely upsetting events often precipitate withdrawal from the activities of everyday life by the victims of bereavement, crime or war (NHSME n.d.: i 188). Not everyone recovers from this and some that do, produce adjustment reactions.

5 Ability to recognise and consume available satisfiers, neither overconsuming nor underconsuming (cf. ch4§1). Argyle characterises schizophrenia primarily as an incapacity to conduct everyday social relationships (Argyle 1978: 208–12). Certainly this demands non-mental capacities, but often mental capacities too (e.g. to follow a story or to comply with the 'instructions for use'). Besides the perceptual and other cognitive failures noted above, instances include self-neglect during depression, anorexia, bulimia, sexual dysfunction and paraphilia.

6 Whether a person obtains the satisfiers he wants depends on his environment besides him and is never guaranteed. A corollary of obtaining and consuming an available satisfier, or failing to, is a corresponding range of emotional responses (ch3§1). Among emotional 'disorders' the works mentioned cite unwanted, self-damaging or distressing emotions such as excessive fears (phobias, neuroses), extreme changes of mood, anxiety (e.g. post-traumatic stress syndrome), depression, panics; also residual schizophrenia. In the 'double-binds' described by Laing, patients perceived that their circumstances stopped them from taking any unequivocally satisfying actions where certain drives were concerned (Laing 1965: 144f).

At first it might appear that what differentiates mental ill health is simply that it affects a person's consciousness. However, physical ill health often does so too, as consciousness of pain or physical incapacity, or loss of consciousness altogether; or as derangements of sensation (e.g. delirium) or of the consciousness of natural drives (e.g. a raging thirst no matter how much one drinks). Frustrating as it might be to those who seek a sharp, observable dividing line between the mental and the physical, previous arguments suggest a more or less smooth continuum between non-conscious 'physical' and consciously articulated 'mental' activities (Chapters 2–3). What differentiates mental from other natural capacities is that, alone among our natural capacities, our conscious capacities are evaluated by epistemic rather than, say, biochemical or mechanical criteria (ch2§§3–4) because of, and insofar as they have, the cognitive elements noted above. The practical reason for this is that satisfying one's drives by one's own conscious action requires a certain degree of valid cognition of oneself and one's environment. The analysis of the cycle of drive, action and satisfaction describes the pursuit of prudential ends (i.e. drive satisfiers). The criteria of valid cognition that are relevant to this are those involved in prudential practical reasoning, in the critical assessment of whether one's drives are also needs (ch3§2); that is, the criteria of prudential 'rationality'.

'Rationality', however, has two senses. One refers to the epistemic and logical status of beliefs, in the present case beliefs about actions and the beliefs that drives implicitly embody (ch3§3). To ask whether such beliefs are rational in this sense is to ask such questions as 'are they true?' and 'are they consistent?'. The other sense refers to a person's capacity to produce assertions that are 'rational' in the first sense. Different levels of rigour apply to each sense. In its former, strictly logical sense, 'rationality' is an attribute of actions or other means to ends. An action may be classed as 'rational' in this sense if, and only if, four conditions all hold:

1　The putative means produce effects that are logically relevant to realising a given end.
2　The causal propositions that the means will produce the stated effects are true.
3　The putative means to realise a given end are compatible with the agent's other ends and activities to realise them.
4　The agent actually has the ends in question (here conceptualised as drives and needs).

This is a specific application of generic epistemic 'values': truth, consistency, validity (ch3§2). Whether putative actions or states of affairs are 'rational' in this sense is an all-or-nothing matter. The differentiation between needs and drives relies on a concept of rationality in the first sense for the purposes of practical reasoning.

To use the term 'rationality' to refer to our natural intellectual capacities is to make a general, dispositional attribution instead of a strictly all-or-nothing attribution. In the present context, it applies to a person who is generally intellectually capable of identifying need satisfiers and the means to produce, obtain and consume them, as noted above. Occasional lapses or mistakes do not prevent us describing a person as 'rational' in this sense, making it a dilute version of the first sense. Its connection with the first sense is that a person may be considered rational in this second sense if he acts on premises that he thinks satisfy the four conditions above, even if he is actually mistaken. (Londoners' slaughter of cats and dogs during the great plague of 1666 counts as rational in this sense once one realises that they thought, mistakenly, that these animals transmit bubonic plague to humans.) It is in this second sense of 'rationality' that a mentally healthy person can be described as 'rational'.

Cognitive failure *per se* is not necessarily incapacitating, occurring with many degrees of comprehensiveness. Walker mentions several cases where 'criminal insanity' was due to a very specific delusion. M'Naghten himself concluded that Sir Robert Peel had caused all his misfortunes; otherwise his mental faculties appear to have functioned much as normally (Walker 1968: i 91f). A minor non-disabling intellectual incapacity (e.g. occasional forgetfulness, malapropisms, inattentiveness, neologisms or errors of fact of logic) would not constitute mental ill health. (Of course, historical drives founded upon mistakes cannot count as needs under the present theory, but that is another question.) But where a person knowingly refuses a minor treatment such as a blood transfusion or an abortion even when that could save a limb or their life (e.g. Dobson 1994), the question arises of how to define where seemingly ill-founded beliefs become not merely heterodoxies but delusions. It is obviously possible to judge a person's cognitive mental capacities in terms of 'rationality' in either sense, for instance whether his beliefs are in fact delusions. How the other two types of mental capacity mentioned above, motivations and emotions, can be evaluated in terms of rationality, hence in cognitive terms, requires explanation.

Beyond the point when natural drives become conscious, their 'working up' begins with the choice of satisfier. A choice or pursuit of an object outside the physically possible range of satisfiers is clearly a cognitive failure, as is incapacity to perceive that one has an occurrent natural drive (as very young children sometimes do). Historical drives arise through the 'working up' of natural drives. Natural drives cathect other objects through the cognitive process of association, above all through associating (or misassociating) satisfiers with putative means to get them (ch3§1). This implies that conflicts of historical drives stem, *inter alia*, from cognitive failures. The case of someone who represses some of their drives (or displaces or projects them) is one illustration. Freud's case histories include well-known instances (e.g. Freud 1977b). The patient has the drive but because the drive is distressing as it conflicts with his other drives (strong religious or moral convictions, say), he will not expressly acknowledge its occurrence even to himself, which is what differentiates this case from the 'ordinary' inhibition of a drive. The refusal, however, is tantamount to contradicting what one implicitly recognises. That is a logical, hence a cognitive, failure. Incapacity to inhibit action betokens, on the previous account of drives, a failure to 'work up' the compulsive drive in a way with less counterproductive effects on satisfying other drives: another cognitive failure.

Emotions were earlier analysed as affective, sometimes motivational, responses to the effects of *faits accomplis* on the satisfaction of our drives (ch3§2). Here too a cognitive element is causally prior to the affective and motivational elements. Just as the cathexis of drives ranges from strong to negligible, so does the (converse) affective and emotional loading of cognitions. This suggests an account of emotional ill health in terms of a mismatch between the cognition and the affective response. One way to conceive this mismatch is to say that in some cases the emotional signs and symptoms noted above might prove to be affective and motivational responses that embody a distorted or a false view of the actual practical importance of events for the sufferer's drives: a cognitive failure. A panicking person or a phobic, for instance, exaggerates the risk of harm from the object of her fears; a depressive exaggerates the scale and intractability of her imaginary or real misfortunes. Alternatively, one might take the cognition as given, and describe the emotional response as so large, or small, as to prevent a prudentially rational response. In effect such a description would regard this failure as the emotional analogue to an extreme over- or undersensitivity to physical pain. To illustrate this, consider a recent trial of a 13-year-old boy for murder. A newspaper report mentions that psychiatric 'Reports showed the boy was prone to violence, especially when he felt provoked, and was unable to cope with jeering and teasing, let alone bullying at school' (anon. 1994d: 4).

As an indirect response to his frustrations at school and elsewhere he opportunistically killed an elderly woman. (His psychiatrist attributed this to 'Asperger's syndrome with a related schizoid personality disorder' and the boy was convicted of manslaughter, not murder, on grounds of diminished responsibility.)

Less dramatically Laing and Freud (among others) saw functional mental ill health as the emotional and motivational product of the patient's social relations, either in placing incompatible practical demands on her (reflected in incompatible historical drives) or in so frustrating her as to cause an emotional overload. Some people fall mentally ill of emotional pressures against which others struggle more successfully or which they do not face (Freud 1972: 82). Pre-1991 allocation formulae for NHS psychiatry budgets explicitly recognised that the prevalence of mental illness and demand for psychiatric services is greater among married than among unmarried women, and less among married than among unmarried men (DHSS 1976: 24). As for social relations outside the family, it is known that in Britain the prevalence of poverty and unemployment coincide with the incidence of mental ill health (DHSS 1980; Smith 1987: 67–85).

By contrast there is no cognitive failure when a person's emotional response is also incapacitatingly large, but large because the practical seriousness of the event to which the person is responding is correspondingly large; for example, when a person feels overwhelmed by grief, anxiety and similar emotions in contemplating their own imminent death. Typically the emotional response results from an all-too-successful cognition; a cognitive overload rather than a cognitive failure. Kubler-Ross (1970: 99–100) regards such responses as initiating a process in which the sufferer gradually takes stock of the new situation, adjusts her knowledge, desires and future plans accordingly and resumes something like her usual activities. Although its affective and motivational effects are large, this is essentially a cognitive process of coming to recognise, at a pace that one can emotionally manage, the full implications of what has happened and adjusting one's future plans accordingly. Here too there is a threshold beyond which a person's emotional response becomes practically incapacitating.

To distinguish those failures that could be described as failures of health, rather than everyday error or eccentricity or emotions, we must resort to the needs-based definition of 'health' proposed earlier (ch4§1). It noted general criteria which a change in a person's natural capacities would have to satisfy to count as an instance of ill health:

1 The condition must impede the operation of the cycle of drive, action and satisfaction, or cause gratuitous pains, or both. Only then would a person need healthcare as a means to restoring her conscious functioning as one of the 'natural capacities' that she needs in order to act upon and satisfy her drives (ch3§1). This implies that the resulting condition must be non-transient and non-trivial (ch4§1).

2 The immediate cause of the condition must be literally within the person herself, even when further causes lie beyond (ch4§1).

So to indicate mental ill health, a complex of signs and symptoms must satisfy three conditions. The signs and symptoms must:

1 Concern the mental, i.e. amount to a failure of rationality by grossly contradicting the publicly available evidence or requirements of logic in respect of everyday matters of fact and prudential reasoning (we are not yet entitled to include moral logic).

2 Practically hinder a person in pursuing the activities of daily life (cp. Shepherd 1983: 122–5). Many of the putative instances of mental ill health listed above do disrupt a person's natural capacities to satisfy her needs, and do so in neither trivial nor transient ways. Many also cause the mental equivalent of pains. A mental incapacity that is disabling in some social settings will not necessarily disable in others (e.g. dyslexic reading does not disable in a non-literate society; a phobia of large fish barely disables the resident of a modern city); but some will disable in any society (e.g. catatonia).

3 Immediately result from a personal incapacity for cognition, whether or not this has further causes such as physical disease, degeneration, external events, trauma or other causes within consciousness itself. Learning disability, for example, can occur either congenitally or traumatically or degeneratively.

Unlike many accounts of mental health needs, the present account does not propose a substantive list of 'good' motives and emotions by which to stipulate humans' mental health needs. (Ramsay cites many examples – 1992: 170–8.) Many of these substantive frameworks could stand within the theory proposed here as special, even individual, cases. Condition 3 implies that this account of mental health can accommodate the concepts both of organic and of functional mental ill health. A description of the effects of the above events on the sufferer's capacities is logically prior to specifications of the causes of these events, as is the case with ill health generally (ch4§1). This leaves open whether the theory-laden diagnostic terms for these disorders ('schizophrenia', 'transference', etc.) logically rest upon scientifically valid theories, and hence which diagnostic lexicon to apply to the signs and symptoms in question.

Under this conceptualisation a particular instance of mental ill health logically could be caused by any combination of many causes: the sufferer herself; social events; the physical environment; genes, ill health or trauma. Which combination applies in a particular case will obviously determine what mental healthcare a person needs – or what other interventions.

§2 DISORDERS AND DISORDER

Violence towards oneself or others is a standard justification in English law for treating allegedly mentally unhealthy people involuntarily, as an alternative to punishing them. Such measures are often warranted on grounds of needs. Walker lists the grounds on which English law has recognised mental ill health as either mitigating punishment or excusing the offender from it altogether (Walker 1968: i 247–50). Condensing his list and rearranging it to correspond to the cycle of drive, action and satisfaction, the grounds are as follows:

1 Automatism, such as uncontrollable action due to an epileptic fugue or brain tumour (Walker 1968: i 117,173).
2 Motivational factors, whether a strengthening of a drive to the point that no one could resist (e.g. abnormal sexual drives) (Walker 1968: i 105, 155), a weakening of self-control, the occurrence of an 'abnormal' motive (e.g. coprophilia), or violent behaviour to avoid reminders or stimuli of other mental disorders.
3 Gross cognitive error (delusion or partial delusion) as to: the nature of the act (e.g. when a person imagines that stabbing someone will not much harm them); its legality (e.g. imagining that one is killing in self-defence) or legal penalties (Walker 1968: i 89, 99); the identity of the victim (e.g. mistaking one's child for a dangerous animal); the situation (e.g. imagining that one's house is on fire); or the likelihood of escaping detection.
4 Low intelligence, or where a person's mental ill health puts him in situations in which anyone would be tempted to break the law (e.g. being hungry and homeless).

5 'Moral defect' (Walker 1968: i 104) such as a misconception that it is morally acceptable to murder one's wife; or when somebody calculates that he can cite his pre-existing mental ill health in order to escape punishment.

Inability to tell right from wrong (point 5) has been one of the most durable excuses in English law, dating from the reign of Edward II (Walker 1968: i 28). However, this presupposes an analysis of moral right and wrong, and of how one would know what is morally right and wrong, which the present account of needs and mental health does not yet contain. The other four points refer to types of incapacity that would indeed count as mental ill health on the conceptualisation outlined above (ch6§1). Whether a person is suffering a neurological disorder or is of low intelligence is *comparatively* easy to settle empirically. It is less easy to determine whether an act of violence can be attributed to a disorder of motivation or cognition rather than treated as a rational act. The present account of drives and need implies a distinction between several different types of violent act, some of which indicate that the agent might need mental healthcare and some of which do not.

Violence towards oneself is usually taken to refer to attempted suicide, active self-harm and parasuicide although more passive self-neglect or exposure to danger would achieve the same results and are also often taken as signs of mental ill health. Ordinarily these would count as signs of mental ill health on the above definition but there are three complications. First, risk-taking is not irrational *per se*, for instance if the only actions open to one are either a risky action (e.g. jumping into the sea) or a still riskier one (e.g. staying on the burning ship). Sometimes it is prudent to risk one's life. Here too there is no well-defined border at which exposing oneself to risks goes beyond the exposure to risk that is unavoidable in the activities of daily life. Second, suicide is not always an imprudent step (in the circumstances listed in ch5§2). Only if these circumstances obviously do not obtain could a suicide attempt be taken as prima-facie evidence of mental ill health. Third, a more controversial scenario is where a patient makes only the most irrational-seeming, health-damaging and needs-frustrating decisions, for example the transfusion-refusing Jehovah's witness.

The relations between drives, needs and mental ill health are more complex in the case of violence directed against others. So-called *crimes passionelles* are essentially motivated by a strong drive (for instance, sexual jealousy, revenge) under considerable emotional 'provocation'. The victim is one particular person and the attacker's close motivational and emotional involvement with him or her is what motivates the attack. The attacker's motives for attacking are fairly clearly defined. The present account of drives and their rationality (ch3§§1–3) implies that from the attacker's standpoint such a crime is rather rational. It satisfies a natural or a historical drive (in Mrs Bobbit's case, to stop further assaults). Were it not for the 'side effects' (punishment, losing the lover or friend whom it was the point of the crime not to lose) one might conclude that the attacker needed to commit the *crime passionelle*. His main irrationality would be in overreacting or in employing means that were disproportionate to his ends, defeating this or his other drives and incurring the side effects mentioned. Recognition of this ambivalence perhaps partly explains why *crimes passionelles* have sometimes been held juridically to warrant either a mitigation of punishment or none (e.g. in nineteenth-century French law). Although the attacker's judgement may be 'diminished' in the heat of the moment or because of the strength of the drives or emotions involved, this hardly amounts to incapacitation nor, therefore, to mental ill health. In terms of drives and needs there seems little to distinguish *crimes passionelles* from other cases where a person overreacts and misjudges, with a violent outcome.

Another case is when violence serves only as a means to obtaining satisfiers which in other circumstances are not intrinsically violent (e.g. robbery with extreme violence) although the attacker was mentally capable pursuing these satisfiers non-violently. Our theory rules out excuses on grounds of mental ill health here. This differs from the case where the attacker lacks the mental capacities for the non-invasive pursuit of his drives although the satisfiers themselves are not intrinsically violent (e.g. someone mentally incapable of more or less normal social relationships). He then satisfies his drives by the only, and violent, means remaining. In a secure mental hospital, for example, I once met a young man whose only means of expressing frustration to his parents was through physical violence, ending in his burning them to death. His case clearly falls under the definition of mental ill health proposed above.

A last category of violent act is the opposite of a *crime passionelle* in two ways. The attacker's method of satisfying his drive tends to be more narrowly determined because he strongly associates violence with the satisfier itself (sadism is the standard example). His violence towards others occurs either as a fairly stable constituent of a person's sexuality (masochism, sadism, etc.) or results from an equally stable drive attributed to a 'personality disorder' or 'psychopathy' (e.g. the Moors murderers, Peter Sutcliffe). (Without a further explanation of the 'disorder' or 'pathology', however, such classifications do little more than re-describe the case.) The attacker has developed such a structure of drives that he is motivated only to pursue satisfiers with this violent constituent, although his other mental capacities are more or less healthy. Into this category fall people who make instrumentally rational plans to satisfy their drives towards, say, bestiality or torture (a connection with certain types of Nazi functionary). Even if he is irrational in the sense of not choosing the most effective means of satisfying his drives, this does not amount to mental ill health by the above criteria unless he pursues objects outside the range of physically possible satisfiers. This sort of attacker needs to be violent if his drive satisfies the criteria of rationality outlined earlier (ch3§4). There is no a priori reason that these conditions will never be satisfied, in the case of some individuals. However, his choice of victim is underdetermined; for instance, anyone sexually attractive to him may serve the sadist, and in analogous cases any eligible, fortuitously available victim will satisfy. What the attacker needs is one thing and what others, especially the victims and potential victims, need is quite another.

Such attackers are not, on the present account, mentally unhealthy; just dangerous to others, much as an unusually aggressive or reckless driver might be. It is not the attacker who needs to be contained, on grounds of mental ill health, but his potential victims who need him to be contained in pursuit of their own needs to avoid pain, injury or death. Szasz is right to argue that it is spurious to medicalise the control of this type of deviant, who have – and pose – 'life problems', not mental health problems (Szasz 1986). This raises the question of whether threats of punishment are a response relevant to this kind of attacker. Our earlier account of drives (ch3§1) explains quite simply how punishment works. Compressing an argument that deserves fuller exploration, instituting punishments is a crude way of artificially altering, even reversing, the balance of prudential advantage between the practical options confronting a person. Deterrent punishing relies upon the potential offender re-working his historical drives to take account of the additional, punitive consequences that have now been added to some of these options. This presupposes that he is rational enough (see ch6§1) to recognise the new balance of prudential advantage between offending and not offending, and to decide and act accordingly. Of course these are mental capacities, and ones whose possession is necessary for a person to meet the 'local' standard of mental health in a society that punishes (ch4§1). Punishment is gratuitous as a means of changing the actions of people mentally incapable of this much prudential rationality. Other means, such as involuntary mental healthcare, may be necessary for changing the way that they act. Insofar as the phrase 'diminished responsibility' refers to diminished amenability to punishment, it also implies a failure of mental capacities (Walker 1968: i 152), and to that extent mental ill health. Someone who is mentally unable to change his actions in response to threats of punishment is also likely to be mentally unable to attempt many other activities of daily life, although this is a contingent, not a logical, connection. So diminished responsibility is, on the present theory, a prima-facie indicator that a person does need mental healthcare. Diminished responsibility is logically neither necessary nor sufficient to establish that a person needs involuntary mental healthcare. What is?

§3   INVOLUNTARY HEALTHCARE

Now we can analyse when (if ever) and why patients need involuntary healthcare. Involuntary treatment differs from non-voluntary treatment because it is not a matter only of substituting for an absent mental capacity but of overriding epistemically defective decisions of the patient's own. Again, a relativist theory of needs forbids us simply to assume that the different parties to proposed involuntary treatment all have compatible needs. Take the case of someone who is only a carrier of a highly infectious, often fatal disease (HIV/AIDS, in a recent case) but who experiences no ill effects from it and therefore refuses to be treated. His potential sexual partners or needle-sharers, and their contacts, would need this carrier to receive involuntary treatment but because of their own health needs, not his. Because the carrier is (suppose) mentally healthy, there can be no pretence that mental ill health is what legitimates treating him involuntarily. Like the case of some of the violent offenders discussed above, this case differs from one in which a person really does need involuntary treatment on his own account. Using our analyses of mental health (ch6§2) and informed consent (ch5§2) we can now say what conditions must hold, to sustain a valid paternalist argument for overriding a patient's desires because he needs involuntary healthcare but is mentally incapable of deciding.

A first condition is that the person actually does need healthcare for his ill health (whether mental or non-mental) so as to prevent or remedy non-transient and non-trivial loss of natural capacities (chs4§1, 6§2) which practically limit his ability to satisfy his drives through the activities of daily life and whose immediate causes lie within the person himself (whether disease, degeneration, trauma or mental events). The nearest one can come to justifying involuntary pain control on grounds of the patient's needs is when involuntary treatment is indicated for the other reasons noted here and pain control is a technical corollary. Being defined in terms of natural capacities, actions and drives, these criteria of need for healthcare apply to voluntary, non-voluntary and involuntary healthcare alike. This implies that, even if other people need them to be controlled in some way (even medical ways), certain categories of offender do not need mental healthcare, for instance some of those violent offenders discussed above (ch6§2). To them must be added three other categories of 'deviant' who do not need mental healthcare.

People who satisfy their drives, even their needs, in eccentric, repellent, socially proscribed or immoral ways constitute one of these categories. As Harris points out, such practices as homosexuality or even necrophilia prompt more questions about the reasons and motives of the people who wish to suppress them than they raise doubts about whether their practitioners find them satisfying and, to that extent, instrumentally rational (Harris 1985: 180–8). A relativist theory of needs clearly separates judgements about what homosexuals or necrophiles enjoy from judgements about whether and why you or I (or the government) might want homosexuality or necrophilia to be suppressed (see ch4§3). Many feminists make similar criticisms of 'normalisation' as a therapeutic goal, regarding normalisation as a spuriously medicalised way of getting women to 'fit into' social roles that men, especially male doctors, might want but women patients definitely do not need. Szasz makes similar points about the relations between child and family, and between individual and state (Szasz 1971: 64, 274n, 285n). Such 'disturbances of conduct' *per se* do not count as mental ill health on the view advanced here (*pace* NHSME n.d.: i 208).

Drug addicts are often treated as mentally ill. But could there be such a thing as a 'rational addiction' (cf. Becker and Murphy 1988: 674–700)? If so, addicts themselves would not need healthcare or any other means of ending their addiction, even if other people wanted to use healthcare as a means of suppressing the use of addictive drugs. We already noted some parallels between paradigm natural drives, which usually qualify as natural needs, and addictions (ch3§1). Thomson argues that we cannot avoid acquiring non-addictive natural needs nor voluntarily give them up (Thomson 1987: 24, 48, 201, 127). Yet we can avoid acquiring some natural needs, for instance by not getting pregnant or by avoiding activities whose consequences will probably include a need for pain relief. Both paradigm natural needs and addictions can be suppressed artificially or by sheer will power, although often only with difficulty and pain. Both appear and abate at different stages in the life cycle. Over-consuming certain types or quantities of addictive product (heroin, alcohol, crack) impairs the addict's body systems (brain damage, liver failure, etc.), eventually disabling him; but so does over-consuming many foods (fats, salt, sugars).

A difference between some addictions (e.g. alcohol, cocaine, heroin, tobacco) and other natural drives is that the effect of satisfying the drive is to impair, not reproduce, the consumer's mental and non-mental capacities (although popular belief exaggerates the impairment) (Griffin 1992: 8, 16, 18, 23–4, 26–7, 36–8). Someone deprived of their preferred food or drink or even sexual partner can, in principle, find a substitute. Some addictive products also show this 'cross-tolerance': alcohol can be taken in many forms; methadone partly substitutes for heroin. Nevertheless addictive products usually have very limited cross-tolerance, which accentuates three incompatibilities between an addiction and other drives. Pursuing the addictive satisfier often reduces or crowds out other activities and drives (e.g. some heroin addicts can eat ice-cream but little else), especially when increasing doses are necessary to produce a given effect (as with heroin). A second incompatibility arises when the addict takes risks (e.g. prostitution, theft) to obtain expensive supplies, and a third through the iatrogenic methods of administering addictive drugs, especially by needle with its risks of hepatitis B and HIV infection. However, many of these difficulties arise more from the difficulty of obtaining cheap, safe, legal supplies (e.g. through health services) than from the nature of addiction.

Whether the addict needs healthcare therefore depends upon whether her addiction already does incapacitate her, or will do so. If so, she needs healthcare as a means of weakening or eliminating the addiction. Since addictions are acquired natural drives, they no more instantiate a problem of peculiarly mental ill health than the occurrence of other acquired, conscious natural drives does. Otherwise the addict's health need is not for healthcare but for effective, cheap, safe supplies of the drug. There is a closer parallel here with consuming food than with consuming intrinsically unhealthy addictive substances such as tobacco. In some instances, such as pain relief for terminally ill patients, addictive drugs may actually meet another health need, while also creating (but then satisfying) the additional natural drive which the addiction is.

The second condition necessary for sustaining a claim that someone needs involuntary healthcare is that the patient is capable of deciding voluntarily but not validly. She is not 'rational' in the weaker sense of 'rational' (ch6§2). In healthcare contexts this implies that she is incapable of informed consent, being unable to understand the following (ch5§2):

1 that her health has already deteriorated so far that she needs treatment, or that without preventive treatment now it will deteriorate that far;
2 what treatments are available and how they differ in their effects on her pain, natural capacities and activities of daily life, their side effects and risks;
3 any factors irrelevant to the patient's healthcare needs that might influence the doctor's choice of referral or treatment.

Because the failure of the patient's rationality is defined in epistemic terms (ch6§2), two things have to be established under each of these three headings. One is the facts of the patient's case. Assessment of the patient's health, of the availability of treatments and their effects are matters of clinical judgement. Disclosing conflicts of interest is a matter for factual declaration or some other institutional safeguard to protect vulnerable patients (ch5§2). Only if the patient lacks the mental capacity to understand all this and to decide accordingly (cf. Faulder 1985: 122–8) is this second condition satisfied. This is a judgement of whether he can perceive, think and decide more or less in conformity with the publicly available standards of truth, consistency and explicitness noted earlier (chs3§4, 6§1). Anyone who is also capable of that much rationality can in principle judge this, although here too there are no sharp qualitative borderlines between capability and incapability. A health worker can do so as competently as anyone else, although by virtue of his lay intelligence, not his clinical expertise. One risk is that the patient's eccentricities of taste, crimes or moral lapses are mistaken for evidence relevant to this judgement although they are irrelevant to the attribution of mental health (see above). It is no wonder that judgements about patients' rationality are sometimes so contestable and open to charges of moralising (or worse) interference. Clinical judgement is required in judging whether the patient's failure to perceive, think and decide in these ways is a failure of capacity due to the patient's ill health. There is a clear difference here between the contributions of (lay) epistemic judgement, clinical judgement and moral judgement.

A third condition is that the patient needs treatment to begin sooner than his rationality is likely to return, whether spontaneously or as a result of voluntary healthcare (for the same reasons as support the analogous principle in non-voluntary treatment). The timescale requirement is probably harder to satisfy in the case of mental ill health. Sedgwick and others report the episodic nature of mental ill health, with periods of ill health punctuated by periods of 'lucidity' in which the patient can give informed consent. Nevertheless in some rather clear-cut cases timescale factors pose no objection to involuntary treatment on the grounds of a patient's need. Among these are suicide prevention (unless suicide is warranted); compulsory removal of health-damaging addictions, provided that the addiction will otherwise lead to loss of health without spontaneous respite; and preventing irreversible self-injury (parasuicide) where it would irretrievably damage the person's natural capacities.

Fourth, a treatment must be both available and likely to be effective when applied involuntarily. Still fewer treatments are likely to be effective in the involuntary than the non-voluntary and voluntary cases because treatments depending on patient compliance are not now available (e.g. because the patient would tear out stitches or tubes) and the placebo effect cannot be relied upon. Since non-treatment is always an option, the converse of involuntary treatment is involuntary non-treatment, including paternalistically refusing a patient's request for unnecessary or harmful treatment (see also on markets). The onus of proof is on the doctor to show that treatment is available and likely to succeed (see ch5§2). Treating a patient involuntarily on grounds of his mental ill health actually involves two courses of treatment: one to address the original ill health (e.g. the infective disease, in the above example); and one to remedy the mental incapacity causing the patient either to refuse treatment that he palpably needs or (in the von Munchhausen syndrome) to seek treatment that he patently does not.

Compatibilism (chs2§§3–4, 3§1) seems to imply that in mental healthcare two therapeutic strategies are available. One is physically to manipulate the thinking body through surgical, pharmaceutical or other physical interventions. The other is to use cognitive methods, supplying the patient with further self-knowledge, new beliefs and ways of thinking, and reconstructing the social relations through which the patient learns.

Physical interventions could, in principle, restore a person's rationality by producing new, valid contents of consciousness and by restoring the cognitive reliability of the processes of perception, motivation, thinking and emotion. Already this can be done crudely with drugs (e.g. Prozac and other anti-depressants) and in theory the same effects might be produced by psychosurgery. At present the great obstacle is sheer ignorance of precisely how our possession of specific contents of consciousness and the mental processes analysed earlier is physiologically constituted. Even if we knew, present-day pharmacology, ECT, therapies and surgery are far too coarse to target particular substantive thought associations, affects, etc. at neurone level or below. No existing physical therapies can yet produce any but the grossest alterations of perception and mood. As Flew remarks, what is objectionable in, say, psychosurgery is not that it is logically impossible, but practically possible and a bad thing (cf. Flew 1978: 103).

Flew's reasons for saying so are different to ours, however. They concern the logical status of the beliefs that precise physical treatments of consciousness would produce if they became available. Being externally produced, Flew assumes, such beliefs could not be true. This assumption seems dubious. Certainly the truth or falsity of (non-self-referential) beliefs does not depend on the source of those beliefs. (The opposite view is the so-called 'genetic fallacy'.) No one complains that a person's vision does not impart genuinely valid knowledge of the 'external' world because he owes his vision to surgery or drugs instead of being born with good sight, or that his arithmetic must be wrong because he can only do long division while under sedation. A more plausible objection would be that when beliefs have not been produced cognitively, the thinker does not know upon what evidence and reasoning those beliefs logically rest. He believes something without knowing why what he believes is true. Inducing beliefs by drugs or surgery might deprive their recipient of the heuristic or pedagogic benefits of learning the grounds for the beliefs for oneself (but even this would depend on exactly what beliefs were induced and how). Yet in that respect these artificially induced beliefs would not differ at all from the many beliefs that we acquire piecemeal and with slender evidence or weak reasons; virtually on authority, 'by description' (Russell 1936: 72–92).

Similar doubts arise about dispositions of character. Flew argues that we would not call truthful a person who, under the effects of hypnosis or drugs, would never tell a lie. One can only reply that such a person would be unusually truthful, and of unusually truthful disposition (while the hypnosis or drugs lasted). The only objection to saying as much would be if one insisted on defining a person's truthfulness, not in terms of whether he wanted to tell the truth or usually did, but according to whether he had further reasons supporting his motive for truth-telling. But there seems to be no reason that someone with what we must call a natural drive to be truthful ('natural', because *sui generis* to consciousness but with non-conscious antecedents) should be disqualified from counting as truthful while someone did qualify who had a phenomenologically and substantively identical motive producing exactly the same actions but learnt it as what we have called a historical drive (as a means to please his parents, say).

So mentally ill patients are unlikely to need involuntary psychosurgery for the same reason as they are unlikely to need voluntary psychosurgery: because it is so ineffective at correcting contents of consciousness or mental processes. Cognitive treatments that appear more likely to be effective in voluntary settings are hampered in involuntary settings by the requirement for treatment efficacy in the face of patient non-compliance. That probably makes involuntary behaviour modification or psychotherapy impracticable (unless the patient can be made to comply by threatening a less agreeable alternative such as longer hospitalisation). All this does not rule out a priori the possibility of effective involuntary treatment of mental ill health but it does suggest that at present the range of effective involuntary treatments is probably small. How small is an empirical question whose answer is not really known.

That suicide is not warranted in terms of the patient's needs (ch5§2) is the fifth condition. Suicide is not always irrational (see ch5§2) and the conditions warranting it – unbearable, intractable, incessant pain or the emotional equivalents – do not depend on whether the killing is voluntary. However, this can never warrant involuntary euthanasia. The patient has privileged knowledge of his need for pain relief and emotional distress so the patient's decision on whether to try to die expresses his need, not a corrigible desire. Against this no one, not even the doctor, can satisfy the onus of proof to justify that intervention in terms of needs. Conversely, intervention to prevent suicide is, except where the patient so judges in cases of permanent, intractable pain (see ch5§2), always justified in terms of the patient's needs.

151

A sixth condition is that the patient needs involuntary treatment only until his or her own rationality (as defined in ch6§2) is restored, as for non-voluntary treatment. As a proxy for the patient's own defective rationality involuntary treatment becomes, at best, redundant when the patient's intellectual capacity to decide returns.

Last, and as in the case of non-voluntary treatment, the patient needs to be assured that there is no conflict between the needs of those carrying out involuntary treatment and his own needs.

Despite all these exceptions and qualifications there almost certainly remain many people who do, on the above arguments, need involuntary healthcare, although (as Szasz and others say) probably fewer than policy-makers imagine. This is not to say that what they need is psychosurgery or truth drugs; not because such methods could not in principle restore valid cognition or genuine dispositions but simply because present therapies are too crude to help their recipients much. There is also a clear distinction between the needs of mentally unhealthy people and those of the people who decide whether to treat them and how. This brings us to the question of the management and design of health systems themselves.

7

DILEMMAS FOR HEALTH WORKERS

§1 NEEDS AND 'BUSINESS ETHICS' IN HEALTHCARE

As in some other health systems, British health system reform is shifting the balance of power within healthcare organisations from doctors to managers (Holliday 1992: 17, 94). A relativist account of needs (ch3§4) no more guarantees a priori that managers' and patients' needs will coincide than it guarantees that doctors' and patients' needs will, or doctors' and managers'. Having examined how patients' and doctors' needs are related, it is time to add the managers to the picture. For these purposes, the term 'manager' includes the many senior doctors, nurses and paramedical professionals whom it has been UK government policy to involve more fully in NHS management since the early 1980s.

Marketising health system reforms and cost-containment pressures tend to heighten tensions between health managers' and patients' needs. These conflicts occur at several points in the health system.

Like official guidance documents, most health managers in the UK would take the terms 'business ethics' or 'managerial ethics' mainly to concern how managers should manage conflicts of their own personal interests, for instance by declaring any personal or commercial interest in NHS decision-making (NHSME 1993b; Harrison 1994: 161–2). Outright corruption – of which substantial examples have recently been reported (e.g. Millington 1995: 4) – are the extreme manifestation of these problems of 'corporate governance'.

Access to information is another such area. Patients who wish to find out what healthcare they really need, and how to get this healthcare through the health system, need access to information on the relative efficacy of different treatments, different healthcare providers and arguably even of different individual doctors. The obstacles to this are not clinical, technical obstacles (Saltman 1994: 214). Information of this kind – still at an early stage of technical development, admittedly – is already used by health authorities and in clinical audit. One of the main obstacles, apart from doctors' collective professional interests (ch5§3), is the necessity for managers to maintain commercial confidentiality in markets or quasi-markets. One of the earliest and most forceful pieces of official guidance on this states:

> Staff should be particularly careful of using, or making public, internal information of a 'commercial-in-confidence' nature, particularly if its disclosure would prejudice the principle of a purchasing system based on fair competition. This principle applies whether private competitors or other NHS providers are concerned.
>
> (NHSME 1993b)

Politicisation of the health system has followed controversial health system reforms in Britain, placing NHS managers under pressure to promulgate the government's public relations messages legitimising the reforms. In practice some managers have seen this as another reason to crack down on 'whistle-blowing', for instance by including 'gagging clauses' in contracts of employment (Brindle 1992: 5). It also has implications for freedom of information. In UK practice the outright falsification of data is comparatively rare, although there have been cases of managers forging letters of 'public' support for the NHS reforms (Brindle 1991: 3). More often, data are subtly manipulated to inflate reform successes and downplay the failures, for example by measuring hospital activity in 'completed consultant episodes' instead of 'episodes of care', tending to inflate the figures for hospital activity faster than would happen under the old measure (Seng, Lessof and McKee 1993: 16–17). Waiting lists were heavily weeded just before the 1992 general election to ensure that the government's promises appeared to have been honoured. Such measures hardly serve patients' needs to understand the real state of NHS services, either to meet their personal healthcare needs as patients (ch5§2) or to influence health policy as citizens.

The 'government's euthanasia programme' (as John Harris calls the policy of pursuing public spending controls to the point where NHS services are cut with predictably lethal delays in treating people whose health status is marginal) also sets managers' needs against patients' (Harris 1985: 84–6). Health managers and doctors have been known tacitly to collude in this informal 'rationing', sometimes conducted under the guise of exercising 'clinical judgement' (Weale 1988: 1–3 gives an anonymised but real case).

Policies to strengthen patient choice in healthcare raise the question of what managers are to do when patients express preferences or opinions uncongenial to them. Saltman observes that patient satisfaction surveys and the like are of little practical use when managers have (and exercise) discretion to ignore the results (Saltman 1994: 209–10). Yet in respect of some aspects of healthcare, patients' opinions are more likely to represent patients' needs than managers' opinions are (ch5§2). Managers have the peculiar role of mediating the needs of patients and other health workers. When these conflict, managers have to decide which side to take. Such conflicts have been particularly visible in long-stay institutional services (Martin 1983). Sedgwick records how, in a spirit of 'law-and-order populism', health workers in one mental hospital refused to admit patients sent there from the courts (Sedgwick 1982: 232). This is not an isolated dispute. One at Ashworth Hospital is drawing to its end at the time of writing (1994–5).

How are such dilemmas to be analysed and resolved, in terms of needs for healthcare? Such a dilemma occurs to a person as a conflict of, say, moral principles, each of which has an action-initiating character (McMahon 1989: 41). Our previous accounts of consciousness and drives (chs2§3, 3§1) imply that this conflict of moral motives is actually a conflict of drives, but of historical drives which are so highly 'worked up' and lightly cathected as to be close to the cognitive end of the drive-cognition continuum (ch3§1). The health manager (or anyone else) facing such a dilemma confronts, *inter alia*, a conflict between two complicated and overdetermined sets of drives. One set is the drives created during their formation as healthcare professional. This involves learning and cathecting professional codes or ethical codes and the 'service ethic' which ranks patients' needs and health highest among practical priorities, legitimated and reinforced by the sort of policy pronouncements noted at the outset (ch1§1). The other set consists of more immediately personal historical drives, connected with individual performance review and performance-related pay, fixed-term employment contracts and the uses to which these instruments of central control are put. They tie substantial material incentives – promotion, status, pay and re-employment – to complying with, indeed actively implementing, policies that exacerbate the conflicts noted above.

Earlier analyses suggest a hierarchy of methods for resolving conflicts of drives to produce a coherent structure of needs. In descending order of efficacy the methods are as follows:

1 Reconsider the validity of the beliefs embedded in the conflicting historical drives, in pursuit of new beliefs (e.g. new moral principles or new interpretations of professional ethics) which will redefine the conflict or define it away (e.g. by ranking the conflicting beliefs or principles so that one overrides the other), in that sense abolishing it. This is the staple activity of healthcare ethics. However, there is no guarantee that this approach will always resolve the conflict. Some conflicts of belief or principle resist being defined away.

2 This occurs when the conflict of the manager's needs reflects a real conflict of needs in the hospital itself. What the close logical and empirical scrutiny shows is that the means to meet his needs really are incompatible with what patients need. In this case the most effective way to resolve the conflict is to abolish it by changing the external conditions creating it (see below). This too is not always feasible.

3 Then one can rank the conflicting historical drives by exploiting the structured and conditional character of one's drives (ch3§3). (At this point in the argument, we are back to prudential, not moral, ranking.) These characteristics imply that it is prudent to satisfy one's unsatisfied natural drives first, in descending order of urgency (ch3§1).

4 After that, it is prudent to satisfy one's historical drives in ascending order of derivation from one's natural drives.

Since the manager's dilemma concerns only his historical drives, strategy 3 is irrelevant here. The present scenario takes the organisational conditions as practically given, ruling out strategy 2. When strategy 1 fails, only strategy 4 remains.

One effect of health service reform has been to strengthen managers' incentives to implement central policy effectively and the penalties for failure or obstruction (conscientious or not). Focusing on his salary and employment, these incentives relate to what, in a market society, is one of the most highly overdetermined, low-level historical needs a person has. In these circumstances it is fairly evident which of the health manager's conflicting drives have priority in prudential terms. Occasionally health service managers say as much. In 1991 Mr Tony Hill was made responsible for closing a locally well-supported NHS cottage hospital in the Midlands. When a reporter asked him to comment about this controversial closure, Mr Hill's unusually frank answer was, one suspects, one that other managers would sometimes give if they dared: 'I have my mortgage to pay' (Clouston 1991: 2).

This makes the manager look responsible for any resulting harm to patients' needs. After all, it is he who pursues the incentives by acting accordingly. Yet if the foregoing account of drives and needs is correct, to expect him not to do so is to expect prudential irrationality of him (ch3§3). A person's historical drives – and *a fortiori* the corresponding needs – are constituted, in effect, by his pre-existing drives plus the means to realise them (ch3§3). What these means are, depends on the 'external' circumstances, the physical environment and social relations, through which he acts to satisfy his drives. So when a manager pursues his needs by closing hospitals that patients need or tampering with information that citizens need, responsibility for this also lies with whoever or whatever created these incentives and tied them to the closures and other instances of harm to patients' needs noted above. In part, this is of course the health managers themselves; but only in part. They are both also victims of health policy, wider social policies and the wider social relations that comprise the 'external circumstances'. The same circumstances and incentives confront anyone who takes on this kind of job. Responsibility for the existence of these dilemmas lies not with the manager alone (as a naive moralist might suggest) nor with the circumstances alone (as an extreme behaviourist might suggest) but with the combination. Managers often respond by victimising obstructive, 'whistle-blowing' or dissident staff (at the time of writing Sister Pat Cooksley in Plymouth is the current *cause célèbre* – Foot 1994: 16). What victimising actually achieves, on the above account, is to replace individuals who were comparatively perceptive of the above dilemmas with less perceptive or more compliant staff. Managerial incentives that achieve this look to be misconceived or misapplied.

Part of healthcare managers' peculiar role is to influence or even design the incentives, policies and structures of the organisation and health system in which he works. The strategy (2) of changing the circumstances that bring their drives into conflict is more available to them than to the ordinary health worker or patient. This poses the question: what sort of health service organisational designs offer the best prospect of preventing dilemmas of the above types from arising at all, or of minimising them if they cannot completely be avoided?

This raises questions of organisational design which demand attention (Chapter 8).

In similar ways healthcare reform tends to exacerbate conflicts between health workers' needs and health managers' needs (in their official capacities). One locus at which these conflicts become visible is in the managerial relationship itself, between employer and salaried employee. From time to time UK governments ponder whether strikes in health services ought simply to be banned (e.g. Harper 1994: 4). Citing patients' needs would be an obvious way to legitimate such a ban. Would it stand up to critical scrutiny?

Although rare in recent years, industrial action in health services is not unknown, not only by NHS industrial workers or occasionally nurses, but in rare instances of doctors threatening to strike and occasionally doing so. (The BMA leadership threatened that its GP members would not participate in the new NHS, until Bevan out-manoeuvred them.) One reason that health service strikes are rare is that most health workers are very reluctant to endanger patients:

> The actual scope for collective industrial struggle by mental-hospital staff (as with hospital staff in physical medicine) is in any case limited by a serious reckoning of the damage or even death that would be wrought among patients if these workers engaged in serious strike action. When it comes to strike action in hospitals, employees of whatever grade nearly always take a 'professional' rather than a 'trade union' view of their respon-sibilities and will not leave wards unstaffed.
>
> (Sedgwick 1982: 229)

Here too it is easy but naive to think that only the strikers bear responsibility for a strike. Just as managers sometimes face compelling incentives for which they are not wholly responsible to close hospitals officially, health workers occasionally face compelling incentives to do so unofficially. Yet the fact remains that in strikes (but not necessarily in other forms of industrial action) patients often suffer inconvenience or delay of treatments that are not life-saving but will improve their quality of life.

This is a somewhat different problem to the conscientious man-ager's dilemma. That was a conflict between the different needs of one person. The strike is a conflict between the needs of different persons. What do the above decision rules imply here?

At first it might seem that the concept of a hierarchy of needs, derived from a structure of drives, solves this problem too; as though one might decide according to whether a patient's need for healthcare or a health worker's need for better wages was more closely connected with that person's natural needs (analogously to strategies 3 and 4 above). After all, the notion of a hierarchy of needs based on the conditionality of historical drives does enable one to compare, at least approximately, which of two or more people has the greater range of unsatisfied needs and which of these unsatisfied needs have a higher prudential priority. However, that is a false hope. The rationale for the foregoing decision rules (above, and ch3§3) is that they describe how to satisfy one person's drives maximally. The requirements for conditionality, transparency, instrumental rationality, maximising life expectancy and compatibility of drives apply only within a person's drive structure, not across different individuals. Prudential reasoning recognises no unrelativised, 'objective' standpoint from which to arbitrate the conflict. All that this leaves is seeking some strategy to remove the external conditions that have brought the health workers' needs into conflict with the patients' (strategy 2 above).

Whether that can be done depends upon what the substantive conflict is between patients' and health workers' needs, and this depends on the strikers' objectives and methods. To illustrate, consider the hospital closure mentioned above. Suppose there are no special circumstances: the hospital is not providing sub-standard care; its closure is not a preliminary to opening a new, better hospital for the same patients and staff; the building is not about to collapse; and so on. Then both patients and health workers have an interest in keeping the hospital open and in a successful outcome for the strike. It is not hard, either, to conceive of circumstances in which the risks and delays in treating patients because of a strike are less than those caused by closing the hospital permanently. Even from the viewpoint of patients' needs, the strike, provided that it has some probability of success, is a lesser (prudential) evil than the closure; and if the strike fails, the patients are no worse off than before. At the opposite pole are strikes whose objectives are either irrelevant to patients' needs or even harm them; for (contentious) example, a strike to defend private medical practice from absorption by the NHS (as was threatened in 1946) or to preserve professional demarcations (cp. ch5§3).

Similar arguments apply to other forms of industrial action, such as boycotts or working to rule. If doctors perform abortions illegally for women who need them (see ch4§3) or ignore budget over-runs and continue treating patients, industrial action might actually meet patient needs more effectively than 'normal service'. (Staff who occupied the Elizabeth Garrett Anderson Hospital when it was first marked for closure continued to provide services unofficially.) A clear instance, partly because it is usually done in support of patients' needs or to protest against some aspect of health policy rather than for the health workers' direct personal gain, is 'whistle-blowing', whether to expose local management, the local medical establishment, government or corruption in private hospitals (e.g. Reed 1992: 8).

So it all depends on the context, objectives and methods whether a health workers' strike is justifiable, or the opposite, in terms of patients' needs. Contrary to what some NHS Trust managers have recently claimed, what patients sometimes do need is precisely for health workers to place their role in meeting patients' needs above their role in meeting the 'organisation's' or managers' need (*The Times*, 17 November 1994).

There are no valid reasons for assuming a priori that strikes, demarcation disputes, whistle-blowing, boycotts or other forms of industrial action in health services are incompatible with patients' needs for healthcare. Sometimes they are. But the fact that sometimes they are not, and in some circumstances might be the only way of advancing patient needs, conclusively removes that justification for banning all industrial action in healthcare, or even strikes specifically. Where health workers' and patients' needs really do conflict, a relativistic account of needs (ch3§4) implies that any putatively 'neutral' arbitrating standpoint is not what it claims to be. In such conflicts an apocryphal rule applies: 'Where you stand all depends upon where you sit'. Responsibility for these conflicts lies with the combination of a person's own needs and the roles constituted by his organisational position. Replacing a dissident health worker (or manager) with a less rational one is certainly one small-scale resolution of the conflict. In cases of organisational conflicts too, however, prevention might prove better than cure, for the patient, for the health worker, and perhaps for the manager. Organisational redesign of health systems is that means of prevention.

§2 SCARCITY

Enoch Powell allegedly coined the slogan 'infinite demand, finite resources' (Hart 1988: 280) which ministers still use to forestall criticism of seemingly inadequate NHS funding (e.g. Department of Health 1988: iii–ix). NHS resources are intended to be distributed on the basis of needs, not demands (ch1§1) and it is conceivable that people's needs for healthcare are smaller than their demands for it (cp. ch4§3). The question of whether health workers inevitably face the task of trying to meet infinite healthcare needs (Culyer 1976: 9, 38) with finite resources underlies ethical dilemmas not only in clinical practice (who will get the last intensive-care bed?) but for managers (is there any defensible way to ration healthcare?) and in health policy (are markets the most efficient way of allocating scarcities?). Three fundamental questions arise here. In what senses are health resources 'scarce', relative to people's needs for healthcare? If resources are scarce, by what criteria can one decide on grounds of need who will get healthcare and who will not? And how do different types of health system (markets, internal markets, nationalised systems, etc.) compare on these criteria?

Neither health economists nor politicians actually have to establish that healthcare needs are infinite in order to prove that healthcare resources are scarce; only that the amount of healthcare resources that people need exceeds the amount available. That would excuse ministers for failing to provide 'enough' healthcare resources and enable economists to apply their generic theories, which presuppose scarcity, to healthcare (e.g. McGuire, Henderson and Mooney 1988: 1): 'The economist's approach to resource allocation starts with the notion of scarcity of resources: that is, there is not, and never will be, enough resources to achieve all desirable objects. It is axiomatic that choices will be required' (Drummond 1993: 16). Previous chapters cast doubt on both the dramatic ('infinite needs') and the careful ('never will be enough') formulations. Both would hold if needs really were infinite, so let us analyse that assumption first. But if its main defect was that it exaggerates, the more careful formulation might yet stand; so the latter must be examined separately.

Claims that needs for healthcare are infinite derive much of their plausibility by conflating four different senses in which needs for healthcare resources might be called 'infinite'. One is to claim that people have needs whose satisfaction requires infinitely large resources ('infinitely large satisfiers', for short). Whether this claim is true depends on what drives a person has and how they withstand logical and factual criticism (ch3§§1–2). There is an optimum range of satisfaction of natural drives which has a finite upper limit (ch3§2). A similar argument applies to instrumental drives, whose satisfiers are the means of satisfying further drives. Whenever that further drive has a finite satisfier, the means that are necessary and sufficient to satisfy it are also finite and demand finite resources. Then what is needed to satisfy the instrumental drive is also finite. Ultimately all instrumental drives are means, or means to means, to satisfy natural drives whose satisfiers are finite (ch3§1). Instrumental needs are therefore finite. Indeed, many instrumental satisfiers can be consumed in self-defeating quantities, much as the satisfiers of natural drives can; a healthcare example is evolution of resistant bacteria through over-use of antibiotics. This leaves the non-instrumental historical drives associated with natural and instrumental drives. Only some of these even conceivably have infinitely large satisfiers (e.g. the drive to accumulate money – Marx 1976b: i 742); others, although bizarre and luxurious, do not. Non-instrumental historical drives count as needs so long as their satisfaction does not impede the satisfaction of instrumental needs and natural drives (ch3§2). However, a non-instrumental historical drive would so interfere, if it had an infinitely large satisfier and a person actually pursued this without limit. Any such drives would fail the tests of prudential rationality (ch3§2). If 'needs' are defined as they are here, no one has needs that have an infinitely large satisfier. Some people might desire (or 'demand') infinitely large 'satisfiers' but that, paradoxically, would only be evidence of their imprudence.

Another sense of 'infinite need' might be that our drives and needs develop open-endedly, through ever-ramifying causal connections and associations (cp. Hart 1988: 287; and ch3§1). However, this does not imply that a person has an infinite number of drives, nor of needs and need satisfiers at any given time. Neither does it imply that there is no limit to the addition of new drives; we all die in the end.

A third sense might be to say that there is no limit to the qualitative range of needs that a person might acquire. An infinitely diverse range of objects could be proposed as possible objects of needs, as of drives, against which no objection can be raised on grounds of fact or logic (ch3§3). Now the object of a drive is a candidate drive satisfier. However, there are clear empirical, let alone logical, limits as to what could actually satisfy a given natural or instrumental drive. Of course there is no a priori reason that any object at all might not become associated with a natural or a historical drive and thus become a non-instrumental historical drive satisfier. But an infinite range of logical possibilities at this point does not imply that a person would actually come to desire the whole infinitely large range of them. If he did, an earlier consideration applies; drives whose pursuit would crowd out the pursuit of other drives could not qualify as needs.

Lastly it might be suggested that each person's needs are finite but the number of people grows open-endedly, too fast for resource growth to catch up with. However, healthcare development has made family planning technically possible without sacrificing individuals' sexual needs. Evidence from developed capitalist societies suggests that after several generations of industrialisation, the fast population growth during early industrialisation decelerates and output starts growing faster, not slower, than population. Neither is it evident a priori that the increased healthcare needs of an aging population offset this.

Human needs in general are finite. For completeness, consider how this conclusion applies to the healthcare needs of a whole population. As far as health needs are concerned, there is a theoretical upper limit to each person's general level of health (ch4§1) and to their life cycle (ch3§1). This places a finite upper limit on the need for healthcare to meet health needs. However, the resources demanded for any method of producing any form of healthcare, although large, are inherently determinate and finite. For any individual there is a theoretical finite maximum of healthcare resources that he would consume even during a lifetime spent continuously consuming the most resource-intensive healthcare available. This is the worst conceivable scenario in re-source–need terms but in it the total resources that this patient would need are still finite, although huge. Any determinate population of such patients will therefore also have a finite theoretical maximum of healthcare resources that they could consume. To the claim that a population can always continue to grow open-endedly one can reply that only existing people have healthcare needs. This scenario de-molishes the 'infinite demand' slogan and its counterpart, 'infinite needs' (Frankel and West 1993: 50).

As for 'finite resources', managers and ministers sometimes use 'resources' to mean 'real inputs to healthcare', but more often to mean 'budgets' or 'money'. Ironically the one 'resource' that is never finite is money. It can be created without limit by the stroke of a pen. Although it is a truism that real resources on earth are finite, healthcare resources are inevitably scarce only if they are inevitably fewer than the amount necessary to meet everybody's needs for healthcare. Once this suppressed assumption is reinstated, the slogan attributed to Enoch Powell is not an obvious truism. Many real inputs to healthcare (labour power, consumables, scientific knowledge) are reproducible on a very large scale. Indeed a main legitimation of market society itself is that market economies themselves gradually overcome scarcity. This can be illustrated empirically by examples of 'overproduction' and waste in markets in other sectors (e.g. dairy products in many European countries) besides the epidemiological evidence of the over-consumption of fat, sugar, salt, alcohol, tobacco, cars and other goods (Department of Health 1991; Royal Commission on Environmental Pollution 1994). 'Green' writers argue that economic scarcity is not inevitable because it results largely from wasteful methods of production and consumption (needless packaging, planned product obsolescence, disposability, etc.) (e.g. Draper 1991). Further left, Marxists still argue that markets are inherently exploitative and crisis-prone, hence a brake on economic development; a socialist society can remove these characteristics and, with them, scarcity. All three very different political standpoints converge on a conclusion that resource scarcity relative to needs is practically avoidable. These arguments all concern general economic development, largely outside the health sector. Within the health sector 'high' technology developments in medicine are often regarded, even defined (Jennett 1972: 2, 11, 118), as expensive. Yet many new medical technologies cheapen healthcare; for example, when drugs replace sanatorium treatment of TB, contraception replaces abortion, or 'keyhole' surgery replaces radical surgery. *Pace* Russell (1986; see ch4§2), prevention usually is cheaper than curing most diseases.

Some resources, however, are not so readily reproducible. Current medical techniques cannot reproduce most of the human body parts used for transplants, research, assisted reproduction, making blood products and so on. They have to be 'harvested'. Yet even this scarcity is not utterly intractable. Genetic engineering now provides unlimited supplies of some body products (e.g. specially selected cells) and it remains an open question what animal, mechanical, cloned or parthogenetic substitutes might become available in future. Time is the only absolutely non-reproducible resource. The period of fuller health that a patient loses while waiting for treatment can never be repaid and some treatments are effective only if they are timely. However, the political and economic debate rarely concerns these scarcities. Its usual focus is the more mundane resources of labour, equipment, knowledge and, above all, money.

Proving that a population's needs for healthcare resources are finite in principle is much easier than showing that they are satiable in practice. The empirical arguments showing whether they are satiable only hold true for a particular health system at a given time. Nevertheless it is worth outlining how such an argument might be constructed because this gives a clue as to whether it might ever be true. There are at least two ways of reaching an empirical first approximation of how the UK population's healthcare needs relate to the resources required to meet them.

The first would begin by estimating the whole population's need for healthcare. Hart and others estimate the 'iceberg' of concealed healthcare needs by the 'rule of halves'. This empirical rule of thumb states that approximately half the people who need healthcare actually receive it (Hart 1988: 109). Applying the rule crudely and literally to the UK, doubled healthcare spending would equal 12.4 per cent of UK GNP (OECD figures for 1990). This is a high level but certainly achievable; current US healthcare spending is almost exactly this proportion. However, the 'rule of halves' applies more directly to preventive and primary healthcare than to hospital care. Doubling preventive and primary care would not double total healthcare costs, only the 44.9 per cent of UK health budgets spent on primary healthcare in 1990 (OHE 1992: table 2.13) and not by that much if there are any fixed costs at all in primary healthcare. Although more disease would be detected for hospital treatment, some would also be prevented from progressing, as now happens, to the point where the patient needs hospital care (Hart 1988: 109–23). The specific net resource impacts on secondary and tertiary care remain indeterminate without much more evidence than is now available.

Another approach is to calculate the additional resources required for treating patients whose unmet needs are already known to the health system because they are on waiting lists for treatment. Of course there is no reason to assume that these patients have been added to the waiting lists for meeting the very criteria of healthcare need outlined above; a rough match is the most we may assume, and that only insofar as the present account of healthcare needs does articulate the intuitions that health workers in fact use for making clinical decisions. On these assumptions, the additional resources necessary to meet these unmet needs are comparatively modest. Frankel calculates that all present NHS waiting lists for urgent cases waiting over one month do not equal more than 2 per cent of NHS hospital throughput in the last year in which data were collected (1987) although to these must be added patients awaiting their first hospital consultation: the waiting list for the waiting list. The ratio of all waiting lists to throughput has never exceeded 15 per cent since the early 1950s. Three-quarters of waiting lists are accounted for by just five hospital specialties (Frankel and West 1993: 4–6). The resources necessary to meet these proxies for need are small compared with the total NHS budget, let alone GNP.

Here we are speaking of gross increases in resources needed. Against these could be offset gains from reducing health system waste. 'Waste' admits of various definitions for this purpose (see ch8§1) but one form is not using available real resources for which needs evidently exist. Bed and hospital closures are one UK example; the under-use of trained ex-nurses in the working population is another. Official guidance to NHS managers identifies, indeed recommends, yet another type of waste: 'Arrangements must be in place for working with clinicians and other professionals to manage activity "back into line" if over-performance occurs' (NHSME 1993c). 'Over-performance' refers to hospitals completing their contracts or exhausting their budgets before the end of the financial year by treating patients faster than expected. 'Manage activity "back into line" means doing the opposite until the accounts balance, which reportedly is sometimes done (Brindle 1993a).

Ministers' and health economists' assertions of inevitable healthcare resource scarcity is hardly an axiom. At best it is an unsubstantiated empirical claim although the limited evidence and crude methods of estimation available suggest that, in the UK, it is probably false. Intuitively it seems unlikely that most developed capitalist societies face health resource 'scarcity' on a vastly different scale. Nevertheless many health systems do appear to be under-resourced. Even then, the first problem is not how to allocate scarce resources among the individuals who need them. This question arises only after one concedes that all one can do about scarcity is to find a defensible way of allocating it. Before resigning ourselves to that, a prior question is: what resource allocations offer the best prospects of palliating, or even ending, the scarcity itself?

In terms of needs, an under-resourced health system is one only able to produce less healthcare than the amount needed by the population it serves, given its current resources. Its methods of healthcare 'production' cannot convert inputs into needed healthcare at a large enough rate to meet everybody's health needs. Either or both of two assumptions underlie this. One is a technical assumption that existing methods of healthcare production physically can only yield fewer episodes of care than is necessary to satisfy the unmet health needs (for instance, there is a limit to how many operations a theatre can accommodate each session). The other is that the health system's payment and reward structures do not sufficiently stimulate, or enable, healthcare providers or individual health workers to do the kinds or quantity of work that would satisfy the unmet needs for healthcare. This is an assumption about the organisation, management and incentives of the healthcare system. Lastly, it may be suggested that the range of needs that the use of healthcare is to meet is defined too broadly. Four strategies are therefore available in principle for reducing healthcare resource scarcity. They can be ranked in descending order of scope for removing the causes of resource scarcity relative to the need for healthcare.

A preventive strategy is to reduce the amount of unmet need for health services to deal with. Preventive strategies are placed first in order of effectiveness in reducing health resource scarcity for two empirical reasons: prevention is generally cheaper than cure and produces a higher level of health status and less iatrogenesis than treating illness does. However, a preventive strategy faces two big obstacles in implementation. Since the main determinants of health lie in the non-healthcare sectors of the economy, its strategy implies shifting resources from curative to preventive care, indeed outside the health system. This is difficult for politicians to legitimate. It also implies decades of 'double running' while people who already have preventable ill health are treated and preventive work takes place alongside; although large, the resource gains are slow to materialise.

A technological strategy is to increase the rates at which clinical and therapeutic interventions convert resources into health gain. This does not reduce the scale of needs for healthcare but does maximise the extent to which ill health can be remedied from given resources. The strategy is second best because even a complete cure still leaves a period of unmet need (health loss) between the onset of the disease and its cure. A third, resourcing strategy is to increase the quantity of resources available. This strategy neither reduces the need for healthcare nor improves the technical possibilities for meeting it but it does tackle the resource side of the imbalance between needs and resources, maximising the amount of need that can be met, given the inadequacies of methods of prevention and cure. This strategy cannot, on the above arguments, be ruled out a priori by claiming that scarcity is inevitable.

An incentive strategy is to increase the rate at which resources can be converted into numbers of effective interventions by health workers. Given undiminished causes of ill health, inadequate technologies and fixed (but insufficient) total resources, this strategy maximises the extent to which health loss can be remedied in the circumstances. The problem that this poses is whether the patient's health is remedied at the cost of the health worker's needs if the strategy is implemented by reducing the health worker's income or job security.

Only now does one arrive at the point where most ethical, managerial and political discussions start: a ranking strategy. This strategy tacitly accepts the fact of scarcity and the other health system inadequacies noted above, responding by trying to manage the scarcity by devising ranking criteria for allocating scarce resources. The purpose of such criteria is to legitimate meeting some people's healthcare needs by sacrificing others'. As yet, we are still investigating what ranking criteria are implied by a prudential, non-moral concept of 'need for healthcare'. A relativist account of needs implies that when healthcare resources are scarce, each person would be prudent to prioritise resourcing the health services relevant to him, in decreasing order of relevance. 'Relevant' services are either those that prevent or treat a type of ill health that he already suffers or risks suffering (an elderly man potentially needs urology but not gynaecology services); or services relevant to the health needs of other people whose health he needs (e.g. his children's), and thus indirectly relevant to him. There are two ways of identifying which services are relevant to a person.

One applies to those types of ill health whose aetiology is little known. For practical purposes the incidence of this type of ill health must then be regarded as occurring randomly across a whole population because (*ex hypothesi*) no one knows whether he is at atypically small or large risk. The only available evidence of his risk of suffering this type of ill health is its incidence (the proportion of a given population who start to suffer that form of ill health per period). Then the prudent allocation of healthcare resources for a healthy person is to allocate resources first to preventing and treating the form of ill health with highest incidence, then to preventing and treating ill health with the second highest incidence and so on in descending order of incidence until resources are exhausted. In most Western societies this method would probably prioritise resourcing health services for people with rheumatism, incontinence and most cancers (the aetiology of a few cancers and of cardiovascular disease is too well known to attribute random occurrence). This method of prioritisation implies that all members of a given population have a common prudential interest in a single determinate allocation of healthcare resources for preventing and treating those types of ill health that must be assumed, for want of more specific knowledge, to occur randomly. The same applies to types of ill health that really do occur randomly, and to those to which everyone is equally at risk (e.g. infections).

Ever fewer types of ill health are so little understood, however. The human genome project in particular promises to reduce this ignorance much further. It remains prudent for each individual that resources be allocated to the types of ill health to which he is most at risk. But now the size of his risk can be estimated from known 'risk factors' (unemployment, obesity, exposure to carcinogens, etc.). One limiting case is where a person already suffers a form of ill health: a 'risk' of 100 per cent. Its opposite is where a person cannot possibly suffer certain types of ill health, for instance those caused by genetic defects which he does not have, those arising at a life-cycle stage which he has already passed, or those that are sex-specific (e.g. morning sickness). Here a prudential theory of needs implies that no common prudential interest exists, in a single determinate allocation of scarce healthcare resources. Different care groups and risk groups have different needs. Scarcity makes these needs incompatible because they cannot all be satisfied. From this point two ethical perspectives open up.

The conventional view is that here we reach the limits of prudential reasoning. What must be done is to devise an 'impartial' or 'objective' standpoint from which these conflicts can be arbitrated 'fairly' or 'rationally', 'efficiently' or 'equitably', either by constructing special decision rules for health resource allocations (e.g. a minimax rule, Rawls' 'difference principle') or by proposing substantive principles (e.g. to maximise the number of worthwhile lives (but not necessarily maximise an abstract total of happiness) (Glover 1977: 70–1) or to satisfy 'basic' before other needs (chs1§2, 2§1). Since there is no common prudential interest here, these attempts must either separate themselves entirely from prudential assumptions (the moralist's solution) or resort to obfuscation or sleight of hand to misrepresent what is really a person-relative standpoint as though it were in everybody's interests (cp. Chapter 9).

Cost–benefit analysis in health resource allocation questions is a good example. The idea of maximising net gain has a clear and valid prudential use when particular individuals – say, a firm's managers and owners – control a number of activities and can offset their losses in some against their gains from others; and when the 'gain' is of something genuinely amenable to addition and subtraction, as monetary profits and costs are. Obfuscation and sleight of hand set in, when the method is abstracted from this setting and reapplied to entities such as the natural capacities and pains of members of human populations. Not only are these intrinsically non-addable but there is no individual or group of individuals who receives any net gain. Any determinate distribution of scarce healthcare resources implies that some individuals have a gross gain and others a gross loss. Among the latter, if QALYs are used, are old people. Since QALYs are directly 'ageism' they are also indirectly sexist (since women outlive men) (Harris 1992) and probably indirectly racially discriminatory too. Those who lose by this method have a prudential need for healthcare managers not to use QALYs, besides whatever moral claims one wishes to impute. Since they presuppose a single beneficiary of net health gain, QALYs might be validly applicable for judging alternate treatment plans for a single person (although even here there are logical difficulties). However, the assumptions built into cost–benefit analysis in general, and QALY analysis in particular, are simply false in respect of non-additive characteristics such as health and of entities such as populations (ch4§§1–3).

When there are no common prudential interests in a determinate allocation of scarce healthcare resources, an alternative approach is to abandon the pursuit of such a solution as futile. Here too, 'where one stands all depends upon where one sits', as far as one's needs for healthcare resource allocations are concerned. This does not mean that no prudential answers are available, as to how to allocate healthcare resources. If anything there are too many answers; one for each care group, conceivably even one for each person. What are not available are answers common to the whole population. Whatever other disadvantages, even terrors, this perspective has, it at least avoids the appearance of legitimating whatever policy of, in effect, passive euthanasia the government and NHS managers adopt as a 'fair' or 'just' or 'objective' policy.

Which of these perspectives to pursue, and how, is a question to return to (in Chapter 9), having completed the prudential analysis of the need for healthcare.

There remains, lastly, a policy option of restricting the range of needs that health services are to address, for instance by redefining what count as 'genuine' or 'real' healthcare needs; a revisionist strategy. In Britain there are already signs of this in the recent court cases to determine whether long-term care of chronically ill elderly people whose health status cannot be improved should count as healthcare or social care. Many health services either do not meet health needs, or meet health needs only incidentally or for a minority of their users (ch4§3). If a revisionist strategy were to be followed, these services would appear an obvious target for de-prioritisation. Another revisionist strategy is to redefine 'needs' as 'ability to benefit' (see ch1§1, ch4§3). Yet the present account of needs implies that individuals' needs cannot be just defined away by verbal fiat and neither, therefore, can the problem of health resource scarcity. A revisionist strategy involves not just a decision not to satisfy some people's healthcare needs, but a further claim that those needs are no longer recognised as 'genuine' healthcare needs at all. From this would follow a refusal to recognise any need for the preventive, technological, incentive and resourcing strategies either.

There is no theoretical warrant, and in industrialised societies doubtful empirical warrant, for maintaining that healthcare resources are inevitably scarcer than is necessary to satisfy healthcare needs. When healthcare resources are contingently scarce for historical or policy reasons, it is more prudent for potential health system users to allocate the available resources in a way that offers some prospect of palliating and eventually ending the scarcity than to focus solely on seeking criteria by which to allocate scarce resources in perpetuity. One reason that health resource scarcity is so dangerous is that it subverts common interests in patterns of health resource allocation.

Health economists maintain the dubious assumption of inevitable scarcity, not because one cannot analyse markets without it but because nearly all economic theory uses that assumption for legitimating markets as 'efficient'. This brings us to the question of what sort of needs-based arguments would justify the provision of healthcare through markets, or through some other type of health system.

8

WHAT KIND OF HEALTH SYSTEM?

§1 COMPARING HEALTH SYSTEMS

Debates about the marketisation of healthcare usually concentrate on provision of healthcare itself. Important as this question is, its focus is too narrow. The largest determinants of health lie outside the healthcare sector. A rounded assessment of the impact of markets on health needs would also cover the effects of markets in other economic sectors on health (primarily the water, sanitation, food, housing, education, transport and income protection sectors). These, together with health services, comprise the health system proper. Previous chapters also concentrated on how health services meet patients' healthcare needs: the healthcare system. How health services are organised determines whether patients' needs for clinical autonomy can be harmonised with doctors' needs for it. Health system organisation also determines whether patients' needs for healthcare can be harmonised with the imperatives to which managers must respond, and whether the needs of doctors and managers can be aligned with the needs of (other) health workers. Our next task is to consider how to compare types of health system (markets, social insurance, etc.) and particular existing health systems in terms of needs for healthcare.

Healthcare systems consist of five types of ingredient. The first, the 'means of production' of healthcare, include physical means (buildings, equipment, consumables), scientific knowledge, 'human resources', information systems and other media for health promotion (cf. ch4§2). Working relations in the healthcare workplace are the second type of ingredient, constituted by the technical division of labour between different types of health worker (the doctor, the radiographer, the cook, etc.). A third ingredient is a set of property

172

relations: the *de facto* relations of control over the means of healthcare production, for example the financial controls, referral systems, decision-making processes and the boundaries of control defining discrete healthcare organisations. Incentive systems, comprising the criteria for rewarding or punishing health workers, with their behavioural effects, are the fourth ingredient. Lastly, the healthcare system also includes the generic ideological and legal frameworks within which healthcare is produced and which codify and legitimate the property relations and incentive arrangements involved.

A health system thus includes a healthcare system plus methods for influencing health determinants in other sectors. There are two ways to compare health systems as means of satisfying the needs of those who need them. One would be to enumerate all the health services that a person might need during the rest of her life (virtually her whole life, for a neonate) and compare what different healthcare systems provide with this list. Obviously there are large uncertainties and problems of data sufficiency in this approach. A more flexible, less data-hungry way is to regard the health system as a system for responding *ad hoc* to a person's contingent health and healthcare needs during her life. Then it is possible to list the characteristics that individuals need in a healthcare system for it to provide healthcare for them.

As Flew observes, goods must first be produced before they can be allocated and consumed (Flew 1981: 86). A first precondition for people getting the healthcare that they need is therefore that the health system actually produces healthcare at all and does so across the full range of health services that a person is liable to need (ch4§4). For short, we can label this condition 'availability of healthcare'.

People who need healthcare must also have access to it if their health and healthcare needs are to be met. The access condition is satisfied by the mere availability of population-level health promotion activities because they are indivisible and non-excludable (ch4§2). Access is a distinct characteristic only for healthcare which can be made into private or personal property (hospital bed-days, drugs, clinicians' services, etc.). Besides payment systems, access involves referral systems (WHO 1978: 59). Healthcare to which individuals have no access might as well not be produced, as far as meeting their healthcare needs is concerned.

Unless the available, accessible healthcare is also relevant to a person's healthcare needs, it will no more satisfy them than not producing healthcare at all would. (First-rate cosmetic surgery services are irrelevant to the needs of elderly male asthmatics.) The needs to which healthcare is relevant (or not) are, first, individuals' needs for health (ch4§2), and, as a second-order criterion, their non-health needs for healthcare (ch4§3).

Similarly, the available, accessible and relevant healthcare must be effective in actually meeting the user's healthcare needs (as defined in Chapter 4). Placing the onus of proof on those who advocate a healthcare intervention suggests a definition of ineffective healthcare as those procedures for which there is no evidence that they actually increase a person's natural capacities or diminish her pains (Cochrane 1972: 8). Ranade alleges that some 70 per cent of clinical procedures would fail this test (Ranade 1994: 42). Ineffective healthcare also satisfies a person's healthcare needs no more than not producing healthcare at all (and if on balance it is iatrogenic, it satisfies these needs less than not providing healthcare at all).

A fifth criterion by which to evaluate a health system in terms of its users' needs is whether it meets its beneficiaries' needs efficiently. This presupposes that the health system in question meets its recipients' needs at all, i.e. that all four preceding criteria are satisfied. Most studies compare health services in terms of what healthcare needs they actually satisfy. Necessary as this is, various writers remind us that healthcare sometimes also has negative effects on its recipients' needs (e.g. Illich 1976; Taylor 1979). It has a direct cost in terms of needs besides an opportunity cost. So the efficiency of a healthcare system can be defined in terms of needs as the balance between these opposite effects. Among these are loss of patients' time, disruption to their activities of daily life and iatrogenesis. Prices, taxes, insurance premiums, etc., are a monetarised but nearly always inaccurate and incomplete proxy for these real costs. Money costs of healthcare normally exclude patient time, for example. (Health economists try to use cost–benefit analysis to compare the goods and bads of healthcare; fallaciously – ch7§2.) A needs-based concept of efficiency must therefore compare what 'goods' (need satisfiers) a health system produces with its output of 'bads' (non-satisfiers). As we are still using a relativist concept of needs, the relevant needs are those of healthcare users. In descending order of ratio of healthcare 'goods' to 'bads', the 'bads' are as follows:

1 Healthcare that meets healthcare needs but uses more natural resources and health workers' time than is technically necessary, given current techniques of production or organisation, such as services with high 'overhead' costs for administrative or industrial

services, over-costly drugs or over-staffing (rarely a problem in the UK but a considerable one in eastern Europe).

2 Healthcare that meets healthcare needs but frustrates other needs, for example by necessitating work elsewhere to undo its external 'side effects'. This happens when, say, hospitals release biohazardous, chemical or radioactive waste into the local environment or subsidise health workers' cars instead of public transport. (These 'externalities' are 'bads' accruing to people outside the health sector and not reflected in – external to – money flows into and out of the healthcare system.)

3 Completely wasted healthcare, i.e. healthcare that meets neither health nor non-health needs. It makes little direct difference to patients' needs whether or not this production is technically efficient or not, although if patients are having to bear the costs of waste anyhow, cheap waste is a lesser evil for them than expensive waste. Views differ as to how much waste of this kind the health sector produces although few commentators regard it as negligible.

When healthcare resources are scarce, people at risk of not getting healthcare need the form of healthcare system that offers the best prospect of removing the scarcity by removing its causes; that is, the one tending to produce the highest-ranked strategies among those listed in the preceding chapter (ch7§2). This is the sixth criterion by which to evaluate health systems in terms of needs.

To meet healthcare needs at all, a health service must be available, accessible, effective and relevant to needs. Health systems' ability to meet healthcare needs is therefore only as strong as the weakest link in this chain of conditions. A comparison of two healthcare systems in terms of their ability to meet individuals' healthcare needs therefore amounts to a comparison of the two subsets of healthcare systems (from each health system) that satisfy all the first four criteria. These first four criteria can therefore be grouped as a single, compound criterion: that of satisfying present healthcare needs. The efficiency criterion concerns present non-health needs, the scarcity-handling criterion the non-satisfaction of present and satisfaction of future health and healthcare needs.

Still we have only a prudential, not a moral, conception of needs to use as a basis for comparison (ch2§2). The multi-criterion decision method, however, is relevant to prudential comparisons of this type. Applied to the present task, its four steps are as follows:

1 to enumerate the healthcare needs which the given set of people need a healthcare system to meet;
2 to nominate the types of healthcare systems or individual services to be compared;
3 to empirically profile the degree of satisfaction of healthcare needs in each healthcare system (or type);
4 to rank the healthcare system, applying the criteria (from stage 1) to the data (from stage 3) about the healthcare systems nominated at step 2.

Either step 1 or 2 can be completed first but both must precede step 3, which in turn must precede step 4.

A prudential and relativist account of needs implies that different users need the healthcare system for different reasons. To get step 1 started, a standpoint has to be assumed. It has been argued persuasively that health services appear to have been organised as suits business interests (Navarro 1979: xii, 75, 148f, 205), government interests, doctors and other health workers' interests (Foster 1995) and the interest of health-sector suppliers and financiers ('medical–industrial complex') (Wohl 1984). However, the standpoint relevant to most people is that of someone needing the healthcare system for maintaining health and obtaining healthcare. These individuals have many needs for healthcare which are not all reducible to one another (Chapters 4–6). If a person knows his healthcare needs, he can judge health systems in terms of which one makes the healthcare relevant to his needs most available, accessible, effective and efficient. However, the standpoint from which health system comparisons are normally tacitly made is that of a healthy person who is uncertain what types of ill health might befall him. His prudent course is to assume that the relative size of different care groups indicates the relative probability that he will need that kind of care in future (cp. ch7§2). Then he would rank his probable needs for different kinds of healthcare in descending care group size. Within each care group category his sequence of needs for healthcare is that noted earlier: preventive first, then curative and so on through to terminal care (ch4§2). After his healthcare needs, there usually follow (in prudential order) his non-health needs for healthcare, which can also be ranked in their order of derivation from his natural drives (chs3§1, 7§1). This enumerates his needs and ranks them ready for the fourth step. For each type of healthcare needed by the person whose standpoint is taken, the different health systems can be assessed in terms of service availability, access, relevance, effectiveness and efficiency (see above).

The second step is to decide which health systems (or types of them) to compare. To start the analysis simply we can begin with two polar types: predominantly market systems and predominantly command-bureaucracy healthcare systems (cp. Field's schema – Field 1989: 7/ schema 1) although the invention of quasi-markets is making such unidimensional schemas obsolete (Sheaff 1994).

For the third step, one must assemble the data necessary for comparing the health systems. Here, the necessary data are those indicating healthcare availability, access, effectiveness and efficiency for the person (or persons) from whose standpoint (or standpoints) the comparison is made. Many technical problems arise in the choice, definition and validation of empirical indicators to operationalise health status and outcome and in adjusting or standardising data from different sources to make them comparable. (For instance, to compare the efficacy of hospital systems one must abstract from non-hospital influences on patients' health status such as patients' age and sex mix, their income distribution, per capita income and so on.) These problems are more fully explored elsewhere (e.g. Bowling 1995; Holland 1983; Wilkin, Hallam and Doggett 1992). For reasons noted above it is necessary to use real, not monetary, indicators wherever possible. At this step one is collecting and analysing data to reveal the impact that each healthcare system has on satisfying and frustrating the needs of the person or people whose standpoint has been assumed.

The fourth step is to rank the healthcare systems according to how far the data amassed at step 3 indicate that they meet the needs enumerated at stage 1. For a rounded assessment in terms of needs, it is as important to compare which healthcare needs and health needs each healthcare system leaves unsatisfied as to compare those that they satisfy. Earlier chapters gave an account of these needs and their relative priority (ch4§§1–2).

Doyal and Gough doubt that a relativist theory of needs can be used for comparing healthcare systems at all because, they say, relativism implies an incommensurability of needs across cultures (Doyal and Gough 1991: 268). There is less difficulty than they think, however, because their objection conflates three separate points. The present theory is relativist in implying that whatever similarities there are in the satisfiers that different people need, is a contingent matter. If person A is to persuade person B that B needs healthcare system 1 rather than healthcare system 2, A must compare the two systems in terms of B's needs, not A's. Given the necessary data, A can do this whether or not his own needs are similar to B's. It is equally logically possible for A to compare the healthcare systems in terms of A's needs, or for B to do so. What prudential needs each of them have is a matter of fact (ch3§2); each of them can in principle discover these facts, and the comparison will be equally factual either way. Such a comparison is not culture relative.

This is a separate question from whether A and B do in fact have similar historical needs. That does depend (partly) on whether they inhabit similar cultures (ch3§1). From whose standpoint one makes the comparison is yet another separate question. If one compares health systems from the standpoint of one's own needs, one does so from a standpoint that is not just culturally, but personally, relative. This comparison is both objective and person relative. To illustrate: a person who needed a heart transplant would have her needs best satisfied in a health system with elaborate, high technology acute services (e.g. the USA). But unless she were very rich, a person with learning difficulties would have her needs met rather badly in a US-style healthcare system but comparatively well in a health system like, say, that in the Netherlands.

There are two ways of ranking health systems by the multiple needs criteria identified at step 1. In the simpler case one system outdoes another on all criteria. However, the more likely result is that healthcare system 1 outdoes healthcare system 2 on some criteria but for other criteria the reverse holds. Then one must call into play the ranking of needs criteria noted at step 1. The ranking method is then to start with the highest-ranked need criterion and rank the healthcare systems by this. The second-ranked need criterion is then used for breaking any resulting ties, the third to break any still remaining, and so on. To illustrate, most health systems in industrialised capitalist countries have very similar scientific knowledge at their disposal and can produce very similar types of healthcare in all but the marginal areas of healthcare that are currently being researched and developed. In terms of healthcare availability there is therefore little to choose between them. In respect of access, it is a different matter, so the relative assessment turns on access, not availability.

This brings us to the substantive comparison of market and nationalised health systems using the method and some of the concepts outlined above. Now we can determine whether it is question-begging to use a concept of 'need' for such purposes because 'need' is an inherently anti-market concept (see ch2§1). By now it should be clear that neither markets, nor nationalised healthcare, nor any specific type of health (or social) system is presupposed by the concept of 'need' used here. Its assumptions lie in a generic theory of action (ch3§§1–2), a compatibilist account of the mind-brain (chs2§3, 2§4, 3§1), a set of logical requirements (ch3§§3–4) and the conceptualisation of 'health' which these together imply (ch4§1). Certainly a person's drives and hence his needs depend on his social setting and biography. But nothing in that presupposes that any particular social setting is morally or prudentially defensible, nor the opposite (ch4§1). Other people do sometimes know what we need better than we do ourselves (ch3§3) but without further assumptions which have not been made so far these 'other people' might equally be private firms' marketing managers as professional experts or bureaucrats.

We can now compare two stereotypes of health system organisation.

§2 HEALTH NEEDS AND MARKETS

Now we can critically compare how market and nationalised health systems meet healthcare needs, using the method and the criteria of critical comparison outlined earlier (ch8§1). In deciding which health systems to compare (the second step of the method outlined above) we must select the strongest instances of either type to avoid 'straw man' arguments (strongest, that is, in terms of their ability to satisfy the needs mentioned in the preceding section). So the following comparison will be illustrated empirically from the US and Swiss healthcare markets and the pre-1900 UK and Swedish nationalised healthcare systems. Indicators and data follow (step 3), then a ranking of the two health system types (step 4).

Complex and important though the data collation and analysis are, they are not tasks of ethical analysis. Here we shall use ready-made empirical results from other researchers. Although we can only summarise main trends here, the results are enough to indicate a probable conclusion and set the scene for continuing the analysis of needs and health systems. To prevent repetition, we proceed directly to step 4, referring to the relevant empirical data in making the ranking.

Measured crudely in terms of numbers of doctors and hospital beds per 1,000 population, the strongest market and nationalised health-care systems show overlapping ranges of figures for the physical availability of acute curative services, with a wider range for the two nationalised models.* Where market systems do perform strongly is in fast dissemination of new technologies. A classic case is the high number of CAT scanners in the USA compared with the UK as a result of the 'medical arms race' in the US hospital markets in the 1970s and early 1980s. Similarly some high technology treatments which are unavailable in the UK are available in the USA (e.g. multiple transplants – the Laura Davies case – or some types of oncological neurosurgery). This difference partly reflects the market incentive to develop services with high 'added value' because these usually yield the highest profits.

By contrast the availability of health promotion activity appears greater in nationalised than in market systems. However, we must distinguish health promotion through individual activity and health promotion through population-wide measures (ch4§2). Markets tend to make available the physical means to personal self-care as saleable commodities: 'health foods', exercise facilities, smoking preventives, contraceptives, non-prescription drugs, minor equipment and consumables (soap, toothbrushes, etc.). Market provision of health promotion at population level is virtually unknown. The nearest thing is health promotion undertaken by charities and political pressure groups but these are hardly the profit-maximising firms of conventional market theory. At first sight markets seem to give commercial health insurers an incentive to promote health in order to reduce their payments for curative care. Louise Russell, however, corrects this impression. Conventional accounting and discounting systems devalue the long-term benefits but not the present costs of health promotion programmes, making them hard to justify financially (Russell 1986: 73). (She concludes that prevention is justified despite these economic 'disadvantages', without challenging the economists' argument itself.) Besides there is always the risk that consumers will change insurer meanwhile so that the savings accrue to a competing insurer, although in theory an insurer who also provided curative services and was confident of long-term consumer loyalty might escape this risk. This concerns prevention at individual level. Even economists agree that population-level preventive services have to be provided as public goods by the state; and are so provided, after a fashion, in both the USA and Switzerland.

---

*Doctors per 1,000 population 1990: USA = 2.3; Switzerland = 2.9; Sweden (1989 figure) = 3.1; UK = 1.4. Beds per 1,000 population 1990: USA = 4.7; Switzerland = 9.6; Sweden = 13.3; UK (1989 figure) = 6.4. (OECD 1992: 44–5).

Empirically, markets and nationalised systems both have short-comings in making care available for long-standing conditions (learning disability, chronic illness, senescence, physical disability, etc.) which are not at present amenable to curative treatment. Nationalised services have been slow to prioritise these 'Cinderella services' for modernisation, tolerating unnecessarily poor conditions (Martin 1983: 3–27, 80–97). Even in Switzerland and the USA, however, market default has resulted in most of the 'Cinderella services' being financed predominantly from non-market, especially public, sources. Markets are especially ill adapted to fund the involuntary care that some patients need (ch6§3). In terms of the availability of 'Cinderella services', then, the evidence of these four countries appears to favour the nationalised service, if only as a lesser evil.

Health promotion and 'Cinderella services' appear more available in nationalised than in market systems but the opposite applies in respect of some types of high technology curative healthcare. Empirically the two types of system offer two overlapping sets of available services. One set does not unequivocally dominate the other.

The position is clearer in regard to access. People needing healthcare face the market entry problem. The more a person needs healthcare, the less able he usually is to enter markets (typically the labour market, but the same applies to any market) to get the means to buy it. (In market society, market entry is equivalent to Daniels' 'normal opportunity range' – Daniels 1985: 57.) Measured by the proportion of the population having access to 'basic profile' healthcare (e.g. the healthcare needed to prevent irretrievable deterioration in health), a nationalised health system gives everyone access to those services that it has physically available. Although the US figures are contested, it appears that the whole US health system finances access to available services to no more than 85 per cent of people below retirement age (ProPAC 1991: 31; Bodenheimer 1992: 201) and to 85.9 per cent of all Americans (HIAA 1995: 5). Subtracting under-insured people who have only partial access reduces this figure further. Yet even this figure is too generous to the market-based US healthcare because it still includes publicly organised and subsidised health insurance: Medicare and Medicaid predominantly. The same argument would discount the Assistance Publique and similar funding in the Swiss cantons. Excluding these to leave conventional market access, and measuring that by the proxy of percentages of healthcare costs paid from private sources (interpreted generously to include non-public, non-commercial sick funds), access figures fall to just under 60 per cent in the USA and around 61 per cent in Switzerland. Even theoretically 'perfect insurance' (where there are no administration costs, only normal insurer profits and premia strictly reflect risk) would confront poorer people, who have higher health risks, with higher premia. To this access problem, market insurance adds adverse selection, skimming, dumping, co-payment and cover exclusions (e.g. for medical catastrophes). Not only does all this reduce access to healthcare but reduces it most sharply for the people most likely to need healthcare.

A counterargument is that nationalised economies also ration healthcare, and that rationing healthcare by willingness to pay is less arbitrary than rationing by delay (Seldon 1980: 52). We saw (ch5§2) that consumers' preferences are likely to reflect their needs for some aspects of healthcare fairly accurately. However, markets ration not only by willingness to pay but, before that question can even arise, by ability to pay. Patients at the bottom of an NHS waiting list get treatment within two years at worst (and usually within six months). In a market system the patient without insurance or cash either gets treatment charitably (i.e. despite the market, not because of it) or never. Besides, the order in which waiting-list patients are treated is intended, in the UK, to reflect the urgency of their healthcare needs. Even allowing for distortions due to doctors' interests in private practice (Yates 1995) and in treating a clinically interesting mix of cases, such rationing is the opposite of arbitrary in terms of patients' needs (see ch5§3). In both the USA and the UK, patients awaiting transplants do so because of the (biological) scarcity of matched organs and tissues (HIAA 1995: 117). Nationalised health systems also display an 'inverse care law' (Hart 1975: 189–206), meaning that patients who tend to need least healthcare (the rich, professional classes) get most of it and those who most need it (economically marginal people, especially the elderly and children in these families) get least. However, access inversely related to need does more to meet these patients' needs for healthcare than no access at all, which is the market alternative for them.

Another reply is that the narrower access to healthcare in markets is really an economic virtue. It avoids the wasteful 'moral hazard' of 'excess demand' for free health services (cf. Pauly 1988: 31, 36). Economists define 'excess demand' as the excess of the quantity of a good demanded over the quantity supplied when its price is below the market equilibrium price (Lipsey 1970: 106–7). This demand is 'excess' only in the question-begging sense of exceeding both the quantity that profit-maximising firms are willing to produce at that price and the equilibrium level of demand in a perfectly competitive market. It is not a priori 'excess' in terms of needs. Preceding chapters have in effect defined 'needs' as 'informed desires' (in what sense 'informed', ch3§3 explained). Because it uses criteria of informedness that are at least as stringent as those that economists use, this sense of 'informed desires' contains the notion of 'informed demand' which welfare economists use in analysing and legitimising perfectly competitive markets. Because needs have finite maxima (chs4§1, 7§2) a curve representing the total need for healthcare of a given population (in that sense, its informed-demand curve for healthcare) would touch the quantity axis shown in Figure 8.1 when healthcare was free at the point of use (zero price). Although large, the need for healthcare is finite (see ch7§2). A corollary of the theory of general equilibrium under perfect competition is that prices must be positive. The difference between the 'excess' quantity of healthcare demanded when healthcare is free and the quantity of healthcare demanded when the price of healthcare equals its marginal costs (as occurs at perfectly competitive general equilibrium) represents the difference in access to healthcare under market and non-market conditions. It is the theoretical measure of market failure to make needed healthcare available and to provide access to it.

'Moral hazard' and 'excess demand' are therefore positive advantages of free (including nationalised) over market healthcare, from the standpoint of people who need healthcare. Where moral hazard promotes access to health services on grounds other than health needs (ch4§2) or other needs (ch4§3), introducing an informed gate-keeper with incentives to refer according to healthcare need is a response better focused upon healthcare needs than co-payment, discretionary insurance or other market mechanisms.

Before concluding that nationalised systems give greater access to needed healthcare than markets do, one should note two provisos. Which system offers each particular person greater access to healthcare depends on how rich he is. A relativist account of needs implies that for those who can afford it, marketed healthcare provides access without any queuing found in nationalised service systems (in such systems that is the main selling point for private healthcare – Horst 1992: 51; Wiles and Higgins 1992). So it might seem that if one is rich enough to afford private healthcare, and rational enough to buy only the healthcare that one needs, and needs acute care, one needs a market health system. Yet the scale of need for acute care is itself a index of

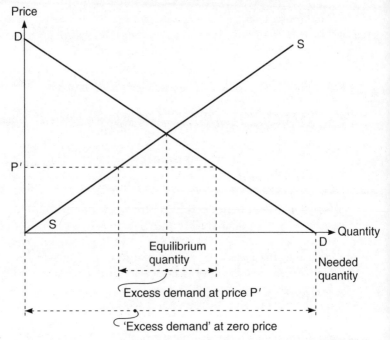

Figure 8.1 Informed demand for free healthcare: how perfectly competitive markets fail to meet the need for healthcare

health system failure (ch4§2). A prior need is for health promotion. Even from the standpoint of the ill and rational rich, their need for market-speed access must be weighed against markets' effects on their health to begin with. Second, even if nationalised healthcare is sufficient for the purpose it might not be necessary for guaranteeing universal access to healthcare (cp. Steiner 1976: 186). State purchasing of healthcare, for instance through a voucher system (Bassett 1993) could also achieve this. Later we must return to this important point, noting only that it too tacitly concedes the inadequacy of conventional markets giving consumers access to the healthcare they need.

Health promotion healthcare, social care, palliation and terminal care techniques are published internationally. Local differences in working practices seem as much to reflect local clinical beliefs as differences in the health system organisation (for example, the availability of radial keratotomy in some countries and not others, or the different policies of English and Russian doctors on anaesthetic type and dose). Any difference in technical efficacy of health system

184

would therefore stem from the ranges of health services that are available (see above). Similarly, there appears empirically little to choose in terms of technical innovation between the best nationalised and market health systems. Nationalised systems such as the pre-reform NHS independently produced major clinical innovations (*in vitro* fertilisation, laminar flow surgery, microsurgical techniques, etc.), as have market systems. Patients need to be able to trust the health worker's selection of treatment, including disclosure of conflicts of interests (ch5§2). Such a relationship is harder to sustain in a commercial setting, as the emergence of ethical codes as a safeguard attests. Nationalised systems at least insulate health workers from the commercial pressures to which markets expose them more directly, especially the self-employed professional.

Relevance to healthcare needs is another area in which market and nationalised-economy health systems appear empirically to have different strengths and weaknesses. Had one to choose between the two profiles or service availability (see above), earlier accounts of the need for healthcare suggest (ch4§2) that, on balance, the nationalised service tends to provide the profile of services more relevant to the health and healthcare needs of most people. For, as the most effective avenue for meeting health needs, health promotion is the touchstone for comparing health service availability in terms of needs. Furthermore, many (not all) of the health services that markets provide and nationalised systems do not (or provide much less of) make little or no impact on health or healthcare needs (cp. ch4§§2–3). Nationalised economies have the ability to prevent direct consumer access to non-emergency secondary services, unlike the conventional market relationship between hospital and patient. This 'gate-keeper' role of the GP (or equivalent primary care doctor) is incidentally an important reason why use and cost of the hospital sector is lower in, say, the UK than in the USA or Switzerland.

In terms of health service relevance to non-health needs, however, the picture is almost the opposite. The US market system has been the source of many new forms of service – day surgery, managed care – as has the non-NHS sector in the UK, although the innovations with the biggest impact on healthcare needs (as defined in ch4§§2–3) have originated from voluntary, not commercial, providers (especially the family planning, abortion and hospice movements). Sometimes nationalised systems have been positively hostile to innovations (e.g. the Peckham experiment in the British NHS – Ashton and Seymour 1988: 32–5). Market healthcare empirically does normally surpass the quality of 'hotel' services and routine administration (convenience of bookings, access to consultants) found in nationalised systems. Another relativistic conclusion emerges. For those rich enough to use it, a market health system empirically tends to meet the non-health needs for healthcare better than a nationalised system does.

Often markets are simply identified with consumer choice (e.g. Lomasky 1981: 87). Defenders of nationalised healthcare tend to reply that informed consumer choice is impossible or undesirable in healthcare, gratuitously conceding their critics' point. Yet 'markets' and 'consumer choice' are not logically equivalent. Whether they are even practically equivalent depends on the range and locus of consumer choice in the market, and the relative bargaining power and knowledge of firms and consumers there (Porter 1985). For example, if all private insurers offer insurance for a range of acute care that excludes, say, cover for mental handicap or HIV/AIDS, the consumer has no practical choice whether to buy cover for these conditions. The locus of competition is restricted to the relative merits of different insurers on what cover they do offer. Besides, there are monopolistic markets in which there is no consumer choice (e.g. the purchaser side of the Canadian health system) and nationalised systems giving consumer choice (e.g. choice of GP in the NHS). What distinguishes market and nationalised systems is not whether there is consumer choice but which aspects of healthcare consumers can practically exercise choice about. That type of health system is more relevant to consumers' needs, in which the loci of consumer choice more closely match those aspects of healthcare about which the consumer is probably the best judge of his own needs (ch5§2). This is partly a matter of enabling consumer choice in those aspects of healthcare where the consumer is likely to know what he needs (e.g. in hospital hotel services), but also of constraining consumer choice in those matters where the expert knows better (ch5§§2–3). In these terms it is far from obvious a priori that a market is superior in terms of providing domains of consumer choice that are relevant to consumer needs.

'Those expending funds for good causes have', Acton once wrote, 'a duty to make their expenditures as economically effective as possible' (Acton 1971: 20). He took it for granted that this implied a duty to use market mechanisms, taking healthcare markets as one application of a general theory that markets make the most efficient use of scarce inputs. The general theory in question is the economists' legitimation of perfectly competitive markets. The standard legitimation starts by formally defining 'utility' in terms of indifference curves. Each curve is taken to represent the amount of benefit resulting from an individual consuming any one of a number of sets of goods, each of which he prefers equally (exactly how to formulate the definition is a long-running dispute in welfare economics – Cirillo 1979: 43, 50–1; Little 1950; Arrow 1951). The standard legitimation takes a set of perfectly competitive markets, all of which eventually reach a 'general equilibrium' purely through the market transactions of 'individuals' (persons, households and firms). These transactions both 'reveal' individuals' 'preferences' and are individuals' means of satisfying them. Algebraic calculations follow, yielding two fundamental theorems: that every position of general equilibrium in a set of perfectly competitive markets is 'Pareto optimal'; and that every Pareto-optimal position is a general equilibrium condition for a set of perfectly competitive markets. These equilibria are defined as 'Pareto optimal' because in them no individual can be made better off without making another worse off. This conception of optimality and sub-optimality combines two distinct assumptions. First, any redistribution that left any 'individual' with less utility than before redistribution is defined as 'sub-optimal' compared with the unadjusted distribution of goods. Second, any move from a sub-optimal to an optimal allocation would, by implication, increase total utility. Accepting Walras's and subsequent mathematical solutions of the simultaneous equations representing all the market variables (prices, quantities, etc.) involved (Walras 1954: 461–82), what do these theorems actually show?

Consider a set of markets at Pareto-optimal equilibrium, which are then subject to a redistribution of goods such that one person loses a little utility and everyone else receives more utility than before. Suppose that even after redistribution the 'loser' is still the utility-richest individual in the economy but all the others have had a large increase in their utility, and that total utility has thus increased. According to the theorems and their underpinning definitions this is a sub-optimal endpoint despite the net increase in utility, because one person has lost utility that he would have had as a result of unadjusted market transactions. This example makes clear that the endpoints excluded as 'sub-optimal' are all those produced by other means than market transactions; that is, any endpoints reached by breaching the property relations found in perfectly competitive markets (which are no different to those in all markets). Similarly, the new endpoint is defined as 'sub-optimal' despite the fact that all individuals save one are better off. So in this definition of 'optimality', maintaining the distribution produced by market transactions counts for more than the maximisation of utility, and for more than the prudential interests of (in this case) all individuals save one. 'Sub-optimal' endpoints include any in which someone loses goods that he would have got by market transactions. The standard arguments alleging the 'efficiency' of perfect competition exclude distributions achieved by other means than market transactions as 'sub-optimal' by *definition*. Implicitly they make the normative assumption that market property relations are both optimal by definition and inviolable.

At most, therefore, the theorems succeed in proving that perfectly competitive markets are more efficient at producing Pareto-optimal equilibria than imperfectly competitive, monopolistic or monopsonistic markets are. This brings us to the second sense in which certain endpoints are defined as 'sub-optimal': in reducing total utility compared with perfectly competitive markets. Utility is defined in terms of individuals' consumption of preferred mixes of goods and services; implicitly, in terms of drive satisfactions. Except for indivisible, non-excludable (and atypical) goods, it is as logically nonsensical to speak of 'aggregate drive satisfaction' and of 'total utility' as it is to speak of 'population health needs' (ch4§2). Arrow long since exposed some of the technical difficulties in describing 'total utility' even in terms of a collective preference (Arrow 1951). Even if utilities could be aggregated, to show that total utility is efficiently maximised is irrelevant (both causally and logically) to showing that any particular, or even a typical, individual's utility is maximised. To demonstrate the Pareto optimality of perfectly competitive markets is not equivalent to demonstrating their prudential optimality even in terms of drives ('ophelimity'), let alone needs (taken as drives withstanding criticism (ch.3§3)). The theorems tell us nothing about how efficiently a perfectly competitive economy matches the goods and services that each individual receives to his drives, neither in general theoretical terms nor in the specific case of healthcare (Stevens and Raftery 1994: i 7). Neither do the theorems show that a bigger quantity of goods, or distribution of them that would more fully satisfy the drives of individual market participants, could not be reached through other types of market, still less through any conceivable non-market economy. The theorems 'proving' the 'efficiency' of perfectly competitive markets stop exactly where a prudential criticism – or defence – of market efficiency should begin.

What the theorems therefore show is that, provided one strictly excludes non-market property relations, perfectly competitive markets are more efficient than other kinds of market at maximising a fictional entity which is logically irrelevant to individual drive satisfaction. It is no wonder that perfectly competitive markets emerge from this reasoning as 'economically efficient', although it is more surprising when the resulting distributions are alleged to be prudentially 'optimal' too. The welfare economists' assertions about the optimising efficiency of perfectly competitive markets are both question-begging and circular.

One response is to relax the definition of 'optimality' so that redistributions from market equilibria still count as Pareto 'optimal' if the gainers collectively could hypothetically (in some versions) or actually (in others) compensate the losers. This weakens the question-begging guarantee that outcomes produced by non-market processes are 'sub-optimal' by definition. In effect, maximisation of total utility replaces the conservation of market property relations as the criterion of economic 'optimality' and hence 'efficiency'. But the resulting claim that markets are efficient in maximising total utility still has the logical flaws noted above. Like many subsequent economists Pareto invoked 'ethical neutrality' as a licence to take the initial and resulting distributions uncritically, as given (Cirillo 1979: 45, 55, 58). The theorems also depend on many other assumptions. For one, perfectly competitive general equilibrium distribution is legitimate if, and only if, the initial distribution of goods and services was legitimate and if all subsequent transactions completely respect individuals' property rights and preferences (cp. Nozick 1974: 151). Force, fraud and luck have played a big enough part in all known societies, and individuals' needs (not to mention moral considerations) a small enough one to make this assumption as nearly guaranteed false as an empirical assumption can be. Many other assumptions (horizontal demand curves facing the individual firm, free market entry and exit, markets clear, etc.) on which the proofs depend are also empirically challengeable. In light of this, the Walrasian mathematical triumph is something of a pyrrhic victory.

An influential and sophisticated objection to nationalised health-care describes non-marketed healthcare as 'unproductive', taking from the 'marketed' sector of the economy funds that would, if invested in the marketable sector, allow that sector to grow faster (and incidentally eventually support a larger publicly funded health sector than now) (Bacon and Eltis 1976: 13–14, 18, 31, 42–3, 84–5, 142, 151–5):

all the money that workers, salary earners and pensioners spend must necessarily go to buy marketed output. *Hence the marketed output of industry and services taken together must supply the total private consumption, investment and export needs of the whole nation.*

(Bacon and Eltis 1976: 27, original emphasis)

This takes the marketed sector as equivalent to the productive base of the economy, from which non-marketed health services take their income and spending. Although Bacon and Eltis do not put it so baldly, this suggests that the scale of non-marketed healthcare should be minimised.

Consider two hospital cleaners. Both work in acute hospitals and both do the same amount of the same kind of cleaning on the same kind of wards for the same wage. According to Bacon and Eltis, the private hospital cleaner contributes to marketed output and therefore counts as 'productive'. The NHS cleaner does not. What difference in what they are 'producing' constitutes this difference in 'productive-ness'? The only possible answer is that the private hospital cleaner is producing (or rather, contributing to producing) a monetarised transaction between hospital and patient and a monetarised profit. In real terms (*pace* Bacon and Eltis) both cleaners make identical contributions to 'the total private consumption, investment and export needs of the whole nation'. To call nationalised health services 'unproductive' amounts to nothing more than the truism that they do not produce monetarised transactions and profits. But this does not tell us which type of health system produces more healthcare need satisfiers and fewer concomitant 'bads' from a given level of resources.

On that point there is little evidence whether private or public health systems are more productive, and only indirect evidence. Mean lengths of hospital stay give little clue: system-wide figures were 14.8 days in the UK (1989), 19 in Sweden, 9.1 in the USA and 24.8 in Switzerland (1989) (OECD 1992: 44–5). Again the ranges overlap, with a greater spread between the two more market-oriented systems. UK hospital occupancy levels tend to be higher in the NHS (at 83 per cent in 1991 – OHE 1992: table 3.23) than in the private sector systems (not published, but reported by those working there to be normally around 65 per cent: a similar level to that in the US system as a whole). Against this, Butler (1992) reports that by December 1987 around 3,000 NHS beds were closed through shortages of cash or staff. This is another, but proportionally much smaller, form of waste when there remain patients needing treatment. As noted, therapeutic and clinical techniques tend to be similar in the two systems. Although it is sometimes alleged that nationalised economies are also more lenient to wasteful, unjustifiable practices at provider level, evidence either way is hard to find. Comparing UK prices of healthcare procedures available in both private and public sectors shows a wide and similar range of prices which probably reflects opportunistic marketing and dubious cost accounting in both sectors rather than systematic differences in production costs.

At the crudest empirical population-level comparison, health indicators are broadly similar in the UK and USA but with a bigger spread in the USA (and Third World levels in the poorest parts of some US cities). If the non-health-sector influences on health status were broadly similar in the two systems, this would indicate greater efficiency in the nationalised service NHS than in the more marketised US health system, which costs a much smaller percentage of a smaller GNP. Yet this understates the margin in efficiency because in the richer economy, the USA, health status indicators benefit from more favourable influences from outside the non-health sector than the UK indicators do.

One reason for this difference in efficiency lies in the considerable transaction costs of financing healthcare privately. Hellander and her collaborators calculate these as 24.7 per cent of all healthcare spending in the US case (Hellander, Himmelstein, Woolhandler and Wolfe 1994: 1–9). In this respect the nationalised service produces far fewer 'bads' of administrative work, although the proportion of these costs are rising as the NHS moves away from the nationalised system towards an internal market (Brindle 1993b: 8; Brindle 1995: 3; Mayston 1992: 47–8). Another difference in efficiency lies in the market incentive to sell services, needed or not. The US health system has been criticised for its levels of unnecessary surgery. For instance, it has been suggested that 36 per cent of US tonsillectomies on children under 5 years old are clinically unnecessary (Scalettar 1993: 33), as are 30.8 per cent of US hysterectomies (Raffel and Raffel 1989); 24 per cent of US women giving birth have a Caesarean section although the American College of Obstetricians and Gynaecologists' consensus is that good clinical practice would normally produce a level between 8.5 and 10 per cent.

When healthcare resources are scarce relative to needs, nationalised economies tend to respond with four of the strategies noted earlier (ch7§2), but primarily with a rationing policy of constraining cash budgets. Health workers, especially doctors, have also tended to lobby publicly for extra health system funding: a resourcing strategy that in the UK provoked Mrs Thatcher to precipitate the 1989 NHS reforms. During the 1980s the NHS also adopted more active prevention and technological (research and development) strategies (see ch7§2). In market systems resource shortage takes the form of a decline in effective demand or of capital. A normal response to either is a resource policy. Where capital is scarce, the usual market-based healthcare provider's response is investment to increase the scale of provision. When demand is tight, healthcare providers in a market system resort to a technical development policy; in the US case, the 'medical arms race' intended not primarily to increase productivity (although this also happens) but to increase the provider's market share and the 'value added' for each patient.

All this explicates the claim that nationalised health services meet healthcare needs more effectively than markets do. In terms of the availability of acute services there is little to choose between markets and nationalised healthcare; empirically the similarities are larger than the differences. When it comes to social care, and *a fortiori* health promotion, a nationalised system offers much larger availability. In respect of access to needed healthcare, nationalised systems win outright, subject to the qualification below. By an unnecessarily small margin they also have an empirical advantage in terms of the relevance of available health services to health and healthcare needs but market services seem better at meeting patients' ancillary non-health needs. For technical effectiveness of the services that are available there appears empirically little to choose between the two types of system. Insofar as their efficiency can be determined empirically, nationalised healthcare appears on balance to produce fewer 'bads' (administrative costs, redundant healthcare) than a market system. The theoretical defences of market efficiency are irrelevant to needs and even to individuals' demands, proving nothing either way. Market-based healthcare providers tend to respond to scarcity with technological and resource strategies, nationalised systems tending to use technological, resourcing prevention and ranking strategies. Earlier arguments suggest that the nationalised system is more defensible as a response to scarcity of needed healthcare resources (ch7§2).

Although nationalised services seem on balance more effective in meeting more and more important health needs for healthcare than markets are (taking examples of both systems at their best), they are far from immune to criticism. Taking nationalised healthcare as a starting point, there remains much scope to improve the health systems' organisational design.

§3 HEALTH SYSTEM DESIGN: SOCIAL ENGINEERING

Superior to markets though they are for meeting most health and healthcare needs, nationalised health systems still have defects of their own. They have often tolerated unnecessarily low quality in the non-clinical aspects of healthcare; unduly limited the range of models of care; been slow to adopt preventive healthcare (ch8§2); and have been accused of being low-paying, exploitative and undemocratic employers (McMahon 1989: 48; Taylor-Gooby 1985: 140). Although they prevent patient choice in matters where patients are not usually competent to choose, they also prevent it in matters where patients are (ch5§2). One cannot maintain that nationalised health systems have nothing positive to learn from the experience of healthcare markets. Even those implacable critics of markets, Marx and Engels, agreed that capitalism had 'created more massive and more colossal productive forces than have all preceding generations together' (Marx and Engels 1969: 48). This dynamism and innovation occurs through a complex system of sometimes self-adjusting, sometimes mutually destabilising incentives and transactions. Dynamism, flexibility and self-adjustment are characteristics that nationalised health systems have found difficult to acquire. All this suggests the project of deliberately redesigning the organisation of nationalised healthcare to contrive a type of health system that retains markets' dynamism and adaptability without their inefficiencies and failures (ch8§2), meeting the healthcare needs noted earlier (ch8§1) still more comprehensively than nationalised healthcare does.

The few texts on organisational 'design' (as opposed to 'development') concern rather limited adjustments to the structures of bureaucracies (e.g. Obel 1981; Simon 1988). A more radical approach is necessary for present purposes. How individuals need to behave, in a given organisational setting, depends upon what type of social relations exist between them and upon what kind of incentives they face (ch3§1). These social relations and incentives depend, *inter alia*, on the character of the organisation's external relations with other organisations (e.g. whether they are competitors, suppliers, legal bodies, etc.). Radical redesign of each organisation necessitates redesigning the relations between them, an organisational redesign of the sector as a whole. Like so-called 'organisation design' but on a larger scale, this is a project of consciously designing social relations to achieve various ends: 'social engineering'. Here the ends in question are fuller satisfaction of the health and healthcare needs outlined earlier (ch4§1).

Although such an organisational redesign is radical, it does not require disregarding all existing health system arrangements and rethinking from scratch. Nationalised health systems illustrate that it is one thing for healthcare providers to know that patients have certain healthcare needs, but quite another for providers to exert themselves to satisfy those needs. This implies that healthcare users need health system incentives to be redesigned for that purpose. Supporters of nationalised healthcare tend to be wary of proposals for incentives, possibly through accepting too readily the assumption that only markets institute economic incentives, possibly because 'incentives' is so often a euphemism for income inequalities having little apparent connection with their beneficiaries' own needs or their contribution to meeting others' needs. Any organisation, however, institutes incentives, if only the feeble or perverse ones found in, say, the later Soviet economy. Although there is no practical choice about whether organisations offer their staff incentives, the questions 'what do healthcare users need there to be incentives for healthcare providers to do?' and 'how are such incentives to be created?' are entirely open. Incentives might be considered as a sort of permanent behaviour modification programme for doctors and managers (cf. ch4§4), here for the purpose of artificially aligning their drives with health system users' needs. Incentives work by making access to rewards conditional upon whatever activity is being 'incentivised'. To be able to use incentives implies that the incentive goods belong initially not to their potential recipients, the healthcare providers, but to whoever (patient or expert non-provider healthcare organisation) decides who shall receive the incentive. Redesigning incentives therefore implies redesigning the property relations among healthcare organisations.

The use of incentives implies some process for judging when the results that the incentive is intended to stimulate have been achieved (here, meeting people's healthcare needs). Some of these needs are usually best understood by the healthcare expert, others by consumers themselves (ch5§2). This implies that a dual incentive system is necessary for matching healthcare provision to users' needs. One set of incentives and judging process is necessary for rewarding those activities whose success in meeting healthcare needs demands clinical expertise to judge; another set of incentives and judging process is necessary for rewarding those activities whose success in meeting patients' needs is most competently judged by patients themselves.

Previous accounts of health needs imply that patients need healthcare providers to face an incentive to minimise the gap between a patient's actual health status and the currently attainable health status for a patient of his type (ch4§1). This would be an incentive for providers to maximise the effectiveness of treatment, select treatment that is relevant to health needs and to pursue both the technological and the health promotion strategies for attenuating any scarcity of healthcare resources (ch7§2). Health promotion demands activity at both population and patient levels (ch4§2). At the population level the necessary incentive to health service providers is simply one reflecting the numbers of people whose health is maintained and their actual health status (or a valid proxy for it). Where causes of ill health lie outside the health system, the principle of incentivising the meeting of health needs can be extended on the 'polluter pays' principle, with the payments large enough to stimulate prevention rather than simply allow the polluter to compensate the damage to health needs and then forget the matter. For health promotion for individual patients, the necessary incentive is one rewarding the provider for each patient whose personal health is maintained at the achievable level, or a valid proxy for this (e.g. whether the patient receives interventions scientifically known to maintain health such as contraception or immunisation). When health promotion fails, and a patient needs curative, social or terminal care (ch4§2), the same incentive to maintain the patient's health status at the fullest achievable level would constitute an incentive to treat all patients whose health status would actually be raised by treatment – and only these.

To complicate matters, many patients need to be referred from health promotion and primary healthcare to secondary or tertiary health services (and often back again) as their ill health, treatment and any recovery take their course. A person also needs to restrict the healthcare he receives to that which is necessary to raise his level of health (ch4§§1–2), so as to minimise iatrogenesis, waste and scarcity (ch7§2). This suggests a correspondingly hierarchical referral structure with incentives matched to it. Since a referral involves two healthcare providers, we must consider the incentives facing each.

For the referring provider, an incentive for restoring the patient to his fullest achievable health status would also constitute a reward for referring effectively treatable patients to other healthcare providers who could do that. One pitfall is that health systems can create perverse incentives to refer patients unnecessarily into secondary or tertiary services. For example, it has been alleged that GPs used to send patients to hospitals for services that, GP fundholding has revealed, can equally effectively be provided at primary care level (Glennister, Matsanganis and Owens 1992: 27–8; Pelta 1992). To avoid this pitfall the incentive for a healthcare provider to treat a patient itself (call this A) must exceed the incentive to refer to another provider (incentive B), even if the latter treats successfully. An obvious way to do this is to reduce the incentive paid when a patient is referred. However, this risks creating a second perverse incentive not to refer treatable patients (as well as untreatable ones) to another provider who could have treated them, even when the first healthcare provider cannot treat them itself. In the first phase of the Leningrad experiment, polyclinics had incentives not to refer patients to hospital, causing hospital referrals to fall dramatically (by some 50 per cent in the case of hernia repairs; so large and sudden a change could not reflect a change in the prevalence of hernias). To avoid this pitfall, the incentives for referring treatable patients must exceed the incentive for not referring them without treating them locally either. An incentive linked to restoration of achievable health status meets the point by paying nothing to a provider who fails to refer a treatable patient (since no health restoration has occurred). However, the incentive for restoring a patient, by one's own treatment, to a lower level of health than another provider could restore the patient to, must always be lower than the incentive for referring to a more effective provider elsewhere. Table 8.1 summarises the logical relation between these incentives.

Table 8.1 Referral incentives to healthcare providers

Health status achieved	Incentives (see text)		
	Treat here		Refer on
Health status 1 (full health):	A1	>	B1
Health status 2:	A2	>	B2
Health status 3:	A3	>	B3
...			
Health status n; viability threshold:	An	>	Bn

and B1 > A2; B2 > A3; and so on.

Note: Health status 1 represents a higher level of health than health status 2; status 2 represents a higher level of health than status 3; and so on.

The obvious way to stimulate healthcare providers to provide healthcare that is relevant to needs about which the patient knows best and effective at satisfying them is to make incentives for healthcare providers depend upon their satisfying patients' preferences in these matters. Allegedly this happens when 'cash follows patients' (Department of Health 1989a: 4). However, that slogan is under-defined in two ways. Patient choice is a valid prima-facie guide to patient needs only in respect of certain aspects of healthcare: whether the patient prima facie needs curative healthcare; his tolerance of risks and side effects; and how healthcare affects the satisfaction of his non-health needs (ch5§2). To meet these needs necessitates an organisational structure that guarantees patient choice in these matters and rewards providers for being chosen by patients; and making these matters the loci of provider competition to attact patients (see below). An obvious way to do this is to make receipt of the incentive conditional on attracting the patient. This, however, poses the further problem of designing structures and incentives that do this without incentivising the treatment of every patient who can be recruited, whether they have health needs for treatment or not (as happens in markets – ch8§2).

Patients also need efficient health services, minimising waste and the production of 'bads' (ch8§1). In markets, providers' incentives to contain the cost of each procedure are countervailed by incentives to maximise the number and 'added value' of procedures sold. There are also incentives to select the patients and treatments where the difference between provider's income and costs (i.e. profit) is largest. This poses a social engineering problem of how to create an incentive for cost minimisation and for technical innovation without perverse effects on the selection of patients and treatment plans. This requires insulating incentives for cost control and innovation from incentives for patient selection and treatment, which we already argued must reflect patients' achievable levels of health status. It also implies that there is no role in a needs-oriented health system for privately financed healthcare, whose pricing necessarily covers all input costs indiscriminately.

Not the least participants in healthcare are patients themselves. They therefore need to face, first, incentives actively to maintain their own health, in face of their own doubts that they can influence it very much (Ranade 1994: 130). At the very least they need health promotion and illness prevention to be available and incentivised. An example of such incentives is the French practice of making social security payments for mothers-to-be depend on their attending antenatal clinics (although this incentive had rather mixed results). They also need incentives to comply with any onerous treatment (or self-treatment) plan recommended by a clinical expert who knows the patient's needs best in such matters (cf. ch5§2). It is also necessary that there be no perverse incentives against self-referral when a patient is unsure or is tolerating mild pain or incapacity, so that any progressive disease can be detected and treated early. Charges to patients for routine examinations or screening would be examples of these perverse incentives. For example, uptake of NHS vision testing fell approximately 20 per cent (2.7 million tests) in the first year after charges were introduced in 1989 (anon. 1991). In these matters, as in more serious ill health, the patient needs there to be no extraneous obstacles preventing access to the healthcare that he needs. To meet prospective patients' needs for access to healthcare, all healthcare should, at least, be free of charge at the point of use.

Two main mechanisms are available for allocating incentives. An administrative method would be for some expert body (e.g. a health ministry or professional body) to research what patients need; to collect data on how different healthcare providers' services compare; and then to allocate incentives accordingly. This would be 'administrative allocation by entitlement'; whoever satisfies the predetermined criteria, receives the incentive. Paying hospitals by reimbursement illustrates the principle, although to the limited extent that the hospital has only to attract and treat the patient to become entitled to payment (e.g. as in the French health system). Alternatively, there can be a competition. But is this not reinstituting the market with all its inefficiencies, failures and perverse incentives (ch8§2)?

Supporters and critics mainly agree that historical experience of markets demonstrates the effectiveness of competition for incentives as means of forcing economic development in determinate directions. Each firm tries to surpass its rivals in the activities that attract incentives, so that firms continually 'leapfrog' each other's product designs and methods of production. The snag, in healthcare markets, is that the directions in which this leapfrogging leads have a decidedly ambivalent relation to consumers' needs (ch8§2). Both critics and supporters of the market economy tend to conflate competition and markets when they debate health system reform. In that context 'managed competition' explicitly means little more than a continually adjusted and restructured market, especially on the insurers' side (e.g. Enthoven 1993: 29). Yet although markets typically are competitive, markets and competition are not synonymous. Many markets are non-competitive (where there are monopolies or monopsonies or both) and competition occurs in many non-market settings (courtship, research, sport and war, to name but a few). One organisational design problem for health system reformers is therefore how to uncouple the mechanism of competition from the perverse consequences it produces in healthcare markets, converting it into a mechanism for meeting healthcare needs. In using competition for this purpose the social engineer can manipulate four main variables:

1   The loci of competition: here, to which characteristics of health services the rewards for competitive success are linked. Economists usually conceptualise the two main loci of competition in markets as 'price' and 'non-price' competition. The task for health system organisational design is one of shifting the loci of competition away from some of those found in markets (e.g. maximising sales, profit and market share; branding; 'me too' products; spurious or trivial product differentiation; convergence on 'middle-brow' products – Sheaff 1991) while retaining others (e.g. technical innovation, new models of service, sensitivity to the non-health needs affected by healthcare).

2   What rewards the winning competitors receive. Money is obviously one but not, preceding chapters imply (ch3§§1–2), the only possibility. Expectancy theory explains incentives using an essentially similar account of drives to the one presupposed here (ch3§1) (Vroom 1964; Handy 1986: 37–42). It argues that to be an effective incentive, the putative reward must be something that its potential recipient actually wants. He must also perceive, with good reason, that whether he gets it depends on what he does, and that there is a high probability of actually receiving the incentive if his actions satisfy the stated conditions. Health workers are certainly susceptible to financial motivation but they have other interests too: professional status, desire for interesting workload, opportunity to learn and to research, and so on (ch5§3). These are 'direct incentives' in that they directly satisfy their recipients' drives.

3   Who the providers have to satisfy in order to receive their incentives; in effect, who judges the competition. One option is to constitute an expert body (e.g. health ministry). Another is to enable healthcare consumers to make the judgement by allowing them 'countervailing power' in the form of 'exit and lateral re-entry' (i.e. choice of healthcare provider – Saltman 1994: 203–4;

Saltman and von Otter 1992: 103, 107) and then linking incentive payments to their choices (much as capitation payments to English GPs). What is necessary is for the incentives that the health provider receives to depend on, say, patient satisfaction. For this it is not necessary for patients actually to hand over the reward personally, only for the payment system to link providers' rewards reliably to patients' preferences.

4 Who may compete. Experience with hospital accreditation systems in the USA, Australia and with hospital 're-authorisation' in France (Mordelet 1992) suggests that in practice a powerful incentive for healthcare providers is winning the opportunity to enter, or re-enter, the market or other arena giving access to direct incentives (financial or real). The reformer has also to decide the number as well as the type of entrants. Allowing more entrants than there are prizes sharpens the pace of competition and gives the adjudicator greater bargaining power (Porter 1985).

Entry conditions for both competition and administrative entitlement can be used to create multiple, sequenced incentives, enabling incentives to be used to produce two or more effects. Providers have to satisfy one set of conditions to enter the system and then another set of conditions to win its rewards. Entry conditions are thus an 'indirect incentive', offering healthcare providers not direct rewards *per se* but access to the means of getting them. Entry conditions too can be satisfied either by competition (as in competitive tendering) or by administrative entitlement (e.g. by state registration or accreditation). They can also be satisfied either by the organisation itself meeting these conditions, or by satisfying patient preferences. Only when the patient has chosen to enter the surgery door can the healthcare provider start to pursue direct rewards.

Its 'leapfrogging' effects make competition an incentivisation method relevant to conditions where there is no a priori upper limit to levels of performance and only practical experience reveals what levels of performance can be achieved and how (e.g. in sports or machine design; or in making innovative models of healthcare available). Competition can be for direct or indirect incentives or both. Where there is an upper limit on standards of performance (e.g. 100 per cent availability of piped oxygen), administrative allocation of incentive by entitlement is applicable and does not create the losers that competition implies.

Experience of healthcare markets indicates another perverse

incentive of competition. In markets the reward of innovation is that the innovator gains competitive advantage by withholding knowledge or free use of the innovation from competitors ('commercial confidentiality' or 'intellectual property' respectively). Competition thus poses the dilemma of either encouraging innovation but preventing its dissemination, or the opposite. This dilemma arises twice in the competition between healthcare providers outlined above: when providers compete to enter the health system and when, having entered, they compete for patient referrals. One solution is to institute large mandatory rewards (e.g. a royalty) for such innovations in return for their mandatory transfer to public domain (cf. Marinker 1994: 37). Now used as seemingly arbitrary medical salary bonuses at the gift of the medical academic establishment, NHS merit awards were originally conceived as an incentive to innovation (Pater 1981). However, a simpler solution would be to allocate the rewards for innovation non-competitively, administratively by entitlement, where possible. Another variable at the social engineer's disposal is to decide how long a period should elapse before such a mechanism comes into play.

Social engineers can therefore adjust two sets of variables in order to 'manage' or 'plan' a health system so that healthcare organisations come to need to meet patients' health and healthcare needs (see ch8§1), and to alter healthcare provision in response to epidemiological changes (e.g. in demography, lifestyles, consumption patterns), new healthcare technologies, and different patterns and causes of health resource scarcity (ch7§2). One set is of structural variables in the health system: its property relations; the use of competition or entitlement for allocating incentives; and, where competition is used, its loci, rewards, entry conditions and judges. The other set is the substantive incentives that healthcare users need healthcare organisations to face: to maximise individuals' health status; to refer all and only patients who need referral; to respond to patient choices in all areas where the patient knows his needs best and not in other matters; to make innovations that increase clinical efficacy or reduce 'bads'; and to pursue the strategies that minimise health resource scarcity (ch7§2). Patients also need to face incentives to maintain their own health. What configuration of all these variables do the preceding arguments suggest?

To insulate the incentives for patient selection and treatment from cost considerations requires separating incentives for improving patients' health from the meeting of direct material costs of care (drugs, bed-days, etc.). This would prevent 'cream skimming' and make the selection of patients cost-neutral, depending only on the scope for raising the patients' level of health. One way to do this would be to supply the physical means of providing healthcare (beds, drugs, etc.) in kind, enabling healthcare providers to 'call off' these goods as required, subject to the usual administrative checks that the resources used were reasonably necessary, as in NHS hospital and community services before 1976, and (for the moment) still in NHS general medical practice. An unexpected effect of GP fundholding in England has been that GPs have spent around half of their fund surpluses on improving their practice premises (anon. 1994a: 2). Conceivably patients gain some benefit from new car parks or GPs having mobile phones or new computers; but the main financial beneficiaries are the GPs who eventually sell the premises. One way to prevent this perverse incentive would be to stipulate that any buildings and equipment to which producers are given access revert to ownership by the expert body at the end of the period.

Since the number of patients could not be controlled by preventing access to healthcare for those who need it, only three ways of reducing the cost, and thus the scarcity and inefficiency, of healthcare would remain. (Here 'reducing inefficiency' still means 'reducing the ratio of "bads" to need satisfiers'.) One way would be to reduce the cost of procuring or producing the physical inputs to healthcare. This could be pursued by stimulating competition among suppliers of these inputs (largely from outside the health sector). Another would be by reducing the need for healthcare (by preventive strategies) and making healthcare more effective (ch.7§2). An incentive for maximising patients' health status would also incentivise this. A third way is by innovating forms of healthcare that reduce healthcare costs ('bads' and waste).

Reducing costs is an open-ended objective, most effectively pursued by competitive 'leapfrogging'. It is also one whose achievement healthcare experts, not consumers, are most competent to judge. Since the main direct incentive to healthcare providers would, on the above arguments, relate to individual patients' health status, competition for the indirect incentive of entering the health system is the remaining way to pursue this objective. The locus of this competition to enter would have to be cost reduction. Its 'prize' would be access to the incentives to maximise patients' health status, including by means of innovating new forms of service and existing healthcare technologies. To make this a standing incentive, it would be necessary to grant prospective healthcare providers only a fixed-term entry to the health system, with periodically renewed competitions for re-entry. (Entrants to the health system could also be required to demonstrate that they satisfied minimum standards of competence and safety, as in existing health systems.) A 'requisite variety' among healthcare providers and a slight over-provision ensure contestability of provision, accommodate a wide range of consumer preferences, and ensure that the balance of negotiating power lay on the side of the health ministry (or equivalent). Since non-market provision is not necessarily equivalent to state provision (Barry 1990: 101, 104, 116), this suggests that entry to the health system should be open not only to state-owned healthcare providers but charities, cooperatives, patient groups, self-employed individuals, pressure groups and so on; but not commercial providers (see above).

Determining what level of health is achievable for a given type of patient, and whether this has been achieved, is something that healthcare experts are usually more competent to judge than patients. Thus the decision whether healthcare providers have earned the incentive for doing so is most competently taken by experts, not consumers. But providers should obviously not judge their own case. Instead the decision to reward could be taken by the local healthcare administration or by another provider who knows the patient, most obviously the person referring the patient. This suggests that an expert, non-providing organisation would judge and reward the work of health promoters; the latter would then judge and reward the work of (primary) curative health services; and so on down the hierarchy of health services outlined earlier (ch4§2). So in terms of health needs for secondary care there are grounds to support the type of payment mechanisms used in English GP fundholding and its Finnish and Russian equivalents, although not necessarily the substantive incentives that they use, which differ from those outlined above. For one thing, we have argued that only incentive payments and not the direct costs of consumables and equipment should be paid this way. To match referrals to patient needs, the incentive to healthcare providers for maximising a patient's level of health would have to be rather highly structured. There is also a ceiling to people's health needs (ch4§1). So this incentive lends itself to being administered by an administrative entitlement system, as do incentives to healthcare users to maintain their own health.

In combination these considerations recommend a health system in which the main direct incentive to healthcare providers is for minimising the differences between patients' actual health status and their

Table 8.2 Needs, incentives and property relations in a socially engineered health system

		Collective health promotion		Meeting individual health needs		
				Expert-defined		Patient-defined
				Primary care	Secondary or later referrals	
Need for healthcare	Availability; Scarcity–attenuation; Effectiveness; Efficiency	Effectiveness; Scarcity–attenuation; Relevance to needs		Access; effectiveness; relevance to needs; Scarcity–attenuation		
Policy objective	Innovation and cost minimisation	Collective health promotion		Meeting individual health needs		
Recipient of incentive	Permitted healthcare providers	Health promotion providers	Non-health sector producers	Healthcare providers		
Loci of competition or entitlement criteria	Effectiveness and cost	Minimise gap actual; attainable health status				Patient preferences
Who determines eligibility to receive incentive	Expert body				Referrer	Patient

Allocation method	Competition	Entitlement criteria	Competition
Who may seek	Any potential provider	(non-optional) Healthcare providers	
Nature of incentive	Entry to system (indirect)	Direct reward to organisation and its staff	
Property relations	Expert body has monopoly control over provider entry; All inputs and incentive payments via control of expert body	Expert body can reward or penalise non-health sector producers	Services free at point of use; Expert body initially owns incentive goods; Incentive goods follow referrals; Expert body owns other inputs and providers 'call off' ad hoc. No sale of health services to users.

achievable health status. This reward is paid by an expert administrative body on entitlement. For divisible (personal) healthcare, a precondition for providers receiving this reward is that the patient to whom it relates has chosen that healthcare provider. Prospective providers periodically compete on grounds of cost (and safety) for the right to enter the health system (or stay in it). Once they have entered, the physical inputs to healthcare production are supplied to them in such a way as not to influence the selection of patients and treatments, preferably being supplied in kind by the same expert administrative body. All this requires that the expert administrative body be one whose main objective is to implement health policy; that is, a public health authority, not a commercial or commercialised 'purchaser'. Table 8.2 summarises the set of incentive and property relations suggested by the above arguments.

Doubtless there are many ways in which this outline can be improved and elaborated. None the less it does show why a polarised choice between nationalised and market health systems looks even more impoverished now than during the cold war. Although it is hard not to believe that many in UK government circles intend 'internal markets' as a furtive first step towards healthcare 'privatisation from within' (Ranade 1994: 50), current health system reforms in many countries are natural experiments in various 'third ways' of organisational design.

9

NEEDS, HEALTH AND MORALITY

When morality has been mentioned at all in preceding chapters it was to insist that so far we have analysed healthcare needs only in prudential, not moral, terms. For at the outset (ch2§2) it was decided not to analyse the moral implications of a theory of needs until its pre-moral basis was sufficiently thoroughly analysed to offer some prospect of avoiding the difficulties that other theories of needs have encountered (ch2§1). Foregoing discussions (Chapters 4–8) have been conducted purely in terms of how individuals can formulate a rational set of desires about healthcare and pursue them effectively. By now the reader might feel entitled to say, 'All very well, but is this really *ethics?*' The needs of healthy people, patients, doctors and other people involved in healthcare have been analysed using what was called (ch3§4) the 'anthropological' (a descriptive and prudential) sense of 'needs'. Its 'expressive' use goes beyond this, making recommendations about whether these people actually ought to have what they need in the 'anthropological' sense. This is what makes health policy debates and healthcare ethics practically interesting.

Initially (ch1§2) we identified four assertions made in expressive claims about needs:

1 An empirical claim that a relation holds between some person and some action or state of affairs. It transpired (chs2§3, 3§3) that this action or state of affairs would be the object of that person's drives, if they were rational.
2 That this relation gives that person (if no one else) a reason for taking that action or obtaining that state of affairs.
3 That the speaker also has reason for this person to get what he putatively needs.

4 That the listener similarly has reason for this person to get what he putatively needs.

In the less common, 'anthropological' uses of 'needs' only the first two claims are made. In its expressive sense, 'A needs X' is true if, and only if, all the following conditions hold (ch3§4). First, X really would be one of A's drive objects if his drives to get X were rational (in the senses outlined in ch3§3). This does not depend on what the speaker or hearer of that sentence himself actually desires or would rationally desire. Next, it would be prudent for the speaker to desire A to have X. Lastly, it would also be prudent for the listener to desire that A has X. In short, the expressive claim 'A needs X' is true if, but only if, A himself, the speaker and the listener would all rationally desire A to have X.

What claims a particular speaker can validly make about specific healthcare needs is therefore comparatively easily settled, when he uses 'needs' in a prudential way. *Previous chapters analysed the needs of various participants in healthcare in 'anthropological', prudential terms.* If these analyses are essentially valid in empirical terms and rest upon essentially sound pieces of economic, health, psychological and organisational theory, all that a given person has to do is to verify which roles he happens to occupy. Then he can conclude that among his needs are those attaching to those roles. For example, whether you or I need what a patient needs (Chapters 5–6) simply depends on whether you or I are a patient. If so, the relevant passages above can be re-read substituting 'you' or 'I' for 'the patient' (or equivalent phrases) throughout. Whether you or I can validly prudentially agree that from our standpoint patient A ought to get what he needs depends on whether what patient A needs is also what you or I prudentially need. Often this will be the case, for instance in respect to the 'public goods' of population-level health promotion (ch4§2).

Moral uses of 'need' are a special case of the expressive uses of 'need'. Used as a moral judgement, 'A needs X' is taken to imply that 'A morally ought to have X'. To call this a moral claim is to imply that it is valid for the speaker, the listener, A and everyone else. It is an inherent characteristic of valid moral judgements that they are valid for everyone.

Reverting for a moment to the prudential use of the word 'need', we previously noted healthcare examples of occasions when people have common need satisfiers and reciprocally need each other's help in obtaining them (chs3§2, 4). Sundry writers therefore argue that it is possible to derive moral judgements about what people morally ought to have from propositions about their prudential needs. Then claims about 'needs' in the moral sense can be explained as specific instances of moral judgements in general, and these in turn can be explained in terms of prudential needs. On that view certain claims about prudential needs imply moral judgements, including moral judgements in the form 'A needs X'. Such a theory would neatly link moral claims about needs to the positions advanced in preceding chapters.

But *is* a claim about prudential needs necessarily a latent moral judgement? This point is important enough to be worth analysing in as cogent a form as we can find. Maureen Ramsay argues:

> If A accepts that she has prudential obligations to meet her needs, then logically she must accept that all other agents have equally strong prudential reasons for meeting their own. Therefore she must acknowledge the obvious point that all persons ought prudentially to meet their needs.
>
> Now, as a matter of empirical fact people cannot meet their needs if other people act to prevent them from being met or do not help them meet them when they cannot be met by individuals acting alone. This means that no agents can meet their needs unless other people refrain from interfering with them or in some cases offer assistance towards their satisfaction. Any agent then who accepts that she has a prudential obligation to meet her needs, and therefore that all other agents do, will then be committed to working towards the general satisfaction of needs . . . . These obligations are moral because the agent must take positive account of other people's interests when the agent acknowledges that all agents have practical interests in satisfying their needs.
>
> (Ramsay 1992: 40–1)

In this elision from needs to morality are three big gaps (and several smaller ones). One is in inferring that 'all persons ought prudentially to meet their needs' because I ought to meet mine. This is true only in the anthropological senses of 'need' and 'ought prudentially', not necessarily from the speaker's own prudential standpoint. It depends upon the speaker's own drives and circumstances whether it is prudent for him to agree that other people's prudential needs ought to be met. Sometimes it is not prudent. For instance, these 'others' might, exceptionally, be the rapist or the starving cannibal whose next victim I am. *They* have prudential reasons for meeting their needs but that does not imply that *I* have prudential reasons for them to do so.

209

Further, the people whose help or forbearance one instrumentally needs in order to satisfy one's own needs are those who are in a practical position to help or forebear. One then needs not the 'general satisfaction' of needs but only for the potential helpers' or hinderers' needs to be satisfied; and then only insofar as is practically necessary for getting them to help (or forebear from obstructing) the satisfaction of one's own needs. Baldly stating a third point that deserves fuller explanation, moral reasoning does indeed 'take positive account of other people's interests' (and needs – Midgley 1980: 78n29) but in a different, more complex and subtle way than transparently prudential arrangements for mutual assistance or non-interference. The Hitler–Stalin pact was not an example of applied moral thinking.

If the account of drives proposed above (chh2§3, 3§1) stands, moral reasoning must also start from individuals' drives and circumstances. Moral reasoning, however, proceeds in a special way with many additions and qualifications, some omissions and other complications. In essence its connection with prudential judgements is as follows. The assumption that it is prudent for individuals to try reciprocally to satisfy one another's prudential needs is not always true. In a developed capitalist society there are genuine, indeed pandemic, conflicts of different individuals' prudential needs. Nevertheless many members of that society do prudentially need that social order to be maintained, and still more want it to be maintained. This necessitates a form of practical reason specifically adapted for reconciling different individuals' conflicting prudential needs, or at least for moderating the potentially socially disruptive practical effects of these conflicts. Morality is this specialised form of practical reason. A form of practical reason that made these conflicts transparently visible would hardly help to maintain the social order. This is the main reason that moral judgements are abstract, in the sense of not being transparently and directly deduced from empirical claims about (*inter alia*) the prudential needs of particular individuals (Sheaff 1979).

All this deserves fuller explanation than I may give here. It implies, however, that a different approach is required for analysing 'need' in its moral than in its prudential uses. Returning to the four elements involved in expressive uses of 'needs', the first of these serves as the empirical criterion for moral as well as for prudential judgements about needs and for the same reasons (ch1§2). What differs is its role in practical reasoning. In the prudential case, it was possible to deduce conclusions about particular individuals' reasons for acting, and specifically about their needs for healthcare, from a description of the empirical conditions satisfying that criterion plus other empirical and theoretical claims about the nature of health and healthcare (Chapters 4–8). In the case of morality, the moral judgement is not deduced immediately and transparently from the empirical criterion. Instead, the moral judgement 'supervenes' on the empirical criterion. What exactly 'supervenience' means in this context is itself a staple controversy in ethical theory. Here the term is used, without accepting all the original prescriptivist theory of supervenience (Hare 1974), to label the fact that the moral judgement is associated with the empirical criterion in a non-deductive way. The moral use of 'needs' also differs because substantive moral judgements are presupposed to be valid for everyone (even if not relevant to their circumstances). This collapses the second, third and fourth elements of an expressive judgement about needs into the single, superficially simple form 'A needs X' which in moral usage implies 'A (morally) ought to get X'.

The claims about prudential needs for healthcare outlined in previous chapters cannot, therefore, simply be restated as moral claims about needs for healthcare. However, this is not such a big limitation on the foregoing, prudential analysis as might first appear. A prudential account of needs in terms of drives answers surprisingly many of the stock problems in healthcare ethics. Many commonly held positions in healthcare ethics (on informed consent, paternalism, viability, what defines the usefulness or harmfulness of healthcare) have been shown to have at least some basis in prudential needs, although the analysis redefines some criteria and occasions for applying those concepts and challenges others outright (e.g. the doctrine of double effect and the argument from potential). This has been done without recourse to substantive moral principles, bizarre decision rules or 'methodologism', metaphysics or species-ism, nor by collapsing morality and prudential reasoning into each other (ch2§2). It has also been done in a way that recognises both biological and social determinants of prudential needs for healthcare, and it stands or falls according to the empirical data about human drives and consciousness that the biological sciences furnish. It conserves the idea that conscious, logical reasoning can and (prudentially) should influence human action, besides yielding concrete health policy conclusions, especially about post-market health systems. All this has been done without recourse to an egoist theory, for we have not assumed that 'what we are trying to bring about is always really some inner state or change in ourselves' (Midgley 1980: 355–6), nor that all social interactions are 'zero sum games'. Neither has it been done by recourse to utilitarianism, for the present account of needs expressly denies that drives are reducible to a single quality, still less that of happiness, pleasure or 'welfare', and denies that they are addable between different individuals.

To address questions that the above analysis does not cover, or where the reader insists upon a moral instead of a merely prudential judgement, one must recall that in moral contexts 'A needs X' implies that 'A (morally) ought to have X'. When 'need' is used to mean 'instrumentally necessary', it is healthcare that is a means to realise other moral goods which have been identified as such on grounds independent of health, drives or prudence (for example, 'flourishing' – Seedhouse 1988). When 'need' is used in an 'absolute', unconditional moral sense the healthcare that people need is healthcare that they ought to have, not as a means but as intrinsically instantiating whatever general moral principles the moralist believes to be valid. More than enough has been written elsewhere to enable the thoughtful reader to consider what applications of healthcare satisfy those more general moral principles. The healthcare that people need, in moral terms, lies within that domain, wherever the moralist judges its borders to lie.

The policy debates about healthcare needs from which we started are, above all, a response to conflicting demands on health policy and healthcare resources, exacerbated by scarcity. Preceding chapters suggest that two ethical responses are available. One is the use of moral reasoning and ethical theory to re-conceptualise and re-define the character, circumstances and causes of the conflicts, logically massaging concepts and definitions to yield consensually acceptable, coherent compromise solutions to the conflicts. Another response is more empirical: that of exposing the causes of the conflicts and, wherever possible, trying to devise institutional and policy solutions to remove them. Healthcare ethics performs its most useful task if, besides producing knowledge, it contributes to discovering these practical ways to help to meet our needs for healthcare.

REFERENCES

Acton, H.B. (1971) *The Morals of Markets: An Ethical Exploration*, London: Longman/Institute of Economic Affairs.

Adams, J.S. (1963) 'Towards an understanding of inequity', *Journal of Abnormal Social Psychology* lxvii: 422–36.

Alderfer, C.P. (1972) *Existence, Relatedness and Growth: Human Needs in Organization*, New York: Free Press.

Alexander, S. (1994) 'Patient gave up hope after misreading medical notes', *Guardian*, 2 September: 9.

Anon. (1991) 'Reluctance to pay eye test fee "leaves illness undiagnosed"', *Guardian*, 13 April.

Anon. (1992) 'Doctor denies attempt to kill suffering patient', *Guardian*, 11 September: 3.

Anon. (1994a) 'NHS surpluses go on surgeries', *Guardian*, 29 August: 2.

Anon. (1994b) 'To cease upon the midnight', *Economist*, 17 September: 21–3.

Anon. (1994c) *Guardian*, 6 October.

Anon. (1994d) 'Boy detained for killing widow 85', *Guardian*, 2 November: 4.

Anon. (1994e) *Daily Telegraph* editorial on Committee on Medical Aspects of Food Policy 1994 report, reported in 'Battle of the bulge', *The Economist*, 20 August: 20.

Anscombe, G.E.M. (1973) 'Modern moral philosophy' in Hudson, W.D. (ed.) *The Is-Ought Question*, London: Macmillan, 175–95.

Argyle, M. (1978) *The Psychology of Interpersonal Behaviour*, Harmondsworth: Penguin (3rd edn).

Armstrong, M. (1988) *A Book of Human Resource Management*, London: Kogan Page.

Arrow, K.J. (1951) *Social Choice and Individual Values*, New York: Wiley.

Ashton, J. and Seymour, H. (1988) *The New Public Health*, Milton Keynes: Open University Press.

Bacon, R. and Eltis, W. (1976) *Britain's Economic Problem: Too Few Producers*, London: Macmillan.

Bamford, T. (1993) 'Rationing: A philosophy of care' in Allen, I. (ed.) *Rationing in Health and Social Care*, London: Policy Studies Institute, 34–9.

Barker, D. (1989) 'The biology of stupidity: Genetics, eugenics and mental

213

deficiency in the inter-war years', *British Journal of Health Studies* xxii: 347–7.

Barry, B. (1990) *Welfare*, Milton Keynes: Open University Press.

Bassett, M. (1993) *A Health Cheque for All: Proposals for a Mixed Market in Health Care*, Manchester: European Policy Forum.

Becker, G.S. and Murphy, K.M. (1988) 'A theory of rational addiction', *Journal of Political Economy* ccclxxxvi: 674–700.

Bentham, J. (1948) *An Introduction to the Principles of Morals and Legislation*, Oxford: Oxford University Press.

BMA (British Medical Association) (1981) *The Handbook of Medical Ethics*, London: BMA.

Bodenheimer, T. (1992) 'Private insurance reform in the 1990s: Can it solve the health care crisis?', *International Journal of Health Services* xxii (2): 197–215.

Boulding, K.E. (1967) 'The concept of need for health services' in Mainland, D. (ed.) *Health Services Research*, New York: Millbank, 464–85.

Bowlby, J. (1965) *Child Care and the Growth of Love*, Harmondsworth: Pelican.

Bowling, A. (1991) *Measuring Health: A Review of Quality of Life Measuring Scales*, Milton Keynes: Open University Press.

Bowling, A. (1995) *Measuring Disease*, Milton Keynes: Open University Press.

Bradshaw, J.S. (1972) 'A taxonomy of social need' in McLachlan, G. (ed.) *Problems and Progress in Medical Care: Essays on Current Research*, Oxford: Oxford University Press.

Brindle, D. (1991) 'Ex-minister to head trust in forgery row', *Guardian*, 2 November: 3.

Brindle, D. (1992) 'NHS staff "must be free to complain"', *Guardian*, 3 July: 5.

Brindle, D. (1993a) 'Minister admits hospitals delay urgent operations', *Guardian*, 27 February: 3.

Brindle, D. (1993b) 'Admin in the "new look" NHS costs extra 1.5bn', *Guardian*, 9 December: 8.

Brindle, D. (1995) 'Spending up £1bn on NHS bureaucrats', *Guardian*, 16 February: 3.

Brown, P.M. (1974) *Towards a Marxist Psychology*, New York: Colophon.

Brown, P.M. (1981) 'The mental patients' rights movement and mental health institutional change', *International Journal of Health Services* xi (4): 523–40.

Bungener, M. (1987) 'Health economics and ethics' in Doxiades, S. (ed.) *Ethical Dilemmas in Health Promotion*, Chichester: Wiley, 117–28.

Butler, J. (1992) *Patients, Politics and Policies*, Buckingham: Open University Press.

Campbell, A.V. (1987) 'Mere words? Problems of definition in medical ethics' in Doxiades, S. (ed.) *Ethical Dilemmas in Health Promotion*, Chichester: Wiley, 15–24.

Campbell, R. and Collinson, D. (1988) *Ending Lives*, Oxford: Blackwell.

Campling, E.A., Devlin, H.B., Hoile, R.W. and Lunn, J.N. (1990 and annually) *The Report of the National Confidential Enquiry into Perioperative Deaths*, London: The Royal Colleges.

Churchland, P.S. (1986) *Neurophilosophy: Towards a Unified Science of the Mind-Brain*, Cambridge, Mass.: MIT.

Cirillo, R. (1979) *The Economics of Vilfredo Pareto*, London: Frank Cass.

Clayton, S. (1983) 'Social need revisited', *Journal of Social Policy* xii: 215–34.

Clouston, E. (1991) 'England's smallest hospital fights for survival', *Guardian* 28 May: 2.

Cochrane, A.L. (1972) *Effectiveness and Efficiency: Random Reflections on Health Services*, London: Nuffield Provincial Hospitals Trust.

Commoner, B. (1991) 'Rapid population growth and environmental stress', *International Journal of Health Services* xxi (2): 199–228.

Condren, C. (1978) 'The quest for a concept of needs' in Fitzgerald, R. (ed.) *Human Needs and Politics*, Oxford: Pergamon, 244–60.

Copeland, J. (1993) *Artificial Intelligence. A Philosophical Introduction*, Oxford: Blackwell.

Culyer, A.J. (1976) *Need and the National Health Service: Economics and Social Choice*, London: Martin Robertson.

Culyer, A. and Wagstaff, A. (1992) *Need, Equity and Equality in Health Care*, York: CHE.

Daniels, N. (1985) *Just Health Care*, Cambridge: Cambridge University Press.

Davenport-Hines, N. (1992) *Sex, Punishment and Death: British Attitudes to Sexuality Since the Renaissance*, London: Penguin.

Dawkins, R. (1978) *The Selfish Gene*, St Albans: Granada.

Dearn, M. (1993) 'Self-inflicted rationing', *The Lancet* cccxli: 1525.

Department of Health (1988) *Community Care: An Agenda for Action*, London: HMSO.

Department of Health (1989a) *Working for Patients*, London: HMSO.

Department of Health (1989b) *Caring for People: Community Care in the Next Decade and Beyond*, London: HMSO.

Department of Health (1991) *The Health of the Nation*, London: HMSO.

Department of Health (1993) *Managing the New NHS*, London: Department of Health.

Department of Health (1994) '£750,000 for projects helping homeless young people', Press Release 94\371, 9 August.

Department of Health Committee of Inquiry into the Future Development of the Public Health Function (1988) *Public Health in England*, London: HMSO Cm. 289 (the Acheson report).

DHSS (Department of Health and Social Security) (1976) *Sharing Resources for Health in England: Report of the Resource Allocation Working Party*, London: HMSO (the RAWP report).

DHSS (1980) *Inequalities in Health*, London: HMSO (the Black report).

Dietzgen, J. (1906) *The Nature of Human Brain-Work*, Chicago (self-published).

Dobson, R. (1994) 'When others suffer for your faith', *Independent*, 25 October.

Donabedian, A. (1973) *Aspects of Medical Care Administration. Specifying Requirements for Health Care*, Cambridge, Mass.: Harvard University Press.

Downie, R.S. and Calman, K.C. (1987) *Healthy Respect: Ethics in Health Care*, London: Faber.

Doyal, L. and Gough, I. (1991) *A Theory of Human Need*, Basingstoke: Macmillan.

Draper, P. (1991) *Health Through Public Policy: The Greening of Public Health*, London: Green Print.

Drummond, M.F. (1993) 'The contribution of health economics to cost-effective health-care delivery', in Drummond, M.F. and Maynard, A. (eds) *Purchasing and Providing Cost-effective Health Care*, Edinburgh: Churchill Livingstone.

Dunning, M. (1992) *Choices in Healthcare*, Zoetermeer: Government Committee on Choices in Health Care, The Netherlands.

Edwards, C.R.W. and Bouchier, I.A.D. (eds) (1991) *Davidson's Principles and Practice of Medicine*, Edinburgh: Churchill Livingstone.

Ehrenreich, B. and English, D. (1979) *For Her Own Good: 150 Years of the Experts' Advice to Women*, London: Pluto.

Eisenberg, L. (1987) 'Value conflicts in social policies for promoting health' in Doxiades, S. (ed.) *Ethical Dilemmas in Health Promotion*, Chichester: Wiley, 99–116.

Engels, F. (1976) *Anti-Dühring*, Pekin: FLPH.

Enthoven, A.C. (1993) 'The history and principles of managed competition', *Health Affairs* xii (supplement): 24–48.

Etzioni, A. (ed.) (1969) *The Semi-Professions*, New York: Free Press.

Faulder, C. (1985) *Whose Body Is It? The Troubling Issue of Informed Consent*, London: Virago.

Festinger, L. (1962) *The Theory of Cognitive Dissonance*, London: Tavistock.

Field, N.G. (ed.) (1989) *Success and Crisis in National Health Systems*, London: Routledge.

Fitzgerald, R. (1978) 'The ambiguity and rhetoric of "need"' in Fitzgerald, R. (ed.) *Human Needs and Politics*, Oxford: Pergamon, 195–212.

Flew, A. (1978) *A Rational Animal and Other Philsophical Essays on the Nature of Man*, Oxford: Clarendon.

Flew, A. (1981) *The Politics of Procrustes: Contradictions of Enforced Equality*, London: Temple Smith.

Foot, P. (1994) 'Time to defy those quangos we don't trust', *Guardian*, 15 August: 16.

Foster, P. (1995) *Women and the Health Care Industry: An Unhealthy Relationship?*, Milton Keynes: Open University Press.

Foster, S., Normand, C. and Sheaff, R. (1994) 'Health-care reform: The issues and the role of donors', *The Lancet* (16 July) cccxxxxiv: 175–7.

Foucault, M. (1965) *Madness and Civilization: A History of Insanity in the Age of Reason*, New York: Pantheon.

Frankel, S. and West, R. (eds) (1993) *Rationing and Rationality in the National Health Service: The Persistence of Waiting Lists*, Basingstoke: Macmillan.

Freeden, M. (1991) *Rights*, Milton Keynes: Open University Press.

Freud, S. (1936) *Inhibition, Symptoms and Anxiety*, London: Hogarth.

Freud, S. (1939) *Civilization and its Discontent*, London: Hogarth.

Freud, S. (1951) *Beyond the Pleasure Principle*, London: Hogarth.

Freud, S. (1959) '"Civilised" sexual morality and modern nervous illness' in

Standard Edition of the Complete Psychological Works, London: Hogarth, ix 181–204.

Freud, S. (1961) *Totem and Taboo*, London: Routledge.

Freud, S. (1972) 'Five lectures on psychoanalysis' in Freud, S., *Two Short Accounts of Psychoanalysis*, Harmondsworth: Penguin.

Freud, S. (1977a) 'Three essays on the theory of sexuality' in *Pelican Freud Library*, Harmondsworth: Penguin, vii 33–170.

Freud, S. (1977b) 'Fragment of an analysis of a case of hysteria ("Dora")' in *Pelican Freud Library*, Harmondsworth: Penguin, viii 31–166.

Friedson, E. (1970) *The Profession of Medicine: A Study in the Sociology of Applied Knowledge*, Chicago: Chicago University Press.

Fromm, E. (1942) *The Fear of Freedom*, London: International Library of Sociology and Social Reconstruction.

Fulford, K.W.M. (1989) *Moral Theory and Medical Practice*, Cambridge: Cambridge University Press.

Galen, R.S. and Gambino, S.R. (1988) *Beyond Normality: The Predictive Value and Efficiency of Medical Diagnosis*, Harlow: Churchill Livingstone.

Georgopoulos, B.S., Mahoney, G.M. and Jones, N.W. (1957) 'A path–goal approach to productivity', *Journal of Applied Psychology*, xxxxi: 345–53.

Gert, B. (1990) 'Rationality and lists', *Ethics* c: 279–300.

Gibbon, E.R. (n.d. but ?1897) *A History of the Decline and Fall of the Roman Empire*, London: Ward Lock.

Glassner, B. (1995) 'In the name of health', in Bunton, R., Nettleton, S. and Burrows, R. (eds) *The Sociology of Health Promotion. Critical Analyses of Consumption, Lifestyle and Risk*, London: Routledge, 159-75.

Glennister, H., Matsanganis, M. and Owens, P. (1992) *A Foothold for Fundholding?*, London: Kings Fund.

Glover, J. (1977) *Causing Death and Saving Lives*, Harmondsworth: Penguin.

Goffman, E. (1984) *Asylums: Essays on the Social Situation of Mental Patients and Other Inmates*, Harmondsworth: Penguin.

Gotzsche, P.C. (1994) 'Is there logic in the placebo?', *The Lancet* (1 October) cccxxxxiv (8927): 925–6.

Grace, V.M. (1991) 'The marketing of empowerment and the construction of the health consumer: A critique of health promotion', *International Journal of Health Services* xxi (2): 339.

Grant, S.C.D., Bennett, D.M., Bray, C.L., Brooks, N.M., Levy, R.D. and Ward, C. (1993) 'Smokers waste valuable resources', *British Medical Journal* (22 May) cccvi: 1408–9.

Gray, J. (1992) *The Moral Foundations of Market Institutions*, London: IEA.

Green, D.G. (1986) *Challenge to the NHS: A Study in Competition in American Health Care and the Lessons for Britain*, London: IEA.

Griffin, J. (1992) *Drug Misuse*, London: OHE.

Griffiths, R. (1983) 'NHS management enquiry', letter of 6 October 1983, under Department of Health Health Notice HN(84)13.

Handy, C.B. (1986) *Understanding Organisations*, Harmondsworth: Penguin.

Hare, R. (1972) *Freedom and Reason*, Oxford: Oxford University Press.

Hare, R. (1974) *The Language of Morals*, Oxford: Oxford University Press.

Harper, K. (1994) 'New threat of strike ban in key services', *Guardian*, 16 July: 4.

Harris, J. (1985) *The Value of Life*, London: RKP.

Harris, J. (1992) 'A philosopher's perspective', Conference on Health Resource Allocation, Manchester University, July 1992.

Harrison, J. (1994) 'NHS corporate governance – myth or reality?' in Malek, M. (ed.) (1994) *Setting Priorities in Health Care*, Chichester: Wiley, 153–68.

Hart, J.T. (1975) 'The inverse care law' in Cox, C. and Mead, A. (eds) *A Sociology of Medical Practice*, London: Collier Macmillan, 189–206.

Hart, J.T. (1988) *A New Kind of Doctor: The General Practitioner's Part in the Health of the Community*, London: Merlin.

Hellander, I., Himmelstein, D.U., Woolhandler, S. and Wolfe, S. (1994) 'Health care paper chase, 1993: The cost to the nation, the states and the district of Colombia', *International Journal of Health Services* xxiv (1): 1–9.

Heller, A. (1976) *The Theory of Need in Marx*, London: Merlin.

Herzberg, F. *et al*. (1959) *The Motivation to Work*, New York: Wiley.

HIAA (Health Insurance Asssociation of America) (1995) *Source Book of Health Insurance Data 1994*, Washington: HIAA.

Hicks, H.G. and Gullett, C.R. (eds) (1981) *Management*, Maidenhead: McGraw-Hill.

Higgins, J. and Wiles, R. (1992) 'A study of patients who chose private health care for treatment', *British Journal of General Practice* xxxxii: 326–9.

Hoffenburg, R. (1987) *Clinical Autonomy*, London: Nuffield Provincial Hospitals Trust.

Holland, W.W. (ed.) (1983) *Evaluation of Health Care*, Oxford: Oxford University Press/EEC.

Holliday, I. (1992) *The NHS Transformed*, Manchester: Baseline.

Horst, E. (1992) 'Denmark' in Leadbeater, N. (ed.) *European Health Services Handbook*, Dublin: EHMA, 48–55.

Ifeachor, E.C. (1993) 'Neural networks and the applications to health care' in Abbott, W. (ed.) *Information Technology in Healthcare: A Handbook*, Harlow: Kluwer and IHSM, A.6.11.

Illich, I. (1976) *Limits to Medicine. Medical Nemesis: The Expropriation of Health*, London: Marion Boyars.

Inglis, B. (1983) *The Diseases of Civilization*, St Albans: Granada.

James, J.H. (1993) 'Health care rationing: Lessons from a district health authority' in Allen, I. (ed.) *Rationing in Health and Social Care*, London: Policy Studies Institute.

Jamous, H. and Pelouille, B. (1970) 'Professions of self-perpetuating systems? Changes in the French hospital system' in Jackson, J.A. (ed.) *Professions and Professionalism*, London: Cambridge University Press.

Jennett, B. (1972) *High Technology Medicine: Benefits and Burdens*, London: NPHT.

Karhausen, L. (1987) 'From ethics to medical ethics' in Doxiades, S. (ed.) *Ethical Dilemmas in Health Promotion*, Chichester: Wiley, 25–34.

Kast, F.E. and Rosenzweig, J.E. (1981) *Organisation and Management: A Systems and Contingency Approach*, Maidenhead: McGraw-Hill.

Kennedy, I. (1981) *The Unmasking of Medicine*, St Albans: Granada.

Kind, P. and Gudex, C. (1993) 'The role of QALYs in assessing health priorities between health-care interventions' in Drummond, M.F. and

Maynard, A. (eds) *Purchasing and Providing Cost-Effective Health Care*, Edinburgh: Churchill Livingstone, 94–108.

Kotler, P. and Clarke, R.N. (1987) *Marketing for Health Care Organisations*, Englewood Cliffs, N.J.: Prentice Hall.

Kubler-Ross, E. (1970) *On Death and Dying*, London: Tavistock.

Labisch, A. (1987) 'The role of the hospital in the health policy of the German social democratic movement before World War I', *International Journal of Health Services* xvii: 279–94.

Laing, R.D. (1965) *The Divided Self: An Existential Study in Sanity and Madness*, Harmondsworth: Penguin.

Lamb, D. (1985) *Death, Brain Death and Ethics*, Beckenham: Croom Helm.

Lipsey, R.G. (1970) *An Introduction to Positive Economics*, London: Weidenfeld & Nicholson (2nd edn).

Little, I.M.D. (1950) *A Critique of Welfare Economics*, Oxford: Oxford University Press.

Loewy, E.H. (1990) 'Commodities, needs and health care: a commercial perspective', in Jensen, U.J. and Mooney, G. (eds) *Changing Values in Medical and Health Care Decision Making*, Chichester: Wiley, 17–31.

Lomasky, L.E. (1981) 'Medical progress and national health care', *Philosophy and Public Affairs* x: 65–88.

McCloskey, H.J. (1975) 'Human needs, rights and political values', *American Philosophical Quarterly* xiii: 1–11.

McDowell, J. (1979) 'Virtue and reason', *The Monist* lxii: 331–50.

McGuire, A., Henderson, J. and Mooney, G. (1988) *The Economics of Health Care: An Introductory Text*, London: Routledge.

McInnes, N. (1978) 'The politics of needs – or, who needs politics?' in Fitzgerald, R. (ed.) *Human Needs and Politics*, Oxford: Pergamon, 229–43.

McKeown, T. (1976) *The Role of Medicine: Dream, Mirage or Nemesis?*, London: NPHT.

MacLagan, W.G. (1951) 'Freedom of the will', *Proceedings of the Aristotelian Society* (supp. vol.), 179–200.

McMahan, J. (1993) 'Killing, letting die and withdrawing aid', *Ethics* ciii: 250–79.

McMahon, C. (1989) 'Managerial authority', *Ethics* c : 33–53.

MacPherson, C.B. (1962) *The Political Theory of Possessive Individualism*, Oxford: Oxford University Press.

Malthus, T.R. (1992) *An Essay on the Principle of Population: or, A View of its Past and Present*, Cambridge: Cambridge University Press.

Manciaux, M. and Sand, E.A. (1987) 'Promotion of child health' in Doxiades, S. (ed.) *Ethical Dilemmas in Health Promotion*, Chichester: Wiley, 157–70.

Marcuse, H. (1968) *One Dimensional Man*, London: Sphere.

Marinker, M. (ed.) (1994) *Controversies in Health Care Policies: Challenges to Practice*, London: BMJ.

Martin, J.P. (1983) *Hospitals in Trouble*, Oxford: Blackwell.

Marx,K. and Engels, F. (1969) *Manifesto of the Communist Party*, Moscow: Progress.

Marx, K. (1973) *Grundrisse: Introduction to the Critique of Political Economy*, Harmondsworth: Penguin.

Marx, K. (1976a) *Preface and Introduction to 'A Contribution to the Critique of Political Economy'*, Pekin: FLPH.

Marx, K. (1976b) *Capital*, Harmondsworth: Penguin.

Marx, K. and Engels, F. (1975) 'The German ideology' in *Marx–Engels: Collected Works*, Moscow: Progress, v 19–537.

Maslow, A. (1954) *Motivation and Personality*, New York: Harper & Row.

Mawhinney, B. and Nichol, D.K. (1993) *Purchasing for Health: A Framework for Action* (speeches; unpublished NHS copies).

Mayston, D. (1992) 'Internal markets, capital and the economics of information', *Public Money and Management* xii (1): 47–52.

Midgley, M. (1980) *Beast and Man: The Roots of Human Nature*, London: Methuen.

Milio, N. (1975) 'Values, social class and community health services' in Cox, C. and Mead, A. (eds) *A Sociology of Medical Practice*, London: Collier Macmillan, 49–61.

Millington, A. (1995) 'Judge halts trial in £400,000 NHS fraud case', *Guardian*, 23 March: 4.

Ministry of Health (1944) *A National Health Service*, London: HMSO.

Mitchell, J. (1975) *Psychoanalysis and Feminism*, Harmondsworth: Pelican.

Montagu, A. (1961) *Man in Process*, New York: Greenwood.

Mooney, G.H. (1986) *Economics, Medicine and Health Care*, Hemel Hempstead: Wheatsheaf.

Moore, G.E. (1929) *Principia Ethica*, Cambridge: Cambridge University Press.

Mordelet, P. (1992) 'The new 1991 French Hospital Act: Autonomy and competition between the public and the private hospital sectors and the use of private sector management in public hospitals', EHMA conference paper, Karlstad, 12 June.

More, E.M. (1992) 'An ethical analysis of the problems derived from the new reproductive technology', Manchester University PhD thesis.

Navarro, V. (1979) *Medicine Under Capitalism*, London: Croom Helm.

NHSME (National Health Service Management Executive) (1991) *Assessing Health Care Needs*, London: NHSME.

NHSME (1993a) *NHS Trusts: A Working Guide*, London: HMSO.

NHSME (1993b) *Health Service Guidance* (93)5, 18 January.

NHSME (1993c) *Executive Letter* (93)10, 12 February.

NHSME (n.d.) *The International Classification of Diseases* (9th revision), London: NHSME and WHO.

NHSME IMG (NHSME Information Management Group) (n.d. but *c*. 1993) *Developing Information Systems to Support Purchasers*, London: NHSME IMG.

Noack, H. and McQueen, D. (1988) 'Towards health promotion indicators', *Health Promotion* iii: 73–8.

Nozick, R. (1974) *Anarchy, State and Utopia*, Oxford: Blackwell.

Oakley, A. (1976) 'Wisewoman and medicine man' in Mitchell, J. and Oakley, A. (eds) *The Rights and Wrongs of Women*, Harmondsworth: Penguin.

Obel, B. (1981) *Issues of Organisational Design*, Oxford: Pergamon.

OECD (Organisation for Economic Cooperation and Development) (1992) *OECD in Figures: Statistics on the Member Countries*, Paris: OECD.

Office of Health Economics (OHE) (1992) *Compendium of Health Statistics 1992*, London: OHE.

Ovretveit, J. (1992) *Health Service Quality*, Oxford: Blackwell.

Pappworth, M.H. (1967) *Human Guinea Pigs: Experimentation on Man*, London: RKP.

Pater, J.E. (1981) *The Making of the NHS*, London: King Edward Hospital Fund for London.

Pauly, M.V. (1988) 'Efficiency, equity and costs in the US health care system' in Havighurst, C.C., Helms, R.B., Bladen, C. and Pauly, M.V., *American Health Care: What are the Lessons for Britain?*, London: IEA.

Pelta, D. (1992) 'GP fundholding', unpublished paper to Anglo-Polish Health Symposium, Jachranka, 4 November.

Pickin, S. and St Leger, S. (1993) *Assessing Health Need Using the Life Cycle Framework*, Buckingham: Open University Press.

Porter, M. (1985) *Competitive Strategy*, London: Collier Macmillan.

ProPAC (Prospective Payment Commission) (1991) *Medicare and the American Health Care System: Report to the Congress*, Washington: ProPAC.

Raffel, M.W. and Raffel, N.K. (1989) *The US Health System*, Chichester: Wiley (3rd edn).

Ramsay, M. (1992) *Human Needs and the Market*, Aldershot: Avebury.

Ranade, W. (1994) *A Future for the NHS? Health Care in the 1990s*, Harlow: Longman.

Rawls, J. (1972) *A Theory of Justice*, Oxford: Oxford University Press.

Reed, C. (1992) 'US hospital fraud hints at wider corruption', *Guardian*, 8 January: 8.

Reiser, S.J. (1978) *Medicine and the Reign of Technology*, Cambridge: Cambridge University Press.

Richman, J. (1987) *Medicine and Health*, Harlow: Longman.

Riddell, P. (1989) *The Thatcher Decade*, Oxford: Blackwell.

Rose, M. (1989) *Industrial Behaviour: Theoretical Development Since Taylor*, Harmondsworth: Penguin.

Royal Commission on Environmental Pollution (1994) *Transport and the Environment*, London: HMSO.

Royal Commission on the National Health Service (1979) *Report of the Royal Commission on the National Health Service*, London: HMSO.

Russell, B. (1936) *The Problems of Philosophy*, London: Butterworth.

Russell, L.B. (1986) *Is Prevention Better than Cure?*, Washington: Brookings Institution.

Sadurski, W. (1983) 'To each according to his (genuine?) needs', *Political Theory*, xi (3): 419–32.

Saltman, R.B. (1994) 'Patient choice and patient empowerment in northern European health systems: A conceptual framework', *International Journal of Health Services*, xxiv (2): 201–29.

Saltman, R.B. and von Otter, C. (1992) *Planned Markets and Public Competition: Strategic Reform in Northern European Health Systems*, Buckingham: Open University Press.

Sartre, J.P. (1977) *Being and Nothingness*, London: Methuen.

Scalettar, R. (1993) 'Clinical quality assurance: Practice parameters', *World Hospitals*, xxix (2): 30–4.

Sedgwick, P. (1982) *Psycho Politics*, London: Pluto.

Seedhouse, D. (1988) *Ethics: The Heart of Health Care*, Chichester: Wiley.

Seldon, A. (ed.) (1980) *The Litmus Papers: A National Health Dis-service*, London: Centre for Policy Studies.

Seng, C., Lessof, L. and McKee, M. (1993) 'Who's on the fiddle?', *Health Services Journal*, 7 January: 16–17.

Shanks, J. and Frater, A. (1993) 'Health status, outcome and attributability: Is a red rose red in the dark?', *Quality in Health Care* ii: 259–62.

Sharkey, A. (1995) 'The doctor prescribes death', *Independent*, 1 February: 21.

Sheaff, R. (1979) 'Marxist political theory's analysis of moral ideology', Oxford University DPhil thesis.

Sheaff, R. (1991) *Marketing for Health Services*, Buckingham: Open University Press.

Sheaff, R. (1994) 'What kind of healthcare "internal market"? A cross-Europe view of the options', *International Journal of Health Planning and Management* ix: 5–24.

Shepherd, M. (1983) 'Social criteria of the outcome of mental disease' in Teeling-Smith, G. (ed.) *Measuring the Social Benefits of Medicine*, London: OHE, 121–7.

Simon, H.A. (1988) 'Decision making and organisational design' in Pugh, D.S. (ed.) *Organization Theory: Selected Readings*, London: Penguin, 213–18.

Skinner, B.F. (1973) *Beyond Freedom and Dignity*, Harmondsworth: Penguin.

Skinner, B.F. (1976) *Walden Two*, New York: Macmillan.

Smith, G. (1980) *Social Need: Policy, Practice and Research*, London: RKP.

Smith, M.B. (1978) 'Metapsychology, politics and human needs' in Fitzgerald, R. (ed.) *Human Needs and Politics*, Oxford: Pergamon, 124–41.

Smith, R. (1987) *Unemployment and Health: A Disaster and a Challenge*, Oxford: Oxford University Press.

Solomon, R.C. (1993) *Ethics and Excellence: Cooperation and Integrity in Business*, Oxford: Oxford University Press.

Sorlin, P. (1969) *The Soviet People and their Society*, London: Pall Mall.

Steiner, H. (1976) 'The just provision of health care: A reply to Elizabeth Telfer', *Journal of Medical Ethics*, ii: 185–9.

Stevens, A. and Raftery, J. (eds) (1994) *Health Care Needs Assessment: The Epidemiologically Based Needs Assessment Reviews*, Oxford: Radcliffe Medical.

Stevens, P.E. and Hall, J.M. (1991) 'A critical historical analysis of the medical construction of lesbianism', *International Journal of Health Services*, xxi (2): 299–300.

Strasser, T., Jeanneret, O. and Raymond, L. (1987) 'Ethical aspects of prevention trials' in Doxiades, S. (ed.) *Ethical Dilemmas in Health Promotion*, Chichester: Wiley, 183–93.

Szasz, T.S. (1971) *The Manufacture of Madness: A Comparative Study of the Inquisition and the Mental Health Movement*, London: RKP.

Szasz, T.S. (1986) interview with Jonathan Miller, BBC2, 19 January.

Tannahill, R. (1971) *Food in History*, London: Eyre Methuen.

Tannahill, R. (1976) *Sex in History*, London: Methuen.

Taylor, R. (1979) *Medicine Out of Control: The Anatomy of a Malignant Technology*, Melbourne: Sun Books.

Taylor-Gooby, P. (1985) *Public Opinion, Ideology and State Welfare*, London: Macmillan.

Thomson, G. (1987) *Needs*, London: RKP.

Thomson, J.J. (1971) 'A defence of abortion', *Philosophy and Public Affairs* i (1).

The Times (1994), Letters to the Editor, 17 November.

Timpanaro, S. (1980) *On Materialism*, London: Verso.

Tolliday, H. (1978) 'Clinical autonomy' in Jaques, E. (ed.) (1978) *Health Services: Their Nature and Organisation and the Role of Patients, Doctors and the Health Professions*, London: Heinemann, 32–52.

Tooley, M. (1972) 'Abortion and infanticide', *Philosophy and Public Affairs* ii (1).

Tuckett, D., Boulton, M., Olson, C. and Williams, A. (1985) *Meetings Between Experts: An Approach to Sharing Ideas in Medical Consultations*, London: Tavistock.

Underwood, M.J. and Bailey, J.S. (1993) 'Coronary bypass surgery should not be offered to smokers', *British Medical Journal* (17 April) cccvi: 1407–8.

Veblen, T. (1994) 'The economic theory of the leisure class: An economic study of institutions' in *Collected Works*, i London: Routledge, i.

Voloshinov, V.N. (1973) *Marxism and the Philosophy of Language*, New York: Seminar.

Von Paczensky, G. and Dünnebier, A. (1995) *Leere Töpfe voller Töpfe. Die Kulturgeschichte des Essens und Trinkens*, Munich: Albrecht Knaus.

Vroom, H.V. (1964) *Work and Motivation*, New York: Wiley.

Walker, N. (1968) *Crime and Insanity in England*, Edinburgh: Edinburgh University Press.

Wall, A (n.d.) *Future Health Care Options: Values and the NHS*, Birmingham: IHSM.

Walras, L. (1954) *Elements of Pure Economics or the Theory of Social Wealth*, London: Allen & Unwin/Royal Economic Society.

Watkins, S. (1987) *Medicine and Labour: The Politics of a Profession*, London: Lawrence & Wishart.

Weale, A. (ed.) (1988) *Cost and Choice in Health Care*, London: Kings Fund.

Weale, S. (1995) 'Dying girl in court fight for treatment', *Guardian*, 10 March: 1.

Wennemo, I. (1993) 'Infant mortality, public policy and inequality: A comparison of 18 industrialised countries 1950–1985', *Sociology of Health and Illness* xv (4): 429–46.

West, R. (1993) 'Joining the queue: Demand and decision-making' in Frankel and West (eds) *Rationing and Rationality in the National Health Service: The Persistence of Waiting Lists*, Basingstoke: Macmillan.

West, R. (1994) *Obesity*, London: OHE.

Whiteis, D. and Salmon, J.W. (1987) 'The proprietarization of health care and the underdevelopment of the public sector', *International Journal of Health Services* xvii (1): 47–64.

WHO (World Health Organisation) (1946) *Constitution*, Geneva: WHO.

WHO (1978) *Alma Ata 1978: Primary Health Care*, Geneva: WHO.

WHO (1979) *Formulating Strategies for Health for All by the Year 2000: Guiding Principles and Essential Issues*, Geneva: WHO.

Wiggins, D. (1985) 'Claims of need' in Honderich, T. (ed.) *Morality and Objectivity: A Tribute to J.L. Mackie*, London: RKP, 149–202.

Wiles, R. and Higgins, J. (n.d.) *Why do Patients Go Private: A Study of Consumerism in Health Care*, Southampton: IHPS.

Wilkin, D., Hallam, L. and Doggett, M.A. (1992) *Measures of Need and Outcome for Primary Health Care*, Oxford: Oxford University Press.

Wilkinson, R.G. (ed.) (1986) *Class and Health: Research and Longitudinal Data*, London: Tavistock.

Williams, B. (1981) *Moral Luck: Philosophical Papers 1973–80*, Cambridge: Cambridge University Press.

Wohl, S. (1984) *The Medical–Industrial Complex*, New York: Harmony.

Yates, J. (1995) *Private Eye, Heart and Hip. Surgical Consultants, the National Health Service and Private Medicine*, Edinburgh: Churchill Livingstone & IHSM.

Young, E. (1994) 'The needs and the damage done', *Guardian*, 20 August: 9–10.

Zola, I.K. (1975) 'Medicine as an instrument of social control' in Cox, C. and Mead, A. (eds) *A Sociology of Medical Practice*, London: Collier Macmillan, 170–85.

INDEX